THE SOCIALIST GOOD LIFE

THE SOCIALIST GOOD LIFE

Desire, Development, and Standards of Living in Eastern Europe

EDITED BY
CRISTOFER SCARBORO, DIANA MINCYTĖ,
AND ZSUZSA GILLE

INDIANA UNIVERSITY PRESS

This book is a publication of

Indiana University Press
Office of Scholarly Publishing
Herman B Wells Library 350
1320 East 10th Street
Bloomington, Indiana 47405 USA

iupress.indiana.edu

© 2020 by Indiana University Press

All rights reserved
No part of this book may be reproduced or utilized in any form or by any means, electronic or mechanical, including photocopying and recording, or by any information storage and retrieval system, without permission in writing from the publisher. The paper used in this publication meets the minimum requirements of the American National Standard for Information Sciences—Permanence of Paper for Printed Library Materials, ANSI Z39.48-1992.

Manufactured in the United States of America

Cataloging information is available from the Library of Congress.

ISBN 978-0-253-04776-2 (hardback)
ISBN 978-0-253-04779-3 (paperback)
ISBN 978-0-253-04781-6 (web PDF)

1 2 3 4 5   26 25 24 23 22 21

To Keith Hitchins, with all best wishes for future success in the study of Southeastern European history.

CONTENTS

Acknowledgments   ix

1. The Pleasures of Backwardness / Zsuzsa Gille, Cristofer Scarboro, and Diana Mincytė   1
2. Consuming Dialogues: Pleasure, Restraint, Backwardness, and Civilization in Eastern Europe / Mary Neuburger   25
3. Just Rewards: The Social Contract and Communism's Hard Bargain with the Citizen-Consumer / Patrick Hyder Patterson   52
4. Conceptualizing Consumption in the Polish People's Republic / Brian Porter-Szűcs   82
5. Oranges and the New Black: Importing, Provisioning, and Consuming Tropical Fruits and Coffee in the GDR, 1971–89 / Anne Dietrich   104
6. VCRs, Modernity, and Consumer Culture in Late State Socialist Poland / Patryk Wasiak   132
7. The Enchantment of Imaginary Europe: Consumer Practices in Post-Soviet Ukraine / Tania Bulakh   162
8. The Late Socialist Good Life and Its Discontents: *Bit, Kultura,* and the Social Life of Goods / Cristofer Scarboro   190
9. The Prosumerist Resonance Machine: Rethinking Political Subjectivity and Consumer Desire in State Socialism / Zsuzsa Gille and Diana Mincytė   218

Index   239

ACKNOWLEDGMENTS

This volume is based on The Pleasures of Backwardness: Consumer Desire and Modernity in Eastern Europe, a conference that took place at the University of California, Berkeley in April 2015. Organized and hosted by Michael Dean, then a graduate student at UC Berkeley, the event brought together an interdisciplinary group of scholars for a lively discussion about the place of consumption in socialist societies and their institutions. The outcomes of these discussions are represented in chapters included in the volume. We gratefully acknowledge the contributions of the authors without whose hard work this volume would not be possible.

THE SOCIALIST GOOD LIFE

ONE

THE PLEASURES OF BACKWARDNESS

ZSUZSA GILLE
CRISTOFER SCARBORO
DIANA MINCYTĖ

Socialism in Eastern Europe was designed to do two things: overcome backwardness and, in so doing, fulfill human needs at ever higher levels. From the beginning, communist readings of political economy were tied to the promise that industrial production would generate plenty and, if properly organized, bring human happiness in its train. This understanding served as the master plot of communism, holding together the Soviet Union and the socialist societies of Eastern Europe from beginning to end. In this reading—a reading shared by Communist Party planners and those writing in the West—Eastern Europe lagged behind the developed states of the industrial heartland. Communism was designed as a means to allow these societies to catch up to and eventually surpass the West in providing a good life increasingly measured in goods.

WHAT KIND OF PLEASURE? WHAT KIND OF BACKWARDNESS?

By both of these measures—pleasure and backwardness—the socialist experiment has generally been found wanting.[1] Collapse and the lingering shadow of the Cold War have served to indict the socialist systems on both counts: in this story, state socialism was neither able to overcome backwardness nor produce pleasure. Our volume asks us to rethink these metrics.

To begin with, it is worth remembering the relatively impressive records of the Eastern European systems in overcoming backwardness and developing modern industrial societies. If socialism was, in large part, a means to replicate the productive capacity of the capitalist West, if not its social structure, much progress was made in the postwar years. Amid great privation and no small amount of terror and coercion, the first decades of the postwar years produced societies in Eastern Europe that echoed their cousins in the West by most measures of development—no small feat considering where East and West stood during the interwar years and the level of destruction wrought by the war itself. Across Eastern Europe, from the early 1960s until the slowdown of the late 1970s, people continued to see their purchasing power, social provisions, and opportunities for leisure advance. All of Europe participated in the "miracle years" that saw a postwar economic boom and resulting social transformation.[2]

As our anthology demonstrates, these transformations were felt and lived differently across the region. In Bulgaria, where industrialization began from a low base, the gap between backwardness and development seemed to close at breakneck speed, ushering in new worlds seemingly overnight. This process was not uncritically experienced, as Mary Neuburger's chapter demonstrates. Development meant worlds gained *and* lost. It also posed the question of what socialism was developing into. To many, "developed socialism" seemed like wishful thinking, and, as an idea, it obscured more than it clarified. It is worth rereading literature emerging from and about what came to be called the late socialist period to recapture the spirit of the age: that of rapid growth (albeit with inflated numbers and suspect reporting). Official growth rates in Bulgaria during the 1960s and 1970s ranged between 7.5 percent and 9 percent annually. The seventh Bulgarian Five-Year Plan (1976–80) called for growth rates of 9.1 percent.[3] This had real results on the ground. From 1965 through 1981, per capita meat consumption rose from 48 to 61 kilograms annually; consumption of milk rose from 148 to 198 liters; eggs from 167 to 203.[4] By 1984, 70,000 apartments were built each year in Bulgaria.[5] In contrast to Bulgaria, Czechoslovakia had a much higher level of industrialization prior to the Second World War—there the question of development and developmental models was much less clear. Even in the more advanced (or less backward) regions of Eastern Europe, however, the development of a socialist middle class was borne out in these statistics and in the lived experience of those in the region.

By the 1960s, the line between first and second worlds was becoming much thinner. Per capita consumption of meat in East and West was comparable between 1950 and 1978. During that period, Greece's meat consumption grew fastest, increasing by a multiple of 6, but Austria's increased by a multiple of 2.8, Belgium and Luxembourg's by 2, and France's by 1.9, while Hungary's increased by 2.09, Yugoslavia's by 3.19, and Czechoslovakia's by 2.5. Lest one thinks this is because their consumption levels were still low in comparison to Westerners', Czechoslovakia's meat consumption level was at 83.4 kilograms,

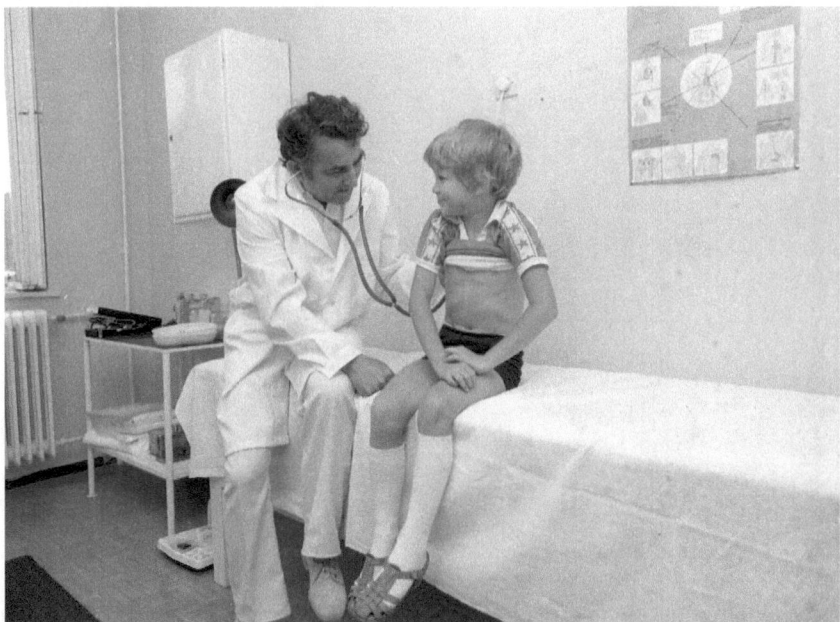

Fig. 1.1. Visit to the pediatrician. Hungary, 1982. Source: Fortepan.

East Germany's (GDR) at 86.2 kilograms, and Hungary's at 71.2 kilograms, while Austria's and Switzerland's was 83 kilograms.[6] The comparison of per capita dairy consumption shows greater growth in the former socialist countries: while between 1950 and 1978 many capitalist countries barely increased or even decreased their dairy intake, Yugoslavia and many other socialist countries more than doubled their dairy consumption. The growth rate of radio and television subscribers per one thousand people between 1960 and 1978 was the largest in the socialist countries.[7]

While it is important to relate these data to how much individuals had to work for them, such comparisons must take into consideration the broader context of collective consumption that was free or heavily subsidized, such as health care, education at all levels, public transportation, meals provided at schools and workplaces, vacation, cultural consumption (movies, theaters, concerts), and other free leisure activities for children and adults alike (see figs. 1.1–1.2). It is telling that Cold War–era American studies on the comparison of living standards between the USSR and the United States came to the conclusion that "everything was cheaper [measured in work time] in the West,

Fig. 1.2. College dorm, collective leisure activities. Hungary, 1949. Source: Fortepan.

except for rent," only by excluding health care costs, vacation, transportation, childcare, and schooling expenses in their consumer basket.[8]

We have data on collective consumption in Hungary in the 1970s, during which time the share of one's income coming from social welfare (in cash and in kind—such as health care, day care, education, vacation and cultural goods, meal plans, and medication subsidies) increased from 22.6 percent to 30.8 percent.[9] While data such as these are selective and come from Communist Party sources, the overall trend was clearly one of continuous elevation of consumption levels—individual and collective—at least until the 1980s, and as such, these data raise questions about the common backwardness narrative.

As Anne Dietrich's chapter notes, the East German experience was complicated by the existence of an alternative Germany emerging to the West. This Western example—a means of assessing success and failure in the East—shadowed the socialist experiment everywhere. This was particularly true in questions of consumption, which increasingly became a space where people in the East and West came to terms with conceptions of the life well lived. By this metric, we have long assumed that Eastern Europeans lived less well than their Western neighbors. Long lines for underpowered cars served as both a marker of progress made and distances yet to be traveled.[10] During the

Cold War, levels of consumption were considered the primary measure of levels of development, the relative merits of communism and capitalism, and whether one could be considered to belong to "Europe." (As Tetiana Bulakh's chapter makes clear, this is still very much the case in postsocialist Eastern Europe.)

Until recently, scholarship has focused on socialist Eastern Europe as a space of dearth and boredom. In both East and West, pleasure is generally understood materially: standards of living helpfully quantified through gross domestic products. If pleasure existed in Eastern Europe, it was bought cheaply through shoddy goods insufficiently distributed. People found pleasure by making do in a world less shiny and compelling than the West. The failure and ultimately the collapse of communism were the results of this lag in development—as Eastern European states abandoned state socialism, they rejoined Europe. History derailed became history confirmed.[11] The years 1989 and 1991 proved that there were no alternatives to the liberal democratic capitalist model, a story that found a welcome audience in the West.

We should take these perspectives seriously but should read them with the understanding that the socialist middle class that developed in Eastern Europe was a *socialist* middle class. Throughout the late socialist period, party leaders and their would-be subjects worked to develop a socialist model of a consumer society. Programs to raise the standard of living (in Bulgaria adopted by the December Plenum of the Bulgarian Communist Party in 1972) became a central plank in what Patrick Hyder Patterson understands as a "hard bargain" between the party and its increasingly demanding citizenry. And the party thought creatively about how to best solve the question of consumption. As Brian Porter-Szűcs notes, party leaders sought to harness the "animal spirits" of consumer desire to create a socialist world rooted in personal consumption. Shortage was an unhappy and dangerous byproduct of state planning within a system that, by many measures, was a success.

If we understand this middle class not in Marxian terms, as defined by its relationship to the means of production, but rather, as it is done in American stratification studies, as a stratum with a comfortable lifestyle, leading a more or less petit bourgeois existence, we might see the irony: a society aimed at transcending, if not eradicating, capitalism ended up incubating a massive social group that was the ideological opposite of the Leninist concept of the working class—that is, collectively minded and whose class consciousness arose out of its productive and collective contribution to society rather than from its ability to achieve individual levels of material comfort.

It is undeniable that it was exactly such a new middle stratum that emerged under late socialism. This socialist middle class expressed and lived their own new visions about what the good life should look like.[12] Often, these visions coincided with the material pleasures of consumption under state socialism—a reduction of working hours, the increased emphasis on private life, and the gratifications of the domestic sphere. The socialist middle class also enjoyed high levels of economic certainty, much like its Western counterparts, but unlike them, this resulted primarily from full employment and from their free access to education, health care, cultural activities, retirement, and various social benefits. Yet experiences of real existing socialism often contradicted and complicated these visions. Old communists bemoaned the lack of voluntary and collective enthusiasm of the postrevolutionary generations;[13] tourists complained about underfunded facilities; and audiences in art galleries fretted about the socialist content of paintings and the meaning and message of an increasingly mechanized world.[14] The pleasures, expectations, and fears of the new socialist middle class emerged in settings familiar yet foreign to the world of liberal democratic capitalism.

Socialism was to be about more than satisfying the material requirements of a good society. It was, equally importantly, to free people from the tyranny of the "alienated, consumerist outlook of bourgeois consumer society," allowing them to become "versatile, harmoniously developed, active, creative individuals."[15] Socialism was designed as an alternative modernity—an improvement on capitalist systems. Ultimately, the socialist projects in Eastern Europe were meant to transform the material base of the country in order to bring about new outlooks and capacities within those living in the new society.[16] The goods were to be a means to an end. A new material culture and new social cosmologies were to emerge from the transformed political economy of the region.

Late socialism was centrally animated by discussions about the relationship between social needs, desires, and the question of pleasure. Baked into these conversations was real fear of social and cultural changes not only among the higher party echelons but also among citizens who loathed the loss of morality and values. In this sense, the proliferation of consumer goods played a central role in the developing social contract undergirding the state socialist system: consumption was a site of negotiating one's place in the socialist state.

Marxist readings of history and development promised that the transformation of the material base in Eastern Europe would lead to new ways of living in the world.[17] Unfortunately for the parties in the region, the gap between material reality and developed consciousness was understood to be both historically determined and resistant to centrally planned education and programs.[18] This did not stop them from trying. States in the region poured tremendous resources into social and cultural programs to cultivate and promote an ideologically sound and profoundly meaningful—perhaps even pleasurable—good life in socialist Eastern Europe.[19] State support of the extra production sphere was profound. In Bulgaria, 1982 saw 811 state-supported art exhibitions (attended by 4.5 million visitors) and 280,000 amateur art performances (including 520,000 performers); 5,300 new books were also published.[20] To be sure, these pleasures are both material and immaterial. Books, after all, are material things. Communing with the sublime, however, is not.

The Committee for Arts and Culture articulated the goals for a newly aestheticized Bulgaria in its Comprehensive Program for Nationwide Aesthetic Education. Among other things, the new culture was to result in "high personal responsibility and a sense of quality in production and public life; a communist collective awareness; pride in socialist gains and intolerance for shortcomings and a materialistic attitude to life; love of beauty in nature, in practical activity and human relations; active struggle against the ugly and the banal; harmony between the physical and spiritual; between the rational and the emotional side of man; an active social stand in the development of and the creative participation of each and every one in the socialist recreation of our life."[21] The tensions here are obvious—even while the conclusions are not. Are rationally planned leisure activities and pleasure mutually exclusive? (And socially constructive planning, like the pursuit of happiness, is a descendent of the Enlightenment.) In other words, can pleasure be teleological?

Under state socialism, needs were separated into objective and subjective categories. Socialism was, from the very beginning, undergirded by the Marxist slogan "from each according to his abilities, to each according to his needs."[22] Individual—not only collective—needs were central for the socialist project. But they are, of course, a moving target—marked by both physiology and desire. What is deemed necessary changes with time and is intensely personal. So what was needed and desirable in the late socialist period? How could pleasure, inherently idiosyncratic, be met by mass production? It was not so simple. People found pleasure and solace in systems designed to provide uniform comfort and pleasure. The failures of the state to meet its own goals in these areas were simultaneously avenues for protest and a means to create a more meaningful life. Needs, desires, and pleasure originating from both "above"—the state—and "below"—the people—were continually emerging, colliding, and mutating.

One element remained constant. In the minds of many in the region (and most outside of it), Western models of development were a vexing measure for those thinking about the good society in Eastern Europe. The state socialist system was never able to fully reproduce the virtues (such as they are) of capitalism in the West. Capitalism was neither met nor transcended. At the same time, the state socialist systems *were* maddeningly reproducing the vices of capitalism—alienation and depoliticization. Late socialism was a period riven through with official consternation and fear: that its promises were not being met *and* that they were. Delivery on the promises of socialism was producing unintended and dangerous results—atomized citizens living only from private pleasure to private pleasure.[23]

BACKWARDNESS AND FORWARDNESS

Our volume begins from the premise that both terms—*pleasure* and *backwardness*—are understood relationally and ambivalently and that they are subject to change over time. Regarding pleasure, we investigate two aspects of relationality. First, that pleasure arises from a unique matrix of effects, which in turn are produced by concrete practices, unique social relations, and institutional structures. These are explored in our next section on political subjectivity. The second aspect of pleasure's relationality is that it is shaped by what Neuburger (in this volume) calls "global consuming dialogues." That is, pleasure and displeasure also arise out of globally circulating images, goods, and practices, in what we may call, following Arjun Appadurai, a transnational *pleasure-scape*.[24] This second angle brings us directly to the question of backwardness. What part of Eastern Europe has been backward and what the nature of the backwardness is are themselves part of a question of relationality. Whether we view Eastern Europe in isolation from the rest of the world, as an entity unto itself, or as enmeshed in a particular and historically determined matrix of connections will imply different conclusions for how we view the progress it made in terms of living standards and the kinds of pleasures it afforded its citizens.[25] Do we compare its level of development to contemporaneous Western capitalist countries, for example, measured in GDP per capita (by which measure it achieved only one-fourth of the record of the West)? Or do we look at its rate of growth, development, gender emancipation, or equality (as measured by a low Gini coefficient, for example) in which it often exceeded Western Europe? Or do we look at different measures of well-being altogether?

Socialist societies of Eastern Europe displayed a much greater variety of consumption pleasures than what is suggested by a simplistic focus on material and individual consumer goods. The spectrum of gratis or heavily subsidized free-time activities—such as chess and sports clubs, music education, two-week vacations, and workplace and school field trips, not to mention theater shows, concerts, movies, and books, all of which were not only cheap but practically foisted upon citizens—created a rather different context in which individual consumer goods (Western or otherwise) came to acquire meaning and significance. While collective consumption (of health care, education, housing, cafeterias, and so on) did not always achieve the quality and quantitative availability the party-state or citizens wished for—and in many areas of consumption, such as transportation, it seemed to have failed—as György Péteri reminds us in discussing the fate of Khrushchev's ideas and policies of the "socialist car,"[26] the dominant presence of collective consumption thoroughly transformed the experience of shortages in individual consumer goods. It did not necessarily make it more bearable; in fact, it may have even created an expectation that the state should increase provisions in all areas of need. However, scholars of consumption simply cannot ignore the difference it made, and we should thus explore further distinctions between collective and immaterial goods, in addition to or, even better, in relation to the usual focus on private and material goods.

Furthermore, if we find consistently low performances on any of these indicators, do we attribute that to the communist ideology/political regime or to the fact that Eastern Europe occupied (occupies?) a particular structural location in the global economic and geopolitical context? Does the region's consumption record make more sense when studied from a Wallersteinian framework, being a semiperiphery region in a capitalist world system? The conflation of these factors is what the sociologist Judit Bodnár has called the "socialism package error": "A popular omission reproduced in the scheme of mirrored comparisons was the lack of global contextualization. Socialism emerged in a less developed part of the world, and due to its ideological weight all previous differences became conflated in the difference that socialism made. This was the second slip of the comparative mind, to which scholars and lay citizens fell prey: life was less glittery in the socialist part of the world not because it had been so even before but because of socialism and, consequently, the lack of free markets. Methodology-conscious comparativists would say the comparison was not controlled."[27] To rephrase our question, then, have Eastern European standards of living been comparatively lower (1) because the measures by which it appeared so reflect Western statistical practices that place capitalist countries in a more appealing light (for example, in terms of individual consumption of material goods, rather than immaterial and collective consumption such as cultural or health care consumption); (2) because Eastern Europe has had to struggle with a historical handicap, which in turn has been beneficial for the West to varying degrees in different periods; or (3) because of communist ideology and central planning that we tended to assume (falsely according to at least two of our authors, Patterson and Porter-Szűcs) was anticonsumption?

The global dialogue, continuing with Neuburger's metaphor, has not been conducted in the same language; commodities and meanings traveling back and forth are inserted in historically and locally specific contexts. There they relate to different understandings of the good life and a definition of the good society. Westerners may have seen tobacco smoking in the Ottoman Empire as barbarian, but, nonetheless, they eventually adopted it in slightly different and now socially consecrated forms. State socialism—with its low level of individual consumption, reliable and cheap public transportation, and quaint commodity-scape—was a coveted pilgrimage destination from the 1970s for Westerners with countercultural or anticapitalist and anticonsumerist leanings.[28] Eastern Europeans have also rejected Western pleasures with different ideological and moral undertones in different periods. Neuburger's claim about Bulgarian communists simultaneously blaming the West for their country's relative underdevelopment while not rejecting the goal of catching up with its standard of living is one example. As outlined by Cristofer Scarboro, Patterson, and Porter-Szűcs, the various discussions and often fierce debates held on all levels of society about the nature and extent of consumption in a socialist society also maintained a critical tone of Western consumerism, mostly fearing its alienating effects leaking through the Iron Curtain.

Yet, even in times of rationing, certain nonbasic commodities, such as tobacco, were seen as a rightful demand of the working class. Later, oranges and VCRs came to be accepted as goods that needed to be supplied routinely. Dietrich argues that complaints about the shortage or low quality of oranges, by then a standard staple of the Western diet, invoked not so much a catching up with relatives on the Western side of the German border but instead focused on the need for vitamin C. This insistence that these dietary needs be met resulted in tropical fruits being added to the list of goods the party-state *had* to deliver in consistent quantity and quality. VCRs were also on this road to being considered a necessity, however. This is evident from the fact that, as Patryk Wasiak demonstrates, Polish companies were instructed to manufacture VCRs to satisfy increasing consumer demand. Similarly, Bulakh's finding from post-Soviet Ukraine argues that the ability to buy certain Western brands, already common elsewhere in postsocialist Europe, has come to be seen as an entitlement or right Ukrainians as Europeans deserve and without which they feel like second-class citizens of the continent. However, even the individual strategies to consume one's way to Europeanness have a paradoxical effect on temporality: by buying only those Western brands that are available used or discounted, Ukrainians actually prefer the atemporality of brands to following the latest fashion.

Mainstream journalism and some scholars may have interpreted Eastern Europeans' seemingly insatiable appetite for Western goods as shallow materialism or as evidence of some innate human penchant for acquisitiveness. Forgotten in such views is the fact that political subject formation is always and everywhere strongly bound up with a sense of belonging and one's ability to participate in various aspects of social existence. Social existence in modern societies, in return, depends on consumption, often beyond the most basic needs. If the Polish sociologist Jadwiga Staniszkis is correct that Leninist ideology prevented citizens in state socialism from becoming political subjects, it is also true, in our view, that efforts to carve out some autonomy for oneself and one's kin often got expressed—however haltingly—in creative if seemingly irrational consumer practices, by which one could also assert one's belongingness to modernity.[29] Zsuzsa Gille and Diana Mincytė go even further in their contribution: they claim that to the extent that successful need satisfaction required active and routine work effort on the part of socialist consumers, their attitude to the world of commodities presaged current Western alternative consumer movements, thus reversing the backwardness claim and complicating the relationship between the socialist state and its subjects. In the next section, we explore this relationship between consumption and political subjectivity.

PLEASURE AND POLITICAL SUBJECTIVITY

However empirically fruitful socialist consumption studies have been, they have failed to incorporate some basic findings of the broader and admittedly West-oriented social science scholarship on consumption. First is the assumption underlying the key claim we referred to above—namely, that dissatisfaction over low consumption levels led to the demise of the communist regimes. Most often the reference point in consumption levels is that of the Western capitalist countries. There are two ways Eastern Europeans could have experienced dissatisfaction over their levels of consumption lagging behind the West's. One is that people on both sides of the Iron Curtain (or, in fact, everywhere) are born with the same needs that they prioritize in the same way. This has been effectively debunked in Western consumption studies, especially in critiques of Maslow's hierarchy of needs, arguing that needs are produced, not born with; that is, they arise in specific social and historical contexts. While people may be born with a certain minimum need for daily calorie intake, how much of that need manifests in a demand for sugar, for example, depends to a large extent on what is available, what is affordable, and what is culturally and socially desirable, all factors that Sidney Mintz carefully dissected in his classic opus on sweetness.[30] We thus need to pay more attention to who produces or directs the population's needs, and to what degree of success. In this volume, Dietrich and Patterson examine the agency and the biopolitical considerations behind need management in socialism.

The other way Eastern Europeans could end up with the same set of needs and same preferences as humans elsewhere is by being informed of the consumption levels of Western middle-class people, key sources of which were the media, Western cultural products (films, TV shows), their own trips to the West, and relatives and tourists visiting them. Of course, we acknowledge the impact that knowledge of or, better said, glimpses of Western consumer goods and lifestyles had on Eastern Europeans' desires—see our section on global consuming dialogues above. However, it is one thing to recognize exposure to the Western consumer world, and it is another to claim that Easterners aspired to achieve it. Empirical evidence of Eastern European tourists shopping in the West and of the food, drink, clothing, music, or home decor items being proudly exhibited only confirms what is obvious: when people travel, they shop. Not tangentially, tourists from Czechoslovakia shopped in Hungary and vice versa as well. To construe this pleasure of acquiring unusual if not exotic commodities abroad as envy, as a desire for capitalism, is a logical fallacy. Many have written about how it was the illicitness of Western goods that made them all the more desirable, not necessarily that they were lacking in the East or that they were better.

To better demonstrate this, I (Zsuzsa Gille) relate a few examples from my childhood in socialist Hungary. We had distant relatives in Canada, who once had sent me a skirt suit. I was probably six years old, and, as you can guess, six-year-old girls never wore nor did they ever desire skirt suits. I was even more baffled by the color of this suit: it was bright pink with light green geometric embroidery that got snagged on something the first time I wore it. I was not eager to don it, however, not only because I had to be extra careful but also because I thought it was just plain ugly. In addition, nobody ever wore hot pink in socialist Hungary, and I felt that I stood out like a sore thumb whenever I wore it. Luckily my mother agreed, so soon the suit got safely tucked away in the back of my closet.

Another strange commodity I received as a gift was from one of my father's colleagues, brought back from a business trip in Paris: banana shake granules. I was about eight. The package looked promising: it was in a wavy see-through plastic jar with a beautifully colored label and bright blue plastic cap on it. The friend translated the preparation instructions to my mother ("Just mix it with either water or milk"). I looked on with much interest as she unscrewed the lid—surprisingly finding an additional barrier of aluminum foil under it—and as she poured a spoonful of granules into a glass. Despite the odd smell I bravely took a sip: I almost spat it out because it tasted so bad. Perhaps if I had had lower expectations of how wonderful it would taste, I wouldn't have reacted so badly. It wasn't just the strangeness of mixing fruit with milk (even if mixed with water the taste was milky), since back then Hungarians had not yet heard of fruit smoothies or shakes. It was also that while I liked bananas and while the drink certainly tasted of banana, I did not quite understand why one would want to drink a banana powder mix when one could just eat a banana. In my recollection, bananas were never quite the shortage items (by the early 1970s) they had once been or as they may have continued to be in other socialist countries. I think my mother may have tried to encourage me to try it again, but since she and my father did not like it either the gorgeous plastic jar with its oddly shaped light-yellow content took up residency on our kitchen counter for many months and then in our cupboard for years.

In both cases, I had a variety of ambivalent feelings surrounding these Western commodities: (1) I was glad to have received something new; (2) I was glad to have something no one had; (3) I was excited to try them; (4) I forced myself to "use" these exotic goods; (5) despite "knowing" that I was supposed to like them because they were from the West, I simply could not bring myself to consume them; (6) I felt guilty for not being able to enjoy them; (7) I, along with my parents, could not bring ourselves to throw them out for many years; (8) since I did not personally meet Westerners until I was fifteen or sixteen, for many years I tried to imagine these odd creatures who wore hot pink and drank banana powder drinks, and I simply could not decide whether there was something wrong with me or with them.

This is, of course, not to say that other Western goods, especially those I later could pick out for myself, were failures as well. It is, however, to illustrate that the pleasures they caused could be moderated by certain ambivalent feelings and that such pleasures resulted more from their novelty than from their quality or their sheer ability to satisfy a need. Of course, we also have much ethnographic evidence of how certain Western goods, or at least their packaging, took on a different meaning and caused different pleasures for non-Westerners than they did for Westerners. People living under socialism proudly exhibited empty bottles of whiskey, occasionally turning them into lamps; children collected and traded wrappers from French chewing gums; women used soap wrappers as scents, placing them in closets and dressers. While these may be seen as examples of idolizing Western consumption, they also demonstrate how the uses of and thus pleasures derived from such products were quite different from what they were originally meant for. One could easily derive such pleasures without actually wanting to drink whiskey or chew bubble gum. (I personally hated the soapy taste of the French brand of chewing gum, but I liked the funnies they were wrapped in.)[31]

As these examples already hint at, such rare Western consumer items caused pleasure by mediating or facilitating social relations—another finding that scholars of consumption studies have tended to ignore. Elizabeth Chin's consumption ethnography beautifully demonstrates how this social function manifests in the United States today. In her study, it is the absence of certain commodities—namely, toys—that prevents poor black children from building friendships or even just interacting with peers.[32] When such goods can be taken for granted, we tend to ignore how they lubricate or sometimes are outright necessary for making connections with others. Owning certain things makes it possible or easier to participate in society, and thus such products are crucial for one's sense of citizenship—whether we like this or not. The late Daphne Berdahl argued this when she analyzed how Ossies (former Eastern German citizens) reacted to not being able to afford shopping on the main street of the town they had always lived in after unification.[33] Similarly, we could say that in state socialism, too, having Western goods—or even just socialist replicas of Western goods, as was increasingly the case from the mid-1970s on (for example, cheeses and jeans in Hungary or VCRs in Poland [see chap. 6])—allowed certain social relationships to develop. Owning a Frank Zappa LP in the early 1980s, as my high-school boyfriend did, allowed for connections with certain youth and allowed new proto subcultures to develop—we then became regular attendees at Hungarian underground music concerts. It was not just following and discussing the lyrics and tasting and retasting the novel musical experience Zappa provided that generated new practices and pleasures; it was the product's very illicitness. My boyfriend's rock band certainly was much inspired by Zappa. Zappa is actually a good example to mention here, because it was the title of his song equating comfortable bourgeois life as lived according to mainstream US consumerist norms with fascism that the Czechoslovakian underground band, the Plastic People of the Universe, took as its name. Václav Havel, as a devout fan, invited Zappa to be his first official foreign guest after being elected the first independent president of Czechoslovakia. Despite the conversion of East and West in producing "plastic people" assumed by this much persecuted band,[34] and despite the transformative effect consumption of Western musical products, even those of a radical critic, such as Zappa, had in his country, Havel would have subscribed to the assumption Patterson in this volume criticizes as the zero sum of consumption and critical political consciousness. Instead, as we will show, consuming certain Western goods could also open up consciousness critical of consumerism, whether in the West or in the East. As this unusual example shows, what political subjectivities may have resulted from the social relationships or the practices such commodities made possible cannot be easily presumed and needs an empirical and theoretically more nuanced study.

To conclude then, the scholarship on the relation between consumer (dis)pleasure and politics in Eastern Europe needs to ask the following: (1) What is the nature of this (dis)pleasure? (2) By what mechanism, if any, does it result in a certain political subjectivity? And (3) what ideological orientation, if any, does such a political subjectivity possess?

Political subjectivity is not only or not directly caused by shortages or a sense of lagging behind the West's levels of consumption. As Gille and Mincytė show, people dealt with shortages or low-quality goods; that is, the practices of making do played a role as well. People's experience of their own capacity to survive and thrive despite shortcomings in state provisions elevated their sense of autonomy in an otherwise oppressive system aimed at creating dependence on a centralized authority. While, as Paulina Bren demonstrates, the dissident intelligentsia of Czechoslovakia was dismissive of these acts of "self-realization," to which they counterpoised their own ethics of "let me be," it is exactly their elitism that doomed their anticonsumerist and antimaterialist agenda. Of course, as we know from studies of the second economy and blat,[35] not all had equal ability to build such independence but that such a capacity was important in people's image of themselves and others cannot be denied. Scarboro demonstrates that the Bulgarian party-state may have indeed encouraged such independence by issuing dozens of publications dedicated to do-it-yourself projects.

As Bulakh shows, consumers, especially young women, take pride in their ability to end their dependency on low-quality mass clothing that most others are forced to buy in the absence of Western fashion chains. There are a variety of practices by which their autonomy—as citizens qua consumers—is expanded, all of which require additional energy, time, and money.

Furthermore, the effect of consumer dissatisfaction cannot be reduced to diminished regime legitimacy. While it is true that the party-state made itself exclusively in charge of providing for the population, people had a rather differentiated view of whom to blame for shortages or shoddy commodities. Articles and letters distinguish between high- and low-level party leadership and economic management, high- and low-level administration, workers and enterprise directors, salespersons and ministry officials. Consumers' own work experience informed and complicated the us-them dichotomy we tended to take for granted in state socialism. My (Gille's) mother, for example, who certainly was taken advantage of at her workplace and who saw a lot of management problems, always argued that it was not the party and its ideology that were at fault but the people who were in charge of realizing the party's objectives. My father, in contrast, criticized the party but not the employees or lower-level administrators.

We also must keep in mind that consumer dissatisfaction was tempered by a series of comparisons. People with memories of prewar or wartime deprivation certainly were aware of the tremendous amount of progress that had been made in elevating living standards and economic certainty in their own lifetime. But even younger people could make certain contrasts, if not with the past, then with other, less fortunate socialist countries. Trips to Romania and later to Poland especially served as stark warnings of how much worse it could be. What Milica Bakić-Hayden termed *nested Orientalisms*—a sense that it is always worse or more backward, if not outright barbaric, further east—was here bolstered by experiences of intrabloc connections.[36] Hungarians who lived under Kádár and many of whom had relatives in Transylvania always talked in tones of lament and pride about how bad things were "over there," and their ability to help kin out with mostly food items (we took bread and coffee to our relatives in Arad) forged ambivalent relations to the regime, while ironically often replicating the Western patronization and condescension that oozed out of Western care packages after the war.

Finally, even if people were aware of how much better most people in Western capitalist countries lived, there was a surprising level of self-reflexivity about socialist consumption. There were regular and public—both official and unofficial—discourses on what legitimate, appropriate, authentic needs were or how much tastes and styles should be allowed to diverge in a society that was working toward communism. In our volume, both Porter-Szűcs and Patterson analyze these instances. The official discourse, as a sui generis understanding of state socialism's self-understanding will readily reveal, made a distinction between objective and subjective needs. While informal everyday (often judgmental) conversations concerning what a neighbor bought for how much money, for example, did not adopt this distinction, people could freely talk not just about shortages and quality problems, as many of the contributors to this volume suggest, but also about what was a fair expectation, what was wasteful luxury, how picky someone could be, and what someone deserved for what performance. While participants in such discourses fell far from the ideal of an always collectively minded *Homo sovieticus*, there usually loomed in the background of such conversations a certain sense of a collective—whether in the form of a utopian highly developed socialist society, the nation, the debt owed to elders and the less fortunate, or at least future generations—that served as a loose reference point in evaluating consumer demands and practices.

―⁂―

To develop the above themes, chapters in this volume explore different aspects of what has constituted a good life in Eastern European societies and how it was experienced during the second half of the twentieth century and the beginning of the twenty-first. The volume begins with three chapters that take a broad view of consumption by locating it in global and political contexts. Neuburger offers a longue durée exploration of consumption in Bulgaria and Eastern Europe by showing how the region has always been a part of global exchanges that included the flows of objects and people. In Neuburger's analysis, Bulgarians emerge as active participants in "global consuming dialogues," where they have engaged with, experienced, and critiqued Western (and Eastern) goods and ideas. Porter-Szűcs's analysis of the role of consumer desire in socialist economics points to surprising parallels between professional economists and policy makers in the Polish People's Republic and their counterparts in the West. By developing consumer behavior theories that resonated with the underlying principles of supply-side economics, as Porter-Szűcs's chapter powerfully shows, socialist economists inadvertently prepared the grounds for the ascendance of neoliberalism far beyond the region.

Patterson's chapter takes us to Yugoslavia to explore the relationship between markets and civic engagement. Patterson asks provocatively, were growing consumption and improving standards of living a Faustian bargain that kept socialist workers from demanding political freedoms, or were they just rewards for hard work? In his reference to Lizabeth Cohen's work on the consumer republic, Patterson argues that unlike in the West, where consumption and citizenship were "conjoined without the total eclipse of citizenship," socialism developed an alternative political space for exercising citizenship—somewhat limited in its reach but also more dynamic and open for negotiations.

Extending the themes developed in the first set of chapters, the following three case studies examine how the political and social imaginaries of the good life have played out on the ground. Dietrich's analysis of coffee and tropical fruit consumption in East Germany examines how these products became politicized. Complementing Patterson's critical analysis of the social contract,

Dietrich tracks consumer coping strategies and institutional efforts to supply socialist citizens with what had become staples of socialist kitchen tables. Dietrich captures the interplays and complicated feedback mechanisms between the state and the daily lives and expectations of its citizens. Similarly, Wasiak studies the social lives of VCRs in 1980s Poland as a site for negotiating the place of consumer desire and the spirit of entrepreneurship in socialism. Wasiak develops the notion of "consumption space" to denote the places and practices through which socialist consumers constructed their identities and belonged to a social milieu. The question of belonging is also key in Bulakh's chapter, which examines clothes shopping in postsocialist Ukraine. Bulakh argues that by consuming global brands, middle-class Ukrainians are negotiating not only their individual social status but also Ukraine's place and its future on the political map of Europe.

The last two chapters, authored by the editors of this volume, combine the insights developed in previous chapters to return to and expand on the themes of modernity (and its different socialist and capitalist incarnations), backwardness, pleasure, and desire. Scarboro shows that the search for beauty was an important ingredient in the larger narrative of the socialist good life in Bulgaria. More broadly, Scarboro's chapter examines surprising parallel developments in capitalism and socialism—the formation of the middle class as defined by acquiescence, consumer pleasures, and the abandonment of the more radical ideals of previous generations. In so doing, this chapter pictures the post–World War II world not as a theater where the Cold War played out but as a space where the new generation grappled with the contradictions and challenges of living in modernity.

Echoing Scarboro, Gille and Mincytė's chapter critiques the teleological view of modernization that portrays Eastern Europe as backward. The authors make a case that socialist consumption was organized in significantly different ways leading to more authentic, postmaterialist experiences of consumption unaccompanied by fetishism or alienation. This chapter points to a paradox in that what were long considered signs of backwardness (DIY culture, recycling/no waste approaches, or collective forms of consumption) have now become the avant garde of the emerging global consumer culture and perhaps even one of the few remaining pathways toward addressing today's challenges.

Taken together, our volume opens up a new line of research inquiry that broadens the meaning of development and of consumption, thereby reinterpreting their relationship with the formation of political subjectivity in state socialism. As such, it provides a solid foundation for future scholarship aimed at a more nuanced and relational approach to postsocialism, globalization, and Europeanization. Our hope is that making newly visible the ethical pillars of socialist development and desire, we will also contribute to empirically grounded but theoretically informed understandings of recent antidemocratic and anti-Western trends in East European politics.

NOTES

1. Crowley and Reid, *Pleasures in Socialism*.
2. Schissler, *Miracle Years*.
3. Bell, *Bulgarian Communist Party*, 133. See also Znepolski, *Narodna Republika Bulgaria*.
4. Bell, *Bulgarian Communist Party*, 134.
5. Dinev, *Socialist Life and Culture*.
6. The source of these data is the Hungarian Central Statistical Bureau (Központi Statisztikai Hivatal); other noncommunist sources seem to confirm these numbers for Western and some Eastern European countries. See for example Kanerva, *Meat Consumption in Europe*; and *The Guardian*, "Meat Consumption per Capita."
7. Központi Statisztikai Hivatal, *A lakossági fogyasztás nemzetközi adatai*.
8. Schapiro and Godson, *Soviet Worker*, quoted in Nintl, "Soviet Union."
9. Béla, *A XX, Század magyar gazdaságpolitikája*.
10. Siegelbaum, *Socialist Car*.
11. Berend, *From the Soviet Bloc*.
12. This is perhaps best outlined in Fehérváry, *Politics in Color*.
13. Scarboro, "Today's Unseen Enthusiasm."
14. Scarboro, *Late Socialist Good Life*.
15. Committee of Culture, *Comprehensive Programme*, 10–11. This understanding of human nature was intended to supplant the conception that prevailed in the liberal democratic capitalist world. As Boris Tsenkov explains: "The bourgeois ideologists and all types of anticommunists assert that the development of the new man under socialism is a sheer utopia. Man, they say and write, is by nature an egoist, thirsting for money and power—in brief, man is an unchangeable quantity." Tsenkov, *Socialist Revolution*, 36.
16. "The development of the socialist productive forces and of the new social relations, though an important task, does not exhaust the content of the socialist revolution and is not the main aim of socialist construction. All that merely serves as a means of emancipating man from all political, economic and spiritual bondage and exploitation. In building up the material foundations of socialist society, socialist construction develops the productive forces on a large scale, forms material conditions for the realization, existence and development of the socialist system which alone achieves man's complete emancipation—the main

aim of the socialist revolution." Obretenov, *Cultural Revolution in Bulgaria*, 17. See also Murawski, "Actually-Existing Success."

17. In *The German Ideology*, Marx pointed the way to the end point of history—a world where one could hunt in the morning, rear cattle in the evening, and criticize after dinner (Marx and Engels, *Collected Works*, vol. 5, *Theses on Feuerbach: The German Ideology and Related Manuscripts*). From the Committee of Culture:

> First, increasing the attraction of labor as a fundamental human activity. The liberation from exploitation, the achievements in socialist construction, the moral and material incentives towards socially useful labor, the Party's overall ideological work, all brought about new material conditions and a new socio-psychological climate, causing a breakthrough in the attitude to labor on the part of all strata of the population. The idea that every able-bodied citizen must work dominates unconditionally through the country. Nevertheless, we are still far from the socio-economic state in which the conditions for labor and the processes of labor itself have an attractive force of their own, on par with that which is now exercised by the sports fields and stadiums, concert halls and other places for free and unrestricted play of man's physical and intellectual powers. Which means that the need for society to consciously orientate its members towards labor and to maintain and evolve a positive attitude to it still exists objectively. The existence of this need is further shown by the diverse expressions of consumerism on the part of some people, especially among teenagers. (Committee of Culture, *Comprehensive Programme*, 76)

18. "Compared to the political and economic revolution, the cultural revolution is more prolonged because the bourgeois ideology, the bourgeois consciousness in general cannot be rapidly replaced by a completely new, socialist ideology and consciousness.... No decrees can compel people to substitute the socialist mode of thinking for the bourgeois one." Tsenkov, *Socialist Revolution*, 10–11.

19. "The socialist state sets aside substantial funds for the development of the extra-production sphere, funds that are roughly equal to one quarter of the national income. The dimensions in absolute terms show that there is a considerable annual increase of funds as a result of the average annual growth of the national income, and parallel with it of the chief source for the maintenance of the extra-production sphere, the social consumption funds. Over the past 40 years there has been a fast increase in the social consumption funds spent on the development of culture, education, science, the public health services, social security, physical education, sport and hiking. In 1952–1978 alone that increase was 15 times against a ten-fold increase in the national income.... The funds set aside for public health services were up 17 times for the same period, for pensions 18 times, for benefits and social security 20 times, for culture 11 times, and for education nearly 10 times." Dinev, *Socialist Life and Culture*, 8–9.

Of particular note were the moves toward education: "Today [1964] more than 1,600,000 people are enrolled in various educational institutions. This means that every fifth citizen in Bulgaria attends a school." During 1944–64, 1,800 new schools were built. That year saw 150,000 students living in new hostels and 120,000 working people taking correspondence courses ("without leaving their work"). The state provided 300 general education evening schools with 40,000 students and 40 evening technical schools with 28,000 students. During 1944–64, more than 500,000 adults enrolled in literacy programs. Denju Vasilev claims that illiteracy was eliminated in Bulgaria by the early 1960s. Vasilev, *Bulgarian Culture*, 10–11.

20. Tsenkov, *Socialist Revolution*, 31.
21. Committee of Culture, *Comprehensive Programme*, 24–25.
22. Marx, *Critique of the Gotha*.
23. Lampland, *Object of Labor*.
24. Appadurai, *Modernity at Large*.
25. Emirbayer, "Manifesto."
26. This would have included a state-owned and operated rental car service and a much denser network of public transportation. See Péteri, "Introduction," 8–9.
27. Bodnár, "Socialism Package Error." See also Murawski, "Actually-Existing Success."
28. See examples in the rightfully critiqued Hollander, *Political Pilgrims*.
29. Staniszkis, *Dynamics of the Breakthrough*.
30. Mintz, *Sweetness and Power*.
31. It is important to note that experiences of the consumption of Western goods were not uniform across the region. Many citizens of the Soviet Union, for example, might have not even tasted a banana or coffee. But, as we argued above, the absence of these food commodities alone tells us little about what was desirable or what generated pleasure in this part of the world.
32. Chin, *Purchasing Power*.
33. Berdahl, *Social Life of Postsocialism*.
34. See Bren, *The Greengrocer and His TV*.
35. See Ledeneva, *Russia's Economy of Favors* and Vihavainen and Bogdanova, eds., *Communism and Consumerism*.
36. Péteri, "Introduction," makes a similar point.

REFERENCES

Appadurai, Arjun. *Modernity at Large: Cultural Dimensions of Globalization*. Minneapolis: University of Minnesota Press, 1996.
Béla, Csikós-Nagy. *A XX. század magyar gazdaságpolitikája*. Budapest: Akadémiai Kiadó, 1996.

Bell, John D. *The Bulgarian Communist Party from Blagoev to Zhivkov.* Stanford, CA: Hoover Institution, 1986.

Berdahl, Daphne. *On the Social Life of Postsocialism: Memory, Consumption, Germany.* Edited by Matti Bunzl. Bloomington: Indiana University Press, 2009.

Berend, Ivan. *From the Soviet Bloc to the European Union: The Economic and Social Transformation of Central and Eastern Europe since 1973.* New York: Cambridge University Press, 2009.

Bodnár, Judit. "The Socialism Package Error." *European Studies Forum* 39, no. 1 (2009): 23–28.

Bren, Paulina. *The Greengrocer and His TV: The Culture of Communism after the 1968 Prague Spring.* Ithaca, NY: Cornell University Press, 2010.

Chin, Elizabeth. *Purchasing Power: Black Kids and American Consumer Culture.* Minneapolis: University of Minnesota Press, 2001.

Committee of Culture. *Comprehensive Programme for Nationwide Aesthetic Education: Adopted at the 8th Extended Plenum of the Committee of Art and Culture, Sofia, December 1975.* Sofia: Sofia Press, 1980.

Crowley, David, and Susan E. Reid, eds. *Pleasures in Socialism: Leisure and Luxury in the Eastern Bloc.* Evanston, IL: Northwestern University Press, 2010.

Dinev, Mihail. *Socialist Life and Culture.* Sofia: Sofia Press, 1984.

Emirbayer, Mustafa. "Manifesto for a Relational Sociology." *American Journal of Sociology* 103, no. 2 (September 1997): 281–317.

Fehérváry, Krisztina. *Politics in Color and Concrete: Socialist Materialities and the Middle Class in Hungary.* Bloomington: Indiana University Press, 2013.

The Guardian. "Meat Consumption per Capita." Datablog, September 2, 2009. https://www.theguardian.com/environment/datablog/2009/sep/02/meat-consumption-per-capita-climate-change.

Hollander, Paul. *Political Pilgrims: Travels of Western Intellectuals to the Soviet Union, China, and Cuba, 1928–1978.* Oxford: Oxford University Press, 1981.

Kanerva, Minna. *Meat Consumption in Europe: Issues, Trends and Debates.* Artec-Paper 187, Universität Bremen, 2013. https://www.uni-bremen.de/fileadmin/user_upload/sites/artec/Publikationen/artec_Paper/187_paper.pdf.

Központi Statisztikai Hivatal (KSH). *A lakossági fogyasztás nemzetközi adatai.* Central Statistical Bureau of Hungary. Budapest: Központi Statisztikai Hivatal, 1980.

Lampland, Martha. *The Object of Labor: Commodification of Socialist Labor.* Chicago: University of Chicago Press, 1995.

Ledeneva, Alena. *Russia's Economy of Favors: Blat, Networking and Informal Exchange.* Cambridge: Cambridge University Press, 1998.

Marx, Karl. *Critique of the Gotha Program.* 1891. New York: International, 1938.

Marx, Karl, and Friedrich Engels, *Collected Works of Karl Marx and Friedrich Engels, 1845–47.* Vol. 5, *Theses on Feuerbach: The German Ideology and Related Manuscripts.* New York: International Publishers, 1976.

Mintz, Sidney W. *Sweetness and Power: The Place of Sugar in Modern History*. New York: Viking Penguin, 1985.
Murawski, Michał. "Actually Existing Success: Economics, Aesthetics, and the Specificity of (Still-)Socialist Urbanism." *Comparative Studies in Society and History* 60, no. 4 (2018): 907–37.
Obretenov, Aleksandur. *The Cultural Revolution in Bulgaria*. Translated by Mihail Shipkov. Sofia: Sofia Press, 1966.
Péteri, György. "Introduction." In *Imagining the West in Eastern Europe and the Soviet Union*, edited by György Péteri, 1–12. Pittsburgh, PA: University of Pittsburgh Press, 2010.
Scarboro, Cristofer. *The Late Socialist Good Life in Bulgaria: Meaning and Living in a Permanent Present Tense*. Lanham, MD: Lexington Books, 2011.
———. "Today's Unseen Enthusiasm: Communist Nostalgia for Communism." In *Post-Communist Nostalgia*, edited by Maria Todorova and Zsuzsa Gille, 46–60. Oxford: Berghahn, 2010.
Schapiro, Leonard, and Joseph Godson, eds. *The Soviet Worker: Illusions and Realities*. London: MacMillan, 1981.
Schissler, Hanna, ed. *The Miracle Years: A Cultural History of West Germany, 1949–1968*. Princeton, NJ: Princeton University Press, 2001.
Siegelbaum, Lewis H., ed. *The Socialist Car: Automobility in the Eastern Bloc*. Ithaca, NY: Cornell University Press, 2011.
Staniszkis, Jadwyga. *Dynamics of the Breakthrough in Eastern Europe: The Polish Experience*. Translated by Chester A. Kisiel. Berkeley: University of California at Berkeley Press, 1991.
Nintl. "The Soviet Union: The Food Consumption Puzzle." Nintl, last modified May 11, 2016. https://nintil.com/2016/05/11/the-soviet-union-food/.
Tsenkov, Boris. *Socialist Revolution and Socialist Culture*. Sofia: Sofia Press, 1971.
Vasilev, Denju. *Bulgarian Culture: Old and New*. Sofia: Foreign Languages, 1964.
Vihavainen, Timo, and Elena Bogdanova, eds. *Communism and Consumerism: The Soviet Alternative to the Affluent Society*. Leiden, Netherlands: Brill Academic, 2016.
Znepolski, Ivaylo, ed. *Narodna Republika Bulgaria: Ot nachaloto do kraia*. Sofia: Ciela Press, 2011.

AUTHOR BIO

ZSUZSA GILLE is Professor of Sociology and Director of Global Studies at the University of Illinois at Urbana-Champaign. She is author of *Paprika, Foie Gras, and Red Mud: The Politics of Materiality in the European Union* (2016) and *From the Cult of Waste to the Trash Heap of History: The Politics of Waste in Socialist and Postsocialist Hungary* (2007—recipient of honorable mention of the AAASS Davis Prize), coeditor of *Post-Communist Nostalgia* with Maria Todorova (2010), and coauthor of *Global Ethnography: Forces, Connections and Imaginations in a Postmodern World* (2000). She was the special guest editor of a thematic cluster on "Nature, Culture, Power" (2009) published in the *Slavic Review*.

CRISTOFER SCARBORO is Professor of History at King's College in Wilkes-Barre, Pennsylvania. He is author of *The Late Socialist Good Life in Bulgaria: Living and Meaning in a Permanent Present Tense* (2011). His current research focuses on consumption and boredom in late socialist Bulgaria.

DIANA MINCYTĖ is Associate Professor of Sociology at the City University of New York's New York City College of Technology. She publishes on environmental and social dimensions of agro-food politics in Eastern Europe. She coedited a number of special issues in journals, including a thematic cluster with Ulrike Plath on environmental and food politics in the Baltic states that received the Vilis Vitols best publication award from the Association for the Advancement of Baltic Studies and was republished as *Food Culture and Politics in the Baltic States* (2017).

TWO

CONSUMING DIALOGUES

Pleasure, Restraint, Backwardness, and Civilization in Eastern Europe

MARY NEUBURGER

Eastern Europe seems to be stuck in a state of perpetual and incomplete transition, or "backwardness."[1] One can refute that such a state has prevailed in certain parts of the region, and of course one can question exactly what it means to be backward.[2] Nevertheless, the state or idea of backwardness has certainly haunted the region as a subject of scholarly study and debate and, perhaps more importantly, as a specter for local actors to lament, embrace, or directly confront.[3] The very notion of backwardness, needless to say, is a modern one, a necessary counterpart to the idea of progress, which is generally measured by a set of economic and social indicators.[4] By these criteria, Eastern Europe—along with most of the rest of the world—is inevitably cast as perpetually unfinished, a descriptor that these states, nations, and regions have grappled with in their own individual ways. But arbitrary and wholly aesthetic considerations have been used to assess modernity as well, immeasurable qualities that were also scrutinized and tracked. Beginning in the eighteenth century, and more widely in the nineteenth, a growing preoccupation with the notion of civilization relied heavily on the patterns and practices of consumption as measures of cultural superiority (reputedly tied to progress).[5] While the notion of civilization was always complex and contested, what people ate and drank and how they dressed were arguably as important as infrastructure, trade, or literacy in external (and in some cases) internal determinations of backwardness and civilization.

Historical transformations in consuming practices are central to what scholars have dubbed the "civilizing process" in Western Europe.[6] The bulk of the scholarship on global consumption has sought to trace the centrality of the emergence of an "exceptional" consumer society in the West and its spread to other parts of the world.[7] Such developments are seen as having been integral to the rise of modern capitalism, or indeed of modernity itself, either explaining it or being explained by it. Efforts to decenter such Eurocentric (and, for a later period, Americentric) scholarly narratives have gained momentum in recent decades. A number of scholars have presented compelling research that refutes the notion of the West as the singular source for the birth, development, or expansion of consumer societies.[8] Yet in spite of such advances, the West remains at the center of the global story of consumption, and Eastern Europe (including Russia) is more often than not omitted.[9] This is no doubt in part because, despite the significant body of work that has been produced on the layered aspects of consumption in the Soviet Union and postwar Eastern Europe, the longer historical trajectory of consumer patterns in the region has not been subjected to intensive study.[10] In addition, at least for historians of commodities and consumption, scholarship connecting the first and second worlds is much weaker than that tying the first and the third. As a result, Eastern Europe and, to a lesser extent, Russia have largely been left out of global studies of consumption, and transnational or globally contextualized work on the region is sparse.[11]

A more integrated look at patterns of consumption in Eastern Europe and how they emerged as part of what I call global "consuming dialogues" can help to shed light on the forms of consumption—consumerist and otherwise—that have shaped the modern world. Here I want to explore the ways in which such dialogues not only led to ever-greater levels of consumption but also worked to delimit the parameters of socially acceptable (and often politicized) modes of consuming.[12] The historical specificity of such culturally constructed checks on consuming practices was arguably as important to the making of modern consumer cultures as the phenomenon that propelled consumer desire and acquisitiveness across time and space. But both, it seems clear, were shaped in a kind of dialogue, or at least an intensive field of global interaction, within which East and West were critical though highly malleable (and arbitrary) operative categories.

Such binaries were especially powerful in much of Eastern Europe, with its particular position of relative scarcity, presumed backwardness, and purported lack of civilization vis-à-vis the West. This peripheral position created fertile ground for a variety of ideologies, movements, and narratives of restraint tied to critiques of the West and modernity and its materialistic consumerist ethos. Marxism, in both its Leninist and Stalinist guises, was one of those ideologies. And although this system was imposed under Soviet occupation in much of the region, socialist experiments were also able to appropriate and capitalize on local resistances to the West. These states implemented redistributive and restrained regimes of consumption under the larger umbrella of "building socialism," tied to condemnation of the West and capitalist consumerism. And yet their own notion of rational consumption allowed for a veritable revolution in consuming practices—in part tied to their own internal modernizing and civilizing processes.

State socialism was established in a wide variety of contexts, each with its own contested notions, narratives, movements, and ideologies around consuming practices—its own culture wars. So even as socialism was "imposed" with varying degrees of force across the region, its message resonated with large segments of the population. Marxism, as locally interpreted and articulated, was seen as reining in injurious and predatory modes of consumption. At the same time, it was able to provide basic consumer goods and services and eventually some luxury items, paving the way for a postwar culture of consent, similar in many respects to the one that developed in the West in the same period. To various degrees, then, these regimes were successful in mobilizing notions of consumer restraint and discontent at the same time that they stoked a desire to acquire new goods on a mass scale. That is to say, consumption was as critical to the ability of such regimes to assume and maintain power as it was to their eventual collapse—when their populations' newly created expectations could no longer be met.

CONSUMING EAST AND WEST

In the past two decades, scholarship has increasingly engaged the question of how the West defined the East, including Eastern Europe and most notably the Balkans.[13] More recently, scholars have begun to look at how Easterners have defined their own nations in relation to the notional West.[14] But few such studies have focused on consumption or the key ways in which consumer patterns, aspirations, and modes of restraint influenced the larger mappings and unwrappings of backwardness and civilization that reinforced or, in some cases, undermined the problematic yet powerful categories of East (or Orient) and West.[15] Consumption was always a powerful subtext of Western narratives on the East and Eastern views of the West, which accelerated and evolved in the modern period, before and during the Cold War.

In consumption studies, much ink has been spilled in explaining the rise and singularity of Western consumerism as an integral part of modernity—as either cause or result.[16] While newer work has done much to complicate such approaches, it has not displaced the tendency to explain consumption in light of Western exceptionalism or, in a more critical vein, dominance. Whether Western consumer patterns are embraced or deplored, in other words, they are seen as having originated, ripened, and then been exported as part of colonial "civilizing missions" or as desired by "imitating" global consumers.[17] Arguments in the consumption literature tend to roughly map onto more general arguments about the West and modernity, which point to favorable geography and other accidents of history but nevertheless rely on a well-worn set of cultural arguments—namely, that the impulses and results of the Renaissance and Reformation, hearkening back to the cradle of the ancients, drove an innovative capitalist Western civilization that was tied to an acquisitive consumer revolution.[18] Of even more significance for thinking about consumption, scholars have argued that the ascendance of the West was in large part a result of its ability not only to foster conditions of abundance but to thriftily manage modes of consumption. In Western Europe and its cultural heir the United States, personal sublimation, thrift, and hard work were the presumed Protestant underpinnings of both the civilizing process and progress.[19] Indeed, some have argued that Western creativity was not born out of an embrace of wanton consumption but, on the contrary, emerged as a result of Western modes or technologies of bodily repression.[20] For scholars of consumption, the Protestant ethos in its Western context was connected to transforming goods and their modes of consumption from "Oriental" or "savage" into "productive" and "modern" forms.[21] Numerous scholars have argued that Western consumer culture emerged and evolved in the shadow of debates about morality, social justice, and the politics of consumption.[22] As the modern West created ever greater abundance and consumer possibilities, various narratives of critique, if not repression, began to crystalize. Historically, a range of critical thinkers, perhaps most famously Thorstein Veblen and Karl Marx, railed against the evils of wasteful consumer culture and "commodity fetishism."[23] As part of a middle-class critique of aristocratic excess, the upper bourgeoisie also became the object of political rancor, given that their new wealth was seen as a cause or symptom of new kinds of inequities.

Yet, as a growing body of scholarship has begun to trace, neither the centrality of consumption in Western culture nor the subsequent criticism of it developed in isolation. Western consumer culture was built on the bedrock of imported Oriental and New World goods and consumer practices, such as smoking tobacco, drinking coffee and tea, and using soap. As greater numbers of people were able to participate in world travel, Westerners consumed the Other abroad and then brought such products and practices home with them.

Arguably, tourism itself was an act of consumption, with consumerist consequences, but so too were the voluminous writings sent back home and served up to hungry publics, who could thereby consume the Other vicariously, if they were not able to experience it directly, through exotic imports. Such writings offered detailed descriptions and assessments of local host cultures and their relative levels of civilization, which in many cases shaped or reinforced notions of Western propriety and restraint. This fueled further denunciations of consumer practices, not just of the upper bourgeoisie but also of the "uncivilized" or unrestrained lower classes. Indeed, the West's critiques of its own consumer practices reflected its experiences with outside cultures. Hence, even as the "savage East" was being delimited in the Western imagination, it became a key subtext for Western notions of propriety and restraint.

Eastern Europe and Russia were definitively part of this East for some, while for others they constituted a puzzling zone of in-betweenness on the outer limits of Europe. As in the larger East, notions of consumer desire and restraint were central to the mapping of Eastern Europe. In *Inventing Eastern Europe*, Larry Wolff describes the French count Louis-Philippe de Ségur's impressions of late eighteenth-century Poland—its "inconceivable mélange" of poverty and riches, of "Oriental luxury" and "scarcity," of "passion for war" and "aversion to discipline."[24] Indeed, for many Western observers in the modern period, "Eastern barbarity" was linked to a purported lack of discipline. Westerners, of course, were divided in the ways in which they characterized or assessed "Oriental luxury," as well as in how they mapped the Orient onto the various subregions of Europe's outer reaches.

The Ottoman Balkans were undeniably the most intertwined with the Orient in the Western mind. Western travelers delighted in and identified with the Oriental luxuries enjoyed by local elites, many of which were gradually appropriated into the Western consumer habitus. Class melded with (often politicized) Turkophile biases that cast elite Muslim consumer patterns as part of acceptable civilized practices.[25] At the same time, a recurring theme in European travel writings on the nineteenth-century Balkans is the image of the lazy "Oriental." Western industriousness was arguably a modern preoccupation, if not invention, that prompted observers to take note of what they saw as the idleness of Balkan men spending hours at the local coffeehouse or tavern.[26] Such observers were largely unaware that in the nineteenth century, the Ottoman coffeehouse was an important setting for cultural interchange and public affairs, a site where commercial transactions, guild meetings, and other kinds of productive activities took place.[27] (See fig. 2.1.) In short, the notion that the men they saw were merely sitting there idly came from a very narrow

Fig. 2.1. A café outside of a Mosque in Karlovo, Bulgaria, in the 1930s. From LostBulgaria.com. http://www.lostbulgaria.com/?p=222.

understanding of Ottoman coffeehouse culture, a culture that expanded from Muslims to Christians and Jews in the Ottoman Empire in the course of the nineteenth century.[28] In the end, however, the broad range of foreign writings and their assessment of Eastern consumption were far from monolithic. They reflect not only powerful narratives about Western superiority but also doubts about and criticism of Western civilization and its consumerist implications.[29]

Equally important, East Europeans were anything but passive recipients of Western demarcations of their relative level of civilization. There were resonances, but resistances also emerged from ongoing encounters (direct and indirect) with the West and its myriad of visitors and imports. In the midst of their own dramatic transformations in consumer practices, Easterners traveled both west and regionally and actively delineated East and West, not to mention their own nations, on and off the terrain of consumer practices. And while many echoed Western characterizations of their own cultures as backward and uncivilized, others saw Western consumer culture as grotesque and barbaric, totally lacking in restraint. Indeed, just as the East became a presumed example for Westerners of unrestrained modes of consumption, the West emerged in the same light under Eastern eyes.[30] While certain aspects of Western practices and narratives fueled local resentment and vehement correctives, others were appropriated or recast. Indeed, Western self-critiques of consumption practices at home provided ready ammunition for East European critiques of the West. For populists, socialists, and Slavophiles alike, the West was the epitome of predatory gluttony, a debased pursuit of the material over the spiritual, which benefited the few instead of contributing to the common good. Moreover, the West was seen as connected to East European excess, promoting imitative local gluttony and conspicuous consumption. Perhaps most importantly, Western indulgence, as connected to the capitalist economy, was seen as coming at the expense of others, including East Europeans.[31] However complicated this might have been given class differences and transnational class collaborations, the West was still the central figure, the insatiable and predatory threat to the East European periphery. Hence, for many, Western excess was largely to blame for East European scarcity and backwardness.

This kind of critique of the West, of course, was not merely (or essentially) East European; it had global reverberations. But for those who inhabited the edge of the chosen continent and could not fully participate in its glories—who were excluded as true citizens of it—the criticism played out in distinct and widely varied ways.[32] Across Eastern Europe, a spectrum of domestic narratives—as part of larger dialogues—explored, critiqued, and embraced a wide range of consumer practices. In each context, social conditions, political circumstances, and a range of cultural impulses colored and set the pace and parameters for responses to the new consumer patterns that were transforming East European life in the nineteenth and early twentieth centuries.

A VIEW FROM THE BULGARIAN PERIPHERY

In Bulgaria, as elsewhere in the region, narratives on consumption and modernity evolved in the shadow of a specific set of political and social concerns and historical dynamics in relation to both West and East. Certainly the new Bulgarian elites of the nineteenth and early twentieth centuries harbored a desire to "catch up" with and in a certain sense emulate the West, including many of its seductive forms of consumption. This longing was deeply connected to their desire to untangle themselves from the East after five hundred years of Ottoman rule.[33] And yet the most powerful Bulgarian narratives from this period were extremely critical of the West and, in particular, of the "aping" of foreign ways.[34] Such critiques were a reaction both to the gradual penetration of Western material forms and to the aspersions cast on Bulgarians in Western writings.

By the mid-1800s, Bulgarian elites had begun to produce their own domestic travel pieces, richly descriptive and opinionated writings in which they mapped the "Bulgarian lands"—responding to, providing correctives for, and sometimes mirroring certain foreign descriptions.[35] Consumption was an important theme in such works, which used foreign writings alternately as sources and as foils with which the authors sought to inculcate a new ethical, moral, and *national* outlook. Ottoman elite consumption was a particular concern and one that mirrored many foreign-produced, generally Orientalist discourses. Bulgarian travel writings or ethnographies of the late Ottoman period (1860s and 1870s) often described rapacious and gluttonous Ottoman elites lording over impoverished Christian peasants.[36] Liuben Karavelov's 1867–68 *Zapiski za Bulgaria i bulgarite* (Notes about Bulgaria and Bulgarians), for example, describes "Turkish beys who are drunk from morning till night" controlling the best arable lands.[37] Karavelov's rather impassioned portrayal of "Turkish" gluttony and drunkenness at the expense of impoverished Bulgarians was foundational to Bulgarian revival narratives around the moral economy of consumption and, in particular, of food consumption.[38] For Karavelov, as for other authors of the national revival period (late eighteenth century to 1878), there was a clear sense that five centuries of Ottoman rule had brought backwardness to the region and economic ruin to the Bulgarian peasantry.

Yet these narratives also generally implicate the Western world in Bulgaria's backwardness or its overall state of poverty. The West was seen as indifferent, as unwilling to intervene against the Ottomans on behalf of Bulgarian autonomy, which was achieved only after the Russian invasion and victory in the Russo-Turkish War of 1877–78. To make matters worse, with the 1878 Treaty of Berlin, the Western powers presided over Bulgaria's massive loss of territories, which they had been awarded in the Treaty of San Stefano. Moreover, in the pre-1878 period, the West had benefited both from Ottoman weakness, via its commercial penetration, and from Ottoman Westernizing reform, which brought an increase in infrastructure and other factors enabling trade. In the writings of the revolutionary poet and essayist Khristo Botev, for example, the Ottomans and the West were conflated as culprits not only in the exploitation of Bulgarians but also in their cultural ruin via consuming practices. Botev lamented that the West had brought poverty to the region, along with debauchery, drunkenness, and other wholly negative "attributes of European civilization."[39] Like other revival writers, he railed against "Turkified" and "Europeanized" Bulgarian elites who lived in luxury as a result of Bulgarian peasant labor.[40] In these seminal Bulgarian texts, critiques of the Ottoman Empire became inseparable from critiques of the West, with the two intertwined as gluttonous and insatiable plunderers.[41]

A range of Bulgarian writings, in contrast, idealize Bulgaria's peasantry as theoretically connected to a "natural" order of producing and consuming.[42] For many, the rural areas of the country represented the unspoiled nation, in contrast to the city, which was infected by "foreign" influences. This view was connected to a broader critique of civilization that evolved in a conversation with populism, socialism, and other ideas and movements coming out of Western Europe, the United States, and other global peripheries, most notably Russia. Indeed, by this period, the self-ascribed Bulgarian elite began to use the term *tsivilizatsia* (civilization) with considerable mockery and outright hostility. Tsivilizatsia signified the foppery, decadence, and superficiality of Europeans and especially Europeanized local elites—particularly in all manners of consumption. It denoted the emulation of European fashion but was also evoked with a clear recognition of the shallow, materialistic nature of modernity.

After the creation of the Principality of Bulgaria in 1878, such narratives continued and proliferated in the shadow of a new set of political and economic conditions. The tumultuous politics and economic hardships of the early post-Ottoman decades led to deep disillusionment among large swaths of Bulgarian society.[43] Even as the independent young principality sought to untangle itself politically, economically, and culturally from the Ottoman East, the West loomed as a far greater threat.[44] An increasingly heavy tax burden, waves of economic crisis, and new levels of peasant debt contributed to the widespread sentiment captured in the popular saying "Ot Turskoto po-losho" (Things are worse than under the Turks).⁴⁵ Bulgaria was largely a peasant nation, with no native aristocracy (they had been eliminated in the period of Ottoman conquest) and only a sparse merchant and urban artisan class, many of whom were devastated by Western competition in this period. The notion of a Western threat, in fact, provoked Bulgarians to argue that "Europe has given us independence but has reserved for itself the right to exploit us.... Political slavery is bad, but economic slavery is worse."⁴⁶ This spurred many statesmen, including the "Bulgarian Bismarck," Prime Minister Stefan Stambolov (1887–94), to make concerted efforts to catch up to the West through increased trade and greater capitalist engagement. Yet even as capitalism gained more of a foothold and Western contact became more frequent, new kinds of global products were being conspicuously consumed by relatively few, with no remedy offered for the continued spread of poverty and inequity.

In this period, the West served as both model and antimodel for its consuming practices, with new voices of restraint against excess audible from both near and far. But so too did Russia, filtering or reacting to the West as part of global consuming dialogues that responded to the ills of modernity. A variety of populist, socialist, Slavophile ("Russophile" in Bulgaria), Tolstoyan, agrarian, and religious sectarian ideas were planted in the fertile soil of post-Ottoman Bulgaria.⁴⁷ The intensification of encounters and dialogues with the West during these years contributed to Bulgaria's transformation, as did the intellectual responses to it. One such source of intensive contact was the educational effort of Anglo-American Protestant missionaries, who were harsh critics of Western decadence and crusaders for temperance.⁴⁸ Interestingly, while the drinking culture was characterized in their temperance writings as a local tradition embedded in Orthodoxy, they also rightly assumed that the burgeoning problem of alcoholism was tied to new capitalist technologies of production and patterns of distribution. In that sense, they at least in part saw it as a social problem connected to the West. Such assumptions found their most audible echo among Bulgarian socialists, who had similar concerns about the devastating effects of excessive alcohol consumption on the toiling classes.⁴⁹ There was certainly some cross-pollination between socialist and Protestant ideas and efforts in this regard, particularly in the advocacy of restraint for higher goals and the imperative of eradicating the consumer ills of Western modernity.

A number of other Bulgarian faith-based local movements emerged at this time that echoed the voices of restraint against Western consuming pleasures. Among them was a Theosophist movement influenced by Buddhism known as the White Brotherhood, or Diunovtsi, founded in 1870 by Petur

Diunov—himself the product of an American Protestant education (in Bulgaria and the United States). The Diunovtsi had a visible presence in interwar Sofia with their distinctive all-white clothing and their communal living arrangements.[50] They were noted for their abstinence, vegetarianism, and annual pilgrimage to a peak in the Rila Mountains, where they performed a ritual circle dance. Somewhat smaller but also noteworthy was the Bulgarian Tolstoyan movement, which was established in 1906 and grew to be the largest outside of Russia. Under the leadership of Georgi Kiosev, its adherents established a colony called Yasna Polyana in the Strandja region of Bulgaria.[51] The late works and life example of Lev Tolstoy created a highly articulated culture of restraint with a convincing urgency that resonated far beyond Russia. For both groups, escape from the evils of civilization (and by extension the West) lay at the heart of another kind of pleasure—spiritual fulfillment.

But escaping from tsivilizatsia was more than just a religious/spiritual endeavor; it was also a secular and even *national* endeavor. The author Ivan Vazov, regarded as the grandfather of Bulgarian literature, hinged a number of his works on what he saw as the need to "return to nature" and "explore the homeland," which he underscored with a critique of the adverse effects of the modern world. In his magisterial *In the Rila Wilderness*, for example, he writes about a journey into the Rila Mountains, for which leaving behind the deleterious effects of civilization was his explicit goal. As Vazov describes, he felt at home with the shepherds, his guide, local peasants, even a brigand—the unspoiled Bulgarians who lived far from tsivilizatsia, which, he noted, had "tamed" the human spirit but also "exhausted and vulgarized it."[52] As a curative, Vazov implored Bulgarians to explore not only the vast natural beauty around them but also the simple and locally connected forms of consuming that their homeland offered, framed by homegrown traditions of restraint. His journey was centered on a pilgrimage to the Rila Monastery and the nearby cave where the renowned monk Ivan Rilski, later Saint Ivan of Rila, lived out much of his life in the ninth and tenth centuries. Known for his extreme piety and fasting—the hallmark of his saintly existence—Rilski, as Vazov noted, "lived exclusively on plants and ate only enough to keep his body and soul together."[53] For Vazov, Rilski was a figure not just to emulate but to revere, in that he emblematized a Bulgarian tradition of restraint that was connected to the natural environment. Through his detailed writings on his travels into the mountainous regions of Bulgaria, Vazov laid the intellectual and symbolic groundwork for the country's tourist movement, which was more formally organized by the turn-of-the-century writer and humorist Aleko Konstantinov.

Aleko, as he is often called, very consciously followed in Vazov's footsteps and famously issued an 1895 appeal in the newspaper to the inhabitants of Sofia to get out of the city and climb the highest peak of nearby Mount Vitosha: "Brothers, set aside for now your thirst for gold, your thirst for power, your vain drive for status, your poisonous pen; leave behind your soft beds, crawl out of your smoky cafes, leave behind the dusty streets and the city, and come here for a few days, to this height of 2,500 meters; experience if only briefly true, pure pleasure, and you will transform, you will become better, healthier, more well-balanced, and more enamored with life."[54] Konstaninov's call to leave behind the creature comforts of the capital, which he openly disparaged, was not soon forgotten; his name, like Vazov's, will forever be associated with the tourist movement in its pre–World War I, interwar, and postwar socialist variants. But Konstantinov, like Vazov, is also one of the most revered and widely read authors in Bulgarian literature. His work carries a strong undercurrent of ambivalence toward the West and, in particular, the spoils of modernity and its consuming passions.[55]

Such narratives would resonate strongly and become increasingly politicized in the twentieth century. Indeed, the more that Western modes of consumption found a place—albeit extremely unevenly—in Bulgarian society, the more that voices and movements coalesced around questioning them. How truly Western such modes were or whether they were different only in form (or aesthetics) but not substance is open for debate. But there is no doubt that intellectual, spiritual, and increasingly political movements blamed many of the problems of post-Ottoman Bulgaria, rightly or wrongly, on the West or the ills of civilization as connected to the Bulgarian city and the nouveau riche. Socialist and agrarian voices, for example, grew in strength in the last decades of the long nineteenth century, as the moral economy of consumption assumed an increasingly urgent form.

As World War I came to a close, Bulgarians were caught up in the "revolutions on the left" that swept much of Europe. While the socialists (in particular the Bulgarian Communist Party [BCP]) and agrarians both had significant support, it was the Bulgarian Agrarian National Union (BANU) that prevailed, holding power in the country from 1918 to 1923.[56] In some respects, the agricultural cooperatives that formed the cornerstone of the agrarian program had enjoyed support from the government and a segment of urban intellectuals since the late nineteenth century.[57] A broad range of Bulgarian thinkers saw cooperatives as the answer to poverty and backwardness and the "peasant question" and also to the perceived ravages of capitalist speculation in the rural areas. Indeed, the widespread resonance of the cooperative idea within

Bulgaria can be explained as a self-defensive reaction by an impoverished and vulnerable peripheral economy to the perceived incursions of capitalism and the West.[58] The agrarians, much like the socialists, espoused a vision of consumer restraint that included abstinence, or at least moderation, as well as the organizing of consumer cooperatives for peasants.[59] But there were also critical disagreements within the movements that spawned deep tensions. Indeed, when BANU's radical agrarianist vision came crashing down with the assassination of its leader, Alexander Stamboliski, in 1923, the BCP took no immediate action. That same year, however, under pressure from the Communist International (Comintern), the BCP staged an insurrection, which was brutally crushed by an ascendant right-wing regime. As elsewhere in Eastern Europe, the Bolshevik threat precipitated a wave of right-wing authoritarianism inspired by European fascism that left no room for the left or for agrarian visions of egalitarian programs. Although the BCP and BANU were decapitated and sent underground, Bulgarian right-wing regimes (and intellectuals) shared some of the concerns of these movements and attempted to mitigate the peasants' problems with their own promises and programs—including, for example, the continued organization of state-regulated agrarian cooperatives. Indeed, the cooperative seemed to provide a solution for the larger issues of the Bulgarian agrarian economy and also to offer an outlet for the search for authenticity among urban intellectuals, for a moral approach to understanding the economy, and for a quest for the "Bulgarian spirit" in capitalist relations.[60]

Hence, even as political criticism of Western-style consumption was driven underground, a variety of related cultural narratives continued to circulate and in some sense prepare the ground for the postwar order. This is not to say that the movements and narratives described above were obvious precursors or created an easy opening for the transition to a radically different political system as World War II came to a close. Numerous factors, including brutal repression under Red Army occupation and brazen opportunism, allowed for the communist takeover in Bulgaria, with variations on this theme across the region. At the same time, communists in Bulgaria, as elsewhere in Eastern Europe, were adept at drawing on local sensibilities and discontents, particularly in relation to the consumer implications of modernity—its gluttony, its voraciousness, its inequalities, and its empty materialism.

CONSUMING REVOLUTIONS

Communism was arguably the first system in Eastern Europe under which the state made comprehensive efforts to control, redirect, and shape consumer habits. The process began in the Soviet Union with the state's consolidation of control over the economy and the radical restructuring of consumer society via the redistribution of resources from elites (liberally defined) to the toiling masses.[61] This was coupled with revolutionary visions of communal kitchens and other avenues for effecting fundamental changes in modes of consumption and of temporary sacrifices for a utopian future characterized by a vague notion of abundance. Such programs and plans were tempered, however, by the reality that the Bolshevik revolution was not followed by the expected global revolution, and various compromise policies became necessary. Lenin's New Economic Policy (1922–29) allowed for small-scale capitalist ventures as a way of mitigating extreme shortages. Stalin then implemented "socialism in one country" and "revolution from above," strengthening the state's control over the Soviet economy and culture and seeking more stable—rather than revolutionary—regimes of consumption. The West was enemy number one in this process, its forms and lackeys to be eradicated but also superseded. In a sense, the Bolshevik, and later Stalinist, program was adept at playing upon local anti-Western sentiments while still playing to desires for Western levels of prosperity.

Under Stalin, the politics of consumption was connected to the new regime of control, as part of which he employed starvation (forced famine) as well as consumer embourgeoisement to consolidate his power.[62] By the mid-1930s, in what many refer to as Stalin's "Great Retreat," official Soviet rhetoric on "abundance" was coupled with the wooing of new elites though mass-produced luxury foods like champagne, caviar, ice cream, and sausages.[63] The more radical voices of restraint from the revolutionary period—for example, those who called for the prohibition of drinking—were pushed aside in favor of a more moderate and realistic approach to regulating consuming habits.[64] For Stalin, the availability of such goods for "deserving workers" was emblematic of socialist achievement. Representations of prosperity were in large part fictional; the famous Soviet cookbook *The Book of Tasty and Healthy Food*, for example, first published in this period, was later compared to socialist realism.[65] Nevertheless, there was a transformation in consumer possibilities and practices in these years, along with new educational and high-cultural offerings. New modes of consuming were directly tied to notions of *kulturnost'* (culturedness), and hence a kind of Soviet "civilizing mission" that was directed especially at "backward" peasants and non-Russian peoples.[66] In short, while Soviet consumption patterns were initially radically altered, revolutionary forms of consumption were largely shelved in favor of a return to a petit bourgeois model, a restrained good life for the still select few, and a projected future of abundance for all.

This model, including the eradication of classes considered to be predatory and gluttonous, was expanded to postwar Eastern Europe. While certain aspects of it undoubtedly resonated with various movements, as described above, that is not meant to suggest that the imposition of communism in Bulgaria, as across Eastern Europe, was somehow preordained or seamless because of the existence there of fertile soil for resistance to the West or a "third way." On the contrary, a number of consuming paths competed for Bulgarians' hearts and minds. As World War II drew to a close, communists were in the minority, with varying levels of support across the region, but they gained followers quickly in those final months of the war for a variety of reasons. And as they consolidated their power, Bulgarian communists were extremely adept at exploiting a range of anti-Western leanings, blaming occupying foreigners and the West more broadly for their country's poverty and backwardness. Hence, communist regimes were able to position themselves in such a way that they could simultaneously reject the West and eject it from the national life—which appealed to widespread anti-Western or anticapitalist sentiments—while still playing to the desires of those who hoped to eventually share in or even exceed its material prosperity.

Across the region, communist regimes appealed to the masses by vowing to take control of the economy on behalf of the people and fulfill basic needs. East European communists established power in large part by mobilizing populations through a kind of social contract that promised access to highly subsidized products and services. This included the provision of not just consumer goods like housing, food, clothing, and furniture to a rapidly urbanizing population but also cultural and social services like education, medical care, and access to the arts. Indeed, the various communist regimes proved successful in many respects in terms of mobilizing their populations under the banner of new consuming possibilities. For rural and underdeveloped countries like Bulgaria, this was enabled by state-directed (and Eastern bloc–connected) postwar economic growth, in which respect Bulgaria far outstripped its capitalist neighbors Greece and Turkey in the 1950s and 1960s.[67] As in the Soviet case, such consumer offerings were part of a more general civilizing process, connected to the larger project of eradicating backwardness and building socialism.[68]

These processes accelerated after Stalin's death in 1953, as postwar recovery and the new imperative of de-Stalinization bolstered Khrushchev's post-1956 "consumer turn."[69] It was not just that his denunciation of Stalinist crimes shook the legitimacy of the bloc, but the ensuing mass protests, including outright revolution in Hungary, made it necessary to reconsolidate socialist citizens' loyalties. Regimes in the Khrushchev era were given the green light to focus more intently on providing consumer goods, with a goal to overtake the West in the consumer domain, along with other spheres of economic and social development. But such pursuits were arguably not tantamount to a turn to capitalist solutions for socialist ills. Instead, the coming of "ripe capitalism" undergirded late socialist narratives of providing unprecedented levels of abundance. These regimes had no way to ensure that their citizenry would consume available goods and services in acceptable "socialist" ways.[70]

Significantly, the process of making new consumer citizens happened in a close and continuous conversation with the West—both real and imagined. This constitutive encounter was critical to the character of both systems. For their leaders, perhaps most visibly since the 1959 "kitchen debates," the ability to fulfill their populations' consumer needs (if not desires) was integral to the Cold War contest. Consuming revolutions took place on both sides of the Iron Curtain and the Atlantic, albeit with different rationales and methods of marshaling resources.[71] Cold War consumer dialogues were initiated by both sides as well—ever curious Peeping Toms wanting to confirm their own superiority or observe and borrow from the other. World's Fairs and trade fairs provided a literal staging for such systemic forensics, but the more individual experiences of travelers also played a part, often codified in travel writings or passed on by word of mouth.[72]

Even into the 1960s and 1970s, travelers to the Eastern bloc still came away impressed by the consumer offerings there. True, many of those visitors were "left leaning, and most were exposed to the best the East had to offer to consumers. In Bulgaria, for example, the Black Sea coast—the so called Red Riviera, arguably the most developed socialist resort zone within the bloc—hosted nearly one million foreigners in 1965 and three million by 1972. Easterners and Westerners came in force to the glimmering new hotels, bars, "folk taverns," casinos, cafés, and restaurants that dotted Bulgaria's long coastline, itself a zone of contact. The state-owned tourist agency, Balkanturist, was attuned to both bloc and Western demands and indeed got constant feedback from visitors from both sides of the Iron Curtain. In Bulgaria, as well as the bloc more generally, Western (or, perhaps more accurately, international) goods, technologies, and standards were also routinely and unproblematically integrated into local consumer practices and offerings. There was considerable leeway, in fact, among industry operatives and regular citizens to creatively pursue a socialist good life in which pleasures were available for all.[73]

To see the world of socialist pleasure as a mere imitation of the West seems to miss a number of key points. One is that a heightened sense and mass fulfillment of consumer desire itself may be modern, but that does not make it somehow "capitalist." Defining consumer desire as capitalist is not as useful as exploring how individuals, cultures, or systems incite, direct, restrain, fulfill, respond to, or shape it. Given that overcoming backwardness was always paramount for communist regimes, confronting and shaping consumers' desires was a central task. Extinguishing such desires was never the goal: they held the potential to drive not just the capitalist dream but also the building of socialism. Communist regimes did, however, continually scrutinize and assess the consumer practices of their citizens. They sought to eliminate irrational forms and excesses of behaviors that were seen as vestiges of the capitalist past, even if there was never complete certainty about the parameters of what was acceptable consumer behavior.[74] Furthermore, the most important opposition voices and movements from the period advocated for a reformed and humane socialism, not for unfettered capitalism.

Still, the Western consumer model was capable of becoming a kind of Trojan horse in the Eastern bloc. While many Eastern Europeans surely imagined the West or saw it firsthand, they also continued to be conscious and critical of the United States' inequities—its homeless, the poverty that mapped onto racist tendencies—and its consumer excesses. Consumers' needs and desires grew over the course of the period, as an educated, professional, urbanized citizenry developed and began to have expectations. Those expectations were dashed in the postrecession era, however, which saw severe shortages across Eastern Europe by the 1980s. Yet, arguably until the bitter end, no opposition movements were coming to the barricades to fight for a Western-style consumer paradise—although for many it admittedly may have been part of their vision of the future.

CONCLUSION

It would be a mistake to underestimate the achievements and the real pleasures of the communist period. Indeed, after the 1989–91 triumph of the imagined West, the transition brought an avalanche of new pleasures to Eastern Europe and Russia—pleasures that have been confronted, scrutinized, and in some cases reined in and managed in new ways. Amid the new abundance, nostalgia for the socialist past has been surprisingly powerful.[75] Capitalism and democracy have brought public disorder and financial insecurity but also new temptations—many of which are out of reach for a large part of the population, for whom it is a serious challenge just to pay their utilities, let alone the costs of health care, education, and food. But beyond a yearning for lost security, one of the more fascinating aspects of nostalgia for communism has been a longing for the goods and services of the communist past—the simple pleasures of that period—which seem to have been trampled underfoot by aggressive globalization, the market, and new kinds of regulatory systems. In Bulgaria, many long for the days when they could afford a month on the Black Sea coast, when the state provided such vacations as a right to the common citizen, when they could smoke freely in public places. But they also remember and long for products such as "real yogurt," which nowadays has been replaced by the flavorless Dannon version. They long for at least certain aspects of the communist era, when life was cheap, simple, and pleasurable. In short, they long for the pleasures of backwardness.

NOTES

1. While I understand the issues surrounding the term *Eastern Europe*, I still find it useful as a term and category for analysis for the region that lies, roughly speaking, between Germany and Russia (and continues south to the Balkans). While this region has many commonalities with Russia in terms of "backwardness" and its relationship to the West, it is also distinct in terms of its predominantly "little" country configurations and shared histories on the periphery of multinational empires or its post-empire fates of being occupied (or in unequal alliances) with Nazi Germany and then the Soviet Union, and being part of the Cold War Eastern bloc (or outside of it but nevertheless socialist as in the case of Yugoslavia and later Albania).

2. The term has been applied, needless to say, not just to Eastern Europe, but to Southern and Central Europe and Russia, not to mention much of the globe. For Eastern Europe, the key (primarily economic) explanations include Chirot, *Origins of Backwardness*; and Berend, *History Derailed*.

3. See, for example, Janos, *Politics of Backwardness*; Jedlicki, *Suburb of Europe*; Bianchini, *Challenges of Modernity*.

4. On progress, see Nisbet, *Idea of Progress*. For a more recent explanation of why backwardness is still a relevant category for Eastern Europe, see Berend and Bugaric, "Unfinished Europe."

5. For an excellent discussion of the broad use and meaning of the term *civilization*, see Fernández-Armesto, *Civilizations*, 11–35. I rely here on Frank Trentmann's definition of *consumption* as "the acquisition, use, and waste of things, taste and desire." This is in contrast to a more normative notion of consumerism that implies "modern" and accelerated modes of circulation of goods. See Trentmann, "Introduction," 1, 8.

6. Elias, *Civilizing Process*.

7. For the best survey of the historiography (and interdisciplinary scholarship) on consumption, see Trentmann, "Introduction," 1–22.

8. See, for example, Trentmann, "Beyond Consumerism"; Hobson, *Eastern Origins*; Prestholdt, *Domesticating the World*; Pomeranz, *Great Divergence*; Quataert, *Consumption Studies*.

9. In part this situation has persisted because of the relative strengths of the field of European and American consumption, which makes it hard to offer balanced, nuanced, and in-depth coverage of the rest of the world. New work in "other" regional and national histories of consumption has certainly helped, but the imbalance is still striking. The balance is beginning to tip, however, as in collections such as Trentmann's *Oxford Handbook*.

10. Crowley and Reid, *Pleasures in Socialism*; Bren and Neuburger, *Communism Unwrapped*; Chernyshova, *Soviet Consumer Culture*; Randall, *Soviet Dream World*.

11. Most of the work that spans the precommunist and communist periods is on Russia. See, for example, Phillips, *Bolsheviks and the Bottle*; Schrad, *Vodka Politics*; Neuburger, *Balkan Smoke*; and edited books such as Romaniello and Starks, *Tobacco in Russian History*; Giants and Toomre, *Food in Russian History*. I am not including scholarship on the postcommunist period.

12. Scholarship on alcohol and tobacco, given the nature of such intoxicants, has gone furthest in dealing with such constraints. See, for example, Schrad, *Vodka Politics*; Neuburger, *Balkan Smoke*; Romaniello and Starks, *Tobacco in Russian History*; Phillips, *Bolsheviks and the Bottle*; and Herlihy, *Alcoholic Empire*. On food, see also Smith, *Recipes for Russia*.

13. Wolff, *Inventing Eastern Europe*; Todorova, *Imagining the Balkans*; Fleming, "Orientalism, the Balkans," 1225; Kostova, *Tales of the Periphery*, 195–96.

14. See Bracewell and Drace-Francis, *Under Eastern Eyes*; Bracewell, *Orientations*; Bracewell and Drace-Francis, *Bibliography*; Bracewell and Drace-Francis, *Balkan Departures*.

15. Such issues are mentioned, of course, but rarely dealt with in depth. A notable exception is the sections on food and drink in nineteenth-century Southeast Europe that can found in Jezernik, *Wild Europe*, 47–55, 147–70.

16. Such works tend to focus on Europe in the seventeenth and eighteenth centuries for "origins," at the turn of the century for a kind of initial "quickening" of such impulses, and after World War II for an Americanized maturity of sorts. See Trentmann, "Introduction," for an excellent survey of the complex and interdisciplinary evolution of this scholarship.

17. Recent examples of this approach are Stearns, *Consumerism in World History*; and de Grazia, *Irresistible Empire*.

18. Work in this vein is so prevalent that it hardly bears citing, but for a recent example, see Ferguson, *Civilization*.

19. This assumption is encoded in too many works to enumerate. A seminal text is Weber, *Protestant Ethic*. For something more recent, see Ferguson, *Civilization*.

20. See, for example, Muchembled, *Orgasm and the West*.
21. See, for example, Schivelbusch, *Tastes of Paradise*.
22. For an excellent transatlantic study on how the West managed and critiqued its own abundance, see Lears, *Fables of Abundance*.
23. Ibid., 2.
24. Wolff, *Inventing Eastern Europe*, 20.
25. See, for example, Todorova, *Imagining the Balkans*, 13.
26. Jezernik argues that after occupying Bosnia-Hercegovina in 1878, the Habsburg administration "took great pains to keep people from lazing about in coffee houses." *Wild Europe*, 152–53, 165.
27. See, for example, Kirli, "Struggle over Space," 11, 156. On this point, see also the classic work of Hattox, *Coffee and Coffeehouses*, 100–101.
28. For more on the coffeehouse in the Ottoman context, see Neuburger, *Balkan Smoke*, 11–42.
29. There is far more work that could be done on this subject, and my suggestions here are largely preliminary.
30. I can't help but think of the amazement, but also disgust in light of Western consumer abundance, expressed by Aleko Konstantinov when he visited the Chicago World's Fair in 1893, particularly after viewing the Chicago slaughterhouses. See Konstantinov, "Do Chikago i nazad," 79.
31. I am keeping the focus here on Eastern Europe—although across the region similar resentments played out in a spectrum of ways. While there are many parallels and obvious links with Russia, Russia also had its own complex of issues, including its stature as an imperial power (rather than a "small" and politically dominated nation), its messianic mission, and its particular idea of the Russian "soul."
32. I am clearly not trying to offer a full comparative survey of such dynamics but rather suggesting avenues for further comparative work that would begin to integrate Eastern Europe into a global history of consumption.
33. See how this played out in various ways in Neuburger, *Orient Within*.
34. Mishkova, "Forms without Substance."
35. Several Bulgarian collections exist of such writings from the pre-1878 Bulgarian revival period, though analysis is rather thin and does not deal with issues surrounding consumption. See, for example, Giurova, *Vŭzrozhdenski pŭtepisi*; and Klisarov and Dinev, *Doosvobozhdenski pŭtepisi*.
36. Giurova, *Vŭzrozhdenski pŭtepisi*, 10–13, 222.
37. Ibid., 245.
38. Here I am referring to the Turkish-speaking Muslim peasantry, but I use quotation marks as this population (like "Bulgarians") generally still lacked a national or even ethnic consciousness as "Turks" in this period.
39. Botev, *Sŭbrani sŭchinenie*, 168.

40. For a rich literature on the cultural, economic, and political dilemmas of "Europeanization," see Daskalov, *Mezhdu iztoka i zapada*; and Daskalov and Marinov, *Entangled Histories*.

41. These later sanctified writings were clearly influenced by Russian populist and various stripes of European socialist thought, layered with clearly Orientalist assumptions.

42. See, for example, Karavelov, *Zapiski za Bŭlgariia i za Bŭlgarete*.

43. Crampton, *Bulgaria*, 159.

44. Although Michael Palairet, John Lampe, and others argue that the "penetration" of the West was relatively insignificant during this period, it is clear that the *perceived* impact was still significant. See Palairet, *Balkan Economies*, 175–78; and Lampe, "Imperial Borderlands," 200–202.

45. For the first iteration see Crampton, *Bulgaria*, 159. For the second, see Elenkov, "Versii za Bŭlgarskata identichnost," 14.

46. Plovdiv okrŭzhen dŭrzhaven arkhiv, F-455, O-1, E-29, L-66.

47. Given the eventual triumph of communism in Bulgaria, the history of the socialist movement has garnered the most attention from historians—though not with an explicit focus on consumer politics.

48. These missionaries were part of the so-called American Great Awakening of the nineteenth century, which witnessed the revival of evangelical movements for whom "saving the world" was paramount. As Ivan Ilchev argues, American missionaries lived in more direct and intimate contact with Bulgarians than any other foreigners during the nineteenth century. Ilchev and Mitev, *Bŭlgaro-Amerikanski kulturni*, 12. By the 1880s, temperance societies had produced and distributed some 100,000 tracts and posters within Bulgaria. Clarke, *Temperance Work in Bulgaria*, 3.

49. Tsentralen Istoricheski Dŭrzhaven Arkhiv (TsIDA) F-1027k, O-1, E-46, L-5. In 1938 the movement was permanently banned because of its apparent communist but also Protestant (and hence foreign) leanings. See also Petkov, *Borbata za trezvenost vŭv Vrachanski okrŭg*, 16–21, 134.

50. See, for example, Slavov, *Izgrevŭt*, 166.

51. Konstantinov, *L. N. Tolstoĭ i vliianieto*; and Dosev, *Blizo do Iasna Poliana*. The colony was named for Tolstoy's estate in Russia, Yasnaya Polyana.

52. Vazov, *Great Rila Wilderness*, 96.

53. Ibid., 36.

54. Konstantinov, *Razkazi i feĭletoni*, 43.

55. There is not room to explore the complexity of Konstantinov's work here, but his most famous work was a novel entitled *Baĭ Ganio*, which lampoons the newly rich in turn-of-the-century Bulgaria, as well as the "Oriental" character of the archetypal Bulgarian—often through his brutish consuming practices.

56. BANU's relationship with the BCP in these years remained uneasy as worker and peasant demands, and the approaches of the two parties, were often

at odds. The rule of Stamboliski is extremely controversial in the historical literature, because while he was popular among the peasant majority, he ruled as a benevolent dictator over competing (mostly urban) interest groups. For an overview, see Bell, *Peasants in Power*.

57. See Avramov, *Stopanskiiat XX vek na Bŭlgariia*, 27–28.

58. For this argument see Avramov, *Komunalniiat kapitalizŭm*, 1, 30.

59. See, for example, *Biuletin na kooperativnoto druzhestvo na sdruzhenite tiutiunoproizvoditeli ot grad Stanimaka i okoliiata*; and *Asenovgrad krepost*, 5.

60. Avramov, *Komunalniiat kapitalizŭm*, 26.

61. For a recent overview of the Soviet case from the perspective of consumption, see Fitzpatrick, "Things under Socialism," 451–66. On Eastern Europe, see Bren and Neuburger, *Communism Unwrapped*.

62. See, for example, Hryn, *Hunger by Design*.

63. See Gronow, *Caviar with Champagne*. See also Fitzpatrick, *Everyday Stalinism*, 90–91.

64. See, for example, Phillips, *Bolsheviks and the Bottle*.

65. Piretto, "Tasty and Healthy," 84. See also Geist, "Cooking Bolshevik"; and Gronow and Zhuravlev, "Book of Tasty and Healthy Food," 24–57.

66. Fitzpatrick, *Everyday Stalinism*, 10; Yuri Slezkine, *Arctic Mirrors*.

67. Haynes, "Rhetoric of Economics," 26–39.

68. See Neuburger, *Orient Within*.

69. Fitzpatrick, "Things under Socialism," 460.

70. For an excellent study on such disjunctures in the Bulgarian case, see Scarboro, *Late Socialist Good Life*.

71. See, for example, Cohen, *Consumers' Republic*.

72. See, for example, a special issue entitled "Between Decolonisation and the Cold War" in the *Journal of Contemporary History*.

73. For more on this, see Crowley and Reid, *Pleasures in Socialism*.

74. On smoking, drinking, and leisure, see Neuburger, *Balkan Smoke*, 167–98.

75. See, for example, Todorova and Gille, *Post-Communist Nostalgia*.

REFERENCES

Asenovgrad krepost, February 15, 1926.

Avramov, Rumen. *Komunalniiat kapitalizŭm: iz Bŭlgarskoto stopansko minalo*. Sofia: Tsentŭr za liberalni strategii, 2007.

———. *Stopanskiiat XX vek na Bŭlgariia*. Sofia: Tsentŭr za liberalni strategii, 2001.

Bell, John. *Peasants in Power: Alexander Stamboliski and the Bulgarian Agrarian National Union, 1899–1923*. Princeton, NJ: Princeton University Press, 1977.

Berend, Ivan. *History Derailed: Central and Eastern Europe in the Long Nineteenth Century*. Berkeley: University of California Press, 2003.

Berend, Ivan T., and Bojan Bugaric. "Unfinished Europe: Transition from Communism to Democracy in Central and Eastern Europe." *Journal of Contemporary History* 50, no. 4 (2015): 768–85.
Bianchini, Stefano. *Eastern Europe and the Challenges of Modernity, 1800–2000*. London: Routledge, 2015.
Druzhestvo na sdruzhenite tiutiunoproizvoditeli ot grad Stanimaka i okoliiata. *Biuletin na kooperativnoto druzhestvo na sdruzhenite tiutiunoproizvoditeli ot grad Stanimaka i okoliiata*, January 28, 1922.
Botev, Khristo. *Sŭbrani sŭchinenie*, vol. 2. Sofia: Bŭlgarski pisatel, 1971.
Bracewell, Wendy, ed. *Orientations: An Anthology of East European Travel Writing*. Budapest: Central European Press, 2009.
Bracewell, Wendy, and Alex Drace-Francis, eds. *A Bibliography of East European Travel Writing*. Budapest: Central European Press, 2008.
———, eds. *Balkan Departures: Travel Writing from Southeastern Europe*. Budapest: Central European Press, 2008.
———, eds. *Under Eastern Eyes: A Comparative Introduction to East European Travel Writing*. Budapest: Central European Press, 2008.
Bren, Paulina, and Mary Neuburger, eds. *Communism Unwrapped: Consumption in Cold War Eastern Europe*. Oxford: Oxford University Press, 2012.
Chernyshova, Natalya. *Soviet Consumer Culture in the Brezhnev Era*. New York: Routledge, 2013.
Chirot, Daniel. *The Origins of Backwardness in Eastern Europe: Economics and Politics from the Middle Ages until the Early Twentieth Century*. Berkeley: University of California Press, 1991.
Clarke, James F. *Temperance Work in Bulgaria: Its Successes*. Samokov, Bulgaria: Evangelical School Press, 1909.
Cohen, Lizabeth. *A Consumers' Republic: The Politics of Mass Consumption in Postwar America*. New York: Knopf, 2003.
Crampton, R. J. *Bulgaria*. New York: Oxford University Press, 2007.
Crowley, David, and Susan E. Reid, eds. *Pleasures in Socialism: Leisure and Luxury in the Eastern Bloc*. Evanston, IL: Northwestern University Press, 2010.
Daskalov, Rumen. *Mezhdu iztoka i zapada: Bŭlgarski kulturni dilemi*. Sofia: Lik, 1998.
Daskalov, Rumen, and Tchavdar Marinov. *Entangled Histories of the Balkans*. Leiden, Netherlands: Brill, 2013.
Dosev, Khristo. *Blizo do Iasna Poliana: 1907–1909 g*. Sofia: Lingua optima consilium, 2010.
Elenkov, Ivan. "Versii za Bŭlgarskata identichnost v modernata epokha." In *Zashto sme takiva? v tŭrcene na Bŭlgarskata kŭlturna identichnost*, edited by Ivan Elenkov and Roumen Daskalov, 5–26. Sofia: Izdatelstvo prosveta, 1994.
Elias, Norbert. *The Civilizing Process*. New York: Urizen Books, 1978.

Ferguson, Niall. *Civilization: The West and the Rest.* New York: Penguin, 2011.
Fernández-Armesto, Felipe. *Civilizations: Culture, Ambition, and the Transformation of Nature.* New York: Free Press, 2001.
Fitzpatrick, Sheila. *Everyday Stalinism: Ordinary Life in Extraordinary Times; Soviet Russia in the 1930s.* New York: Oxford University Press, 1990.
———. "Things under Socialism: The Soviet Experiment." In *The Oxford Handbook of the History of Consumption,* edited by Frank Trentmann, 451–66. Oxford: Oxford University Press, 2012.
Fleming, Katherine. "Orientalism, the Balkans and Balkan Historiography." *American Historical Review* 105, no. 4 (2000): 1218–33.
Geist, Eduard. "Cooking Bolshevik: Anastas Mikoian and the Making of the Book about Delicious and Healthy Food." *Russian Review* 71, no. 2 (2012): 295–313.
Giurova, Svetla. *Vŭzrozhdenski pŭtepisi.* Sofia: Bŭlgarski pisatel, 1969.
Glants, Musya, and Joyce Toomre, eds. *Food in Russian History and Culture.* Bloomington: Indiana University Press, 1997.
Grazia, Victoria de. *Irresistible Empire: America's Advance through Twentieth-Century Europe.* Cambridge, MA: Belknap Press of Harvard University Press, 2005.
Gronow, Jukka. *Caviar with Champagne: Common Luxury and the Ideals of the Good Life in Stalin's Russia.* New York: Berg, 2003.
Gronow, Jukka, and Sergey Zhuravlev. "The Book of Tasty and Healthy Food: The Establishment of Soviet Haute Cuisine." In *Educated Tastes: Food, Drink and Connoisseur Culture,* edited by Jeremy Strong, 24–57. Lincoln: University of Nebraska Press, 2011.
Hattox, Ralph. *Coffee and Coffeehouses: The Origins of a Social Beverage in the Medieval Near East.* Seattle: University of Washington Press, 1985.
Haynes, Michael. "The Rhetoric of Economics: Cold War Representations of Development in the Balkans." In *The Balkans and the West: Constructing the European Other,* edited by Andrew Hammond, 26–39. Burlington, VT: Ashgate, 2004.
Herlihy, Patricia. *Alcoholic Empire: Vodka and Politics in Late Imperial Russia.* Oxford: Oxford University Press, 2003.
Hobson, John. *The Eastern Origins of Western Civilization.* Cambridge: Cambridge University Press, 2004.
Hryn, Halina, ed. *Hunger by Design: The Great Ukrainian Famine and Its Soviet Context.* Boston: Harvard Ukrainian Research Institute, 2009.
Ilchev, Ivan, and Plamen Mitev, eds. *Bŭlgaro-Amerikanski kulturni i politicheski vrŭzki prez XIX–pŭrvata polovina na XX v.* Sofia: Universitetsko izdatelstvo Sv. Kliment Okhridski, 2004.
Janos, Andrew. *The Politics of Backwardness in Hungary, 1825–1945.* Princeton, NJ: Princeton University Press, 1982.

Jedlicki, Jerzy. *A Suburb of Europe: Nineteenth-Century Polish Approaches to Western Civilization.* Budapest: Central European University Press, 1999.
Jezernik, Božidar. *Wild Europe: The Balkans in the Gaze of Western Travellers.* London: Saqi Books, 2003.
Karavelov, Liuben. *Zapiski za Bŭlgariia i za Bŭlgarete.* Sofia: Dŭrzhavna pechatnitsa, 1930.
Kirli, Cengiz. "The Struggle over Space: Coffeehouses of Ottoman Istanbul, 1780–1845." PhD diss., State University of New York, Binghamton, 2001.
Klisarov, Georgi, and Liubomir Dinev. *Doosvobozhdenski pŭtepisi:[sbornik].* Sofia: Nauka i izkustvo, 1969.
Konstantinov, Aleko. *Baĭ Ganio: neveroiatni razkazi na sŭvremenen Bŭlgarin.*
———. "Do Chikago i nazad." In *Sŭbrani sŭchineniia*, vol. 1. Edited by Tikhomir Tikhov. Sofia: Bŭlgarski Pisatel, 1980.
———. *Razkazi i feĭletoni.* Sofia: Knigoizdatesltvo fakel, 1937.
Konstantinov, Georgi. *L. N. Tolstoĭ i vliianieto mu v bŭlgariia.* Sofia: Biblioteka svobodna misŭl, 1968.
Kostova, Ludmilla. *Tales of the Periphery: The Balkans in Nineteenth-Century British Writing.* Veliko Turnovo, Bulgaria: Universitetsko izd-vo Sv. Kiril i Metodii, 1997.
Lampe, John. "Imperial Borderlands or Capitalist Periphery? Redefining Balkan Backwardness, 1520–1914." In *The Origins of Backwardness in Eastern Europe: Economics and Politics from the Middle Ages until the Early Twentieth Century*, edited by Daniel Chirot, 200–202. Berkeley: University of California Press, 1989.
Lears, Jackson. *Fables of Abundance: A Cultural History of Advertising in America.* New York: Basic Books, 1994.
Mishkova, Diana. "Forms without Substance: Debates on the Transfer of Western Models to the Balkans." In *Entangled Histories of the Balkans.* Vol. 2, *Transfers of Political Ideologies and Institutions*, edited by Rumen Daskalov and Diana Mishkova, 1–98. Leiden, Netherlands: Brill, 2014.
Muchembled, Robert. *Orgasm and the West: A History of Pleasure from the Sixteenth Century to the Present.* Cambridge: Polity, 2008.
Neuburger, Mary. *Balkan Smoke: Tobacco and the Making of Modern Bulgaria.* Ithaca, NY: Cornell University Press, 2013.
———. *The Orient Within: Muslim Minorities and the Negotiation of Nationhood in Modern Bulgaria.* Ithaca, NY: Cornell University Press, 2004.
Nisbet, Robert. *History of the Idea of Progress.* New York: Basic Books, 1980.
Palairet, Michael. *The Balkan Economies c. 1800–1914: Evolution without Development.* Cambridge: Cambridge University Press, 2003.
Petkov, Pavel. *Borbata za trezvenost vŭv vrachanski okrŭg, 1920–1980.* Sofia: Izdatelsvo na otechestveniia front, 1982.

Phillips, Laura. *Bolsheviks and the Bottle: Drink and Worker Culture in St. Petersburg, 1900–1929.* DeKalb: Northern Illinois University Press, 2000.

Piretto, Gian Pierro. "Tasty and Healthy: Soviet Happiness in One Book." In *Petrified Utopia: Happiness Soviet Style,* edited by Marina Balina and Evgeny Dobrenko, 79–97. London: Anthem, 2011.

Plovdiv okrŭzhen dŭrzhaven arkhiv, F-455, O-1, E-29, L-66. Plovidv, Bulgaria.

Pomeranz, Kenneth. *The Great Divergence: China, Europe, and the Making of the Modern World Economy.* Princeton, NJ: Princeton University Press, 2000.

Prestholdt, Jeremy. *Domesticating the World: African Consumerism and the Genealogies of Globalization.* Berkeley: University of California Press, 2008.

Quataert, Donald. *Consumption Studies and the History of the Ottoman Empire, 1550–1922: An Introduction.* Albany: State University of New York Press, 2000.

Randall, Amy. *The Soviet Dream World of Retail Trade and Consumption in the 1930s.* Basingstoke, UK: Palgrave Macmillan, 2008.

Romaniello, Matthew, and Tricia Starks. *Tobacco in Russian History and Culture: From the Seventeenth Century to the Present.* New York: Routledge, 2009.

Scarboro, Cristofer. *The Late Socialist Good Life in Bulgaria: Meaning and Living in a Permanent Present Tense.* Lanham, MD: Lexington Books, 2011.

Schivelbusch, Wolfgang. *Tastes of Paradise: A Social History of Spices, Stimulants, and Intoxicants.* New York: Pantheon Books, 1992.

Schrad, Mark. *Vodka Politics: Alcohol, Autocracy, and the Secret History of the Russian State.* New York: Oxford University Press, 2014.

Slavov, Atanas. *Izgrevŭt: kŭm svetskata biografiia na Petŭr Dŭnov.* Sofia: Kheliopol, 2010.

Slezkine, Yuri. *Arctic Mirrors: Russia and the Small Peoples of the North.* Ithaca, NY: Cornell University Press, 1994.

Smith, Alison. *Recipes for Russia: Food and Nationhood under the Tsars.* DeKalb: Northern Illinois University Press, 2011.

Stearns, Peter. *Consumerism in World History: The Global Transformation of Desire.* New York: Routledge, 2001.

Todorova, Maria, and Zsuzsa Gille, eds. *Post-Communist Nostalgia.* New York: Berghahn Books, 2010.

Todorova, Maria. *Imagining the Balkans.* Oxford: Oxford University Press, 1997.

Trentmann, Frank. "Beyond Consumerism: New Historical Perspectives on Consumption." *Journal of Contemporary History* 39 (2004) 377–78.

———. "Introduction." In *The Oxford Handbook of the History of Consumption,* edited by Frank Trentmann, 1–22. Oxford: Oxford University Press, 2012.

———, ed. *The Oxford Handbook of the History of Consumption.* Oxford: Oxford University Press, 2012.

Tsentralen Istoricheski Dŭrzhaven Arkhiv (TsIDA) F-1027k, O-1, E-46, L-5. Sofia, Bulgaria.

Vazov, Ivan. *The Great Rila Wilderness*. Sofia: Sofia Press, 1969.
Weber, Max. *The Protestant Ethic and the Spirit of Capitalism*. New York: Scribner, 1958.
Wolff, Larry. *Inventing Eastern Europe: The Map of Civilization on the Mind of the Enlightenment*. Stanford, CA: Stanford University Press, 1994.

AUTHOR BIO

MARY NEUBURGER is Professor of History; Director of the Center for Russian, East European, and Eurasian Studies (CREEES); and Chair of Slavic and Eurasian Studies at the University of Texas at Austin. Neuburger is author of *The Orient Within: Muslim Minorities and the Negotiation of Nationhood in Modern Bulgaria* (2004) and *Balkan Smoke: Tobacco and the Making of Modern Bulgaria* (2012). Neuburger is also editor with Paulina Bren of *Communism Unwrapped: Consumption in Cold War Eastern Europe* (2012) and has authored numerous articles on Bulgarian and Cold War history. She is currently working on a cultural history of food in Bulgaria and is coeditor of the *Journal of Contemporary History*.

THREE

JUST REWARDS

The Social Contract and Communism's Hard Bargain with the Citizen-Consumer

PATRICK HYDER PATTERSON

Mephistopheles:
Still, my good friend, a time may come,
When one prefers to eat what's good in peace.
Faust:
When I lie quiet in bed, at ease.
Then let my time be done!
If you fool me, with flatteries,
Till my own self's a joy to me,
If you snare me with luxury—
Let that be the last day I see!
That bet I'll make!
Mephistopheles:
Done!

From Johann Wolfgang von Goethe, *Faust* (translated by A. S. Kline)

In the latter decades of European state socialism, a number of influential Western economists, government officials, and political analysts pinned their hopes for an eventual relaxation of Cold War tensions on the introduction of market forces to the communist East. Direct liberalization of the political realm, they assumed, would not be forthcoming. Yet the urgent need for practical material progress—a cure for the lingering "backwardness" of the socialist world—might nevertheless open the gates to economic liberalization and the adoption of market mechanisms, which could in turn gradually clear an opening for something that edged closer toward liberal democracy. With the crises and dislocations that burdened Eastern Europe from the mid-1970s onward, this prescription became increasingly popular, and there is evidence that policy makers concerned with the region had long viewed the welcome "stealth" effects of economic change in precisely such terms.

It was with these concerns in mind, for example, that one declassified State Department assessment from 1965 identified "economic decentralization and liberalization" as one of the four primary aims of US policy in the region and remarked that "the Yugoslav example of independence in foreign affairs and *a relatively freer and more prosperous society* has generated envy within the other Communist countries of Eastern Europe and has *encouraged the movement towards greater independence and internal economic and political change* characteristic of Eastern European Communist countries today."[1] The payoff for the broader aims of Cold War statecraft seemed clear: "In effect," the State Department analyst observed, "Yugoslavia has served the US as a Trojan Horse in Eastern Europe; our policies have produced good results in furthering diversity and some liberalization within the Communist world."[2] From this perspective, the hunger for prosperity required the acknowledgment of consumer demand, while the attempt to meet consumer demand compelled a greater recognition of market forces and a liberalization of business practice, and the emancipation of market-oriented enterprise led, in turn, to the democratization of citizen participation in governmental processes. In other words, economic freedom begat political freedom. And behind it all, as the keys to liberation, were simple human pleasures: the fulfillment of the desires of ordinary consumers and the satisfaction that supposedly would follow.

With the analysis presented here, I hope to invite a deeper consideration of whether, and how, a process rather different from the one envisioned by such Western critics might have been at work in communist Europe during the 1960s and 1970s, in the years when something like a socialist version of the Good Life started to take shape in some of the more prosperous East European societies. In questioning the certainties of the democratizing pathway envisioned by advocates of economic liberalization, I do not mean to claim that the societies of socialist Eastern Europe remained politically unfree because they simply never reached the requisite level of economic freedom. Even less do I posit any direct inverse relationship between the two types of freedom, according to which increases in economic and commercial autonomy would necessarily have led to *decreases* in democratic political liberties. Instead, I want to suggest the need to examine more closely the assumed nexus between *mercatura* and *civitas*—that is, between the economic activities of the market and the political work of citizenship—and thus to look for a variety of more subtle cultural, social, and civic consequences of liberalizing socialist "business." Commerce did indeed have serious effects on political engagement and the meaning of citizenship, but we must remain alert to outcomes that from the theoretical vantage point of the pro-market liberals would have been unwelcome, unanticipated, and certainly unintended. This means, in turn, acknowledging the possibility that what seemed to be and often were meant to be liberalizing moves in socialist economies might actually have resulted in a suppression—or, in less deliberate terms, a weakening—of democratic processes and popular involvement with political questions.[3]

Seen from the distance of more than a quarter century, the complexities of socialist Europe's historical record compel this sort of renewed and deepened inquiry. Recent studies on consumption under socialism have made us increasingly aware of how the consumer experience mattered—and how much it mattered. With this new emphasis on what shoppers and ordinary citizens expected and received, we are also beginning to direct more concern to the markets, marketplaces, and market makers themselves: the businesses, business practices, and businesspeople that delivered (and failed to deliver) the opportunities that consumers desired. On the face of things, at least, what we now know about the history of the socialist states of Eastern Europe raises the possibility that the reorientation of their economies toward either presumed or documented market signals, and especially toward those specific market signals represented by consumer demand, ended up working (perversely, from the liberal point of view) to the detriment of democracy. Even in those instances in which a policy shift toward the market was coupled with the extension of a certain degree of entrepreneurial or quasi-entrepreneurial freedom to producers and sellers, it may be the case that any incremental gains to the political culture of democracy were more than offset by the countervailing effects of a disengaged, politically apathetic, consumerist popular culture.

As explained below, the presumed existence of such trade-offs is one of the most frequent and most important implications of the substantial academic and critical literature on the topic that is the focus of my examination here: the nature and workings of a specific socialist version of the *social contract*, one that, through compromises and concessions regarding popular acceptance of communist rule and the accommodation of the public's expectations for increasing living standards, reflected the outcome of continual tacit "negotiations" between communist leaders and their citizens. Acknowledging the importance of contractual readings of socialist history for a wide variety of countries across the communist world, I argue that such approaches may, despite significant difficulties and weaknesses, have continuing utility for understanding the importance of consumer experience. (Social-contract interpretations may likewise prove useful for understanding other critical aspects of public welfare, such as the provision of health care, education, vacation and leisure opportunities, and retirement security, though these lie beyond the scope of the investigation here.) What is needed in future social-contract analyses, I suggest, is a more nuanced, complex, and open approach than has routinely been the case, one that recognizes useful alternative or parallel ways of construing the "bargains" at issue and tries to respond to the various problems that, as I show, often arise with contractually oriented readings.

There is plenty at stake here, as the costs to democracy and public political engagement of such state-society deals are potentially quite heavy. On this count, however, I maintain that we still do not know enough: in the social-contract literature too much has been asserted, and not enough has been proven. Accordingly, much work remains to be done, and as we continue to examine the complex meanings of the pleasures of progress and the pleasures of backwardness, the critical relationship between freedom and the Good Life (however these admittedly problematic concepts might be defined) will demand more of our care and attention.

Writ simply—too simply—the matter can be made to seem all very stark and grim: seen from the perspective of the harshest versions of the social-contract paradigm, the people of socialist society were bought off by their illegitimate leaders. Seeking to forget the scarcity and ravages of wartime, ordinary folk accepted the contractual terms offered, Faustian though they obviously were. Snared with luxury, seduced by ease, fooled into a belief in the joys of the self by the egoistic flatteries of consumer culture and consumerist culture, East Europeans opted to "lie quiet," as Faust himself put it, and give up the prerogatives of a more genuinely democratic citizenship in favor of full pantries, appealing shops, well-furnished apartments, and attractive wardrobes. Preferring the Mephistophelean offer "to eat what's good in peace," they were glad that the time had come, finally, to do just that—and none too soon for this struggling, habitually impoverished, and, yes, backward part of the European periphery. This is, to be sure, a dim view of the socialist citizen's ultimate fate, one that harmonizes well with some of the most influential critiques of communist rule.

Assertions that this sort of trade-off took place need not be inherently hostile to the socialist project, though often enough they have been. Nevertheless, whether framed as a resentful indictment of communism or, more neutrally, as an objective assessment of competing interests, such formulations about deals with the devil actually underscore the fundamental uncertainty of *both parties'* bargaining positions, a fact that may not be apparent from the outset. Yet even this more balanced judgment ultimately redounds to the detriment of communism, both normatively and analytically: ordinary East Europeans may have shown themselves repeatedly to be too weak to offer true democratic resistance with any success, but the communists were weak in their own way as well, and there were big worries that coercion had reached its limits. Mephistopheles needed the bargain, too.

TRADING PLACES: THE SOCIETIES OF COMMUNIST EUROPE AS SETTINGS FOR A SOCIAL CONTRACT

The idea of an unwritten, unacknowledged state-society accord along these lines is one with a long history, and evidence for it comes from many quarters. Surveying relations between communist governments and their peoples during the period of mature socialism in the 1970s and 1980s, the Czech emigré Antonin J. Liehm read contemporary events as evidence of a "new social contract" that helped guarantee the security of one-party rule. Under this arrangement, Liehm said, the socialist public had "ceded to the authorities its rights to free speech and assembly, its right to organize, and various other basic democratic rights" in a trade-off for "the state's provision of important social services and a degree of social security" along with "assured employment that, even if providing only mediocre wages, permits a standard of living above the poverty level," all of this taking place in circumstances in which "little real effort, personal involvement, or individual initiative is required" and where, as long as the contract holds, "social and political calm prevail, and there is no need for labor camps, revolts, terrorism, or more than a minimal number of political prisoners."[4] This was, to be sure, a pessimistic reading of existing conditions, and Liehm, who was part of the post-1968 exodus from Czechoslovakia, judged the socialist system to be paralyzed by "the generalized laxity, poor workmanship, decline of skills, and indifference that are the obvious and general consequences of the new social contract."[5] Socialism might have been going nowhere, but then again, neither were its communist leaders. Indeed, it was precisely this unshakeable persistence of Marxist-Leninist rule that Václav Havel had in mind in 1978 when he referred to "the historical encounter between dictatorship and the consumer society" as the foundation of the new, updated, "post-totalitarian" form of totalitarianism that he diagnosed as typical of contemporary communist governance, a system that was, according to Havel, grounded in a Faustian compromise made possible by "the general unwillingness of consumption-oriented people to sacrifice some material certainties for the sake of their own spiritual and moral integrity," by "their willingness to surrender higher values when faced with the trivializing temptations of modern civilization," and by "their vulnerability to the attractions of mass indifference."[6]

These observations came from a time when the communist monopoly on power seemed securely entrenched. We now know that it was not. Yet interest in a socialist version of the social contract has not subsided in the intervening years. Indeed, the growing number of post-1989 analyses that highlight the importance of consumption opportunities and consumer culture have, if anything, only heightened the suspicion that communism's stability depended on some underlying compact with the broader public that was tied to material satisfaction (or at the very minimum to material complacency).

As I have explained in an earlier study on the rise and demise of a Yugoslav Dream keyed to the pleasures of abundance, postmortems of the catastrophe that befell Yugoslavia are salted with the more-than-occasional accusation that the citizenry of the various republics had been bought off in just this way: that democratic processes and potentials had been squelched—consciously and even "diabolically," as some contemporary critics claimed—through the Titoist government's pursuit of a consumer-friendly economic policy.[7] In her wonderful, bittersweet lamentations on the Yugoslavs' Not-Quite-Paradise Lost, Slavenka Drakulić talks in this vein about the profound change in material circumstances that marked the country's escape from the shadow of the Second World War. The Good Life only arrived after years of real hardship: "It was my generation," Drakulić writes, "that grew up in times of scarcity when milk and butter, meat and clothes were rationed.... Sometimes we tasted powdered milk from UNRRA packages—it was so sweet that we licked it from our palms like some special kind of sweet. Or we'd eat yellow Cheddar cheese from the cans, or margarine, or 'Truman's eggs' as we called powdered eggs.... Married, we tried different combinations to escape living in crowded communal apartments shared by two or three families."[8] Drakulić goes on to suggest a connection between sacrifice and civic spirit: the immediate postwar generations that suffered these privations did so with a surprising willingness; they were deeply and genuinely involved in a broad-based, hopeful effort to build Yugoslav socialism. They cared about politics. For politics, and specifically socialist politics, seemed to many to give hope for new beginnings, for a more prosperous and just Yugoslavia. This had been, in other words, a society of engaged worker-*citizens*, even if the concept of citizenship that was involved in this new experiment broke with the norms of the liberal democratic tradition stretching back to the French Revolution and beyond.[9]

In stark contrast, those called on to fight the wars of the 1990s came from a generation of more or less oblivious plenty. As things got better, citizenship faded, and the new priorities were different: "career, money, but no politics, please."[10] In this view, newly depoliticized Yugoslav citizens—or had "subjects" become the better word?—undertook *"a kind of contract with the regime*: we realize you are here forever, we don't like you at all but we'll compromise if you let us be, if you don't press too hard."[11] The quid pro quo in this view may not have been stated explicitly, and the social contract involved here may have been harder to recognize in Yugoslavia than in other, more authoritarian societies. But it was a real agreement all the same. Yugoslavs, Drakulić muses, "traded our freedom for Italian shoes."[12]

Although Yugoslavia's embrace of consumerism was the most spectacular, the most whole-hearted, and the most successful, that ill-starred country does not stand alone as a special case when it comes to allegations of devil's bargains and freedoms bartered cheap. Indeed, much the same might be said of the longer postwar trajectories of any of those communist societies that ultimately managed to offer reasonable material progress and comfort. And much the same *is* being said right now about Vietnam and, a fortiori, about China, where the communist leadership seems to have cemented in place a system we might aptly call "Capitalism-Leninism," that is, all the insistence on the vanguard party's monopolistic control and ample authoritarianism but without the burdens and hindrances of any serious Marxist economics and, consequently, with plenty of room for private capital on a massive scale.[13]

Looking back to other socialist histories, we see what appears, at least at the outset, to be considerable evidence for the existence of some fundamental state-society bargain over consumption and material welfare. We should proceed with some caution here, especially in those cases where consumption opportunities remained limited, and material welfare was precarious at best: what we uncover from the deprivations of socialist Romania, for example, may make for another story altogether, while Poland and Bulgaria offer mixed and variable records, intriguing in their own ways despite some doubts about their governments' ability to consistently engage in bargaining with the public on the requisite material terms.[14] Still, as Mary Neuburger has shown for the Bulgarian case, even in an economy marked by considerable limitations, there were many moments of genuine satisfaction for consumers.[15] Here, too, there may well have been the makings of a social contract around consumption. Indeed, Martin Dimitrov's study of citizen complaints takes the existence of such an agreement as a given, notwithstanding the comparatively constrained potentials of the Bulgarian economy. "Communist regimes were bound by a social contract," Dimitrov insists, "and had to attempt to respond to the needs of the people, even when those needs included mundane items like jar lids and salt."[16]

The tumultuous history of socialist Poland likewise lends itself to interpretations in which the provision of basic social welfare benefits and services was the cost of political calm.[17] And while it is possible to read the bloody price-driven protests that led to the ouster of party secretary Władysław Gomułka in 1970 as evidence of "the declining relevance of the 'unwritten social contract,'" it may be best to view these events as a forced renegotiation of the terms of that deal.[18] Seen in this light, it proves very tempting to treat the pro-consumption policies adopted in the early 1970s by Gomułka's replacement Edward Gierek as an example of just this sort of deal—an awkward communist Food for Peace program, as it were. Short-lived as Gierek's successes proved to be, Poland's history is probably less indicative of the absence of any attempt to buy off the masses than of the simple *failure* of the ongoing effort to do so.

Even for the continually overstretched USSR it is possible to read the history of the post-Stalin "thaw" as a time marked not primarily by any principled rejection of terror and coercion as tools of political and social discipline but rather by an acknowledgment that attention to consumer desire might serve the same ends more effectively and with greater benefit to the overall soundness of the Soviet system. Social-contract ideas seem applicable to other periods of Soviet history as well. Just this type of resort to the material as a means of ensuring social stability and acquiescence was, for example, a critical element in Vera Dunham's 1976 account of "the Big Deal" between the leadership of the USSR and the country's middle socioeconomic stratum in the period between 1945 and Stalin's death in 1953.[19] Almost a decade later, James Millar expanded the notion of a state-society compact, arguing that in return for continued citizen compliance the Brezhnev regime concluded its own "Little Deal," a "conscious, if tacit, contract" pursuant to which the government opted to tolerate or disregard various illegal or potentially illegal forms of very small-scale private market activity and interpersonal economic reciprocity in order to increase the wealth of individuals and their households, thereby yielding a distribution of income, goods, and services that more closely meshed with consumer preferences.[20] With time, the idea of ongoing social contracts that both limited the range of state action and afforded citizens some meaningful influence over government by allowing them to grant or withhold consent became one of the most important interpretative paradigms of Soviet studies in the West.[21]

The history of East Germany lends itself readily to an interpretation along much the same lines. Although the GDR always remained to some extent a *Mangelgesellschaft*, a society of shortage and want, the country's leadership nevertheless sought to build social support through the explicit acknowledgment of the value of individual consumption in the development of party priorities.[22]

And though it could never surpass the Federal Republic as was promised, East Germany cultivated the consumerist orientation with some success and with a remarkable penchant for emulating certain ideologically suspect Western styles, models, and techniques.[23]

Here once again the idea of a conscious if unspoken social negotiation finds considerable support. Mark Landsman's careful study of East German consumption policy in the period before the severance of physical ties with the West concludes, for example, that such an exchange, or the perceived need for it, characterized much of the history of the GDR, especially in its final decades. Thus he presents the party leader Erich Honecker as deploying a set of policies "in which, for reasons of political expediency and the legitimation of the new leadership, consumption would enjoy a new autonomy from the hitherto all-important demands of production."[24] Landsman finds in the East German record evidence of still another communist deal as well: "Living standards would improve, albeit modestly; the regime would thereby ensure that its citizens continued to acquiesce to its rule. In short, Honecker was imposing *a trade-off: expanded consumption and material security in return for political quietude, if not loyalty.*"[25] Here the transaction—Food for Peace, or TVs for Peace, or Trabis for Peace—is conceptualized in stark, straightforward terms, and the most profound meanings of the consumerist course appear to lie precisely in the hoped-for potential for pacification. And Landsman is not alone in his interpretation; support for the idea of this sort of social contract in the GDR appears frequently in the literature on this, the best-studied case.

Indeed, the East German state-society bargain stands, as well as any instance does, as an emblem of the deals made, or at least the deals pursued, all across the Soviet sphere of influence, when consumption rose to prominence in the late socialist period as the single most important basis of communism's legitimacy and indeed its survival. As Tony Judt suggests in his grand synthesis of Europe's history after World War II, individual consumption became the key to the socialist system, just as it had for its capitalist rival. And the state-society contract hung in the balance: "Ever since it had become clear by the end of the Sixties that the future promise of 'Socialism' could no longer be counted upon *to bind citizens to the regime,*" Judt concludes, "Communist leaders had *opted instead to treat their subjects as consumers* and replace (socialist) utopia tomorrow with material abundance today."[26] Along these lines, as Judt observes, the promotion of consumer satisfaction was one of the first strategies adopted by the conservative Czechoslovak Central Committee secretary Vasil Bil'ák to deaden the memories of the Warsaw Pact invasion of 1968.[27]

With its comparatively strong manufacturing capacities in the consumer sector and its painful failed attempt to create a genuinely democratic and genuinely socialist reconceptualization of citizenship, Czechoslovakia's experience poses the questions under consideration here in a particularly straightforward and useful way. Along these lines, recent work on the "normalization" policies that followed the suppression of the Prague Spring corroborates and extends our understanding of a new social compact that emerged after 1968. In his work on the consumer advertising used to sell images of material abundance to the Czechoslovak population, Bradley Abrams emphasizes that the Soviet-led military intervention largely ended any prospects for genuine party-state legitimacy anchored in socialist values, with the communist leadership compelled to opt instead for "a strategy of legitimation based on consumption," a move that constituted, in effect, a social contract by which the regime "offered citizens a high standard of living—in comparison to the other countries of the socialist bloc—and strong growth in exchange for their political demobilization and their acceptance of the power of the Party."[28] Similarly, Paulina Bren's rich account of everyday life under normalization finds that a quiet retreat into the private world of consumption—a move that entailed a simultaneous retreat from politics—served as a principal strategy for citizens' self-realization in new and inhospitable circumstances. To seal the deal, the Czechoslovak authorities relied on alluring (and reassuring) visions of the material Good Life, carefully crafted and propagated through the mass media, with representations of comfort and material abundance serving, Bren suggests, as "the very images with which the normalization regime ... would barter over the next few years: images of a normalized Czechoslovakia triumphant in its victory over reform communism, offering capitalist-type consumption and the 'calm and light' that only a return to normality could bring."[29] Here, too, it is hard to escape the impression that a more democratic understanding of citizenship was what had been "bartered," that is, traded off, for increased access to consumer opportunities or at least the promise of some sunnier tomorrow.

In Hungary, public discourse lately seems inclined to treat the post-1956 Kádár era as one in which dreams of freedom were cashed in for well-stocked refrigerators, trendy fashions, cars from East Germany, and the private space of diverting little weekend houses to visit in those private automobiles. Writing in *Élet és Irodalom* (Life and literature), one of Hungary's leading forums for cultural opinion, György Báron has offered up just this sort of warning about the images of consumer delight captured in the films *Budapest Retró* (1998) and *Budapest Retró II* (2003), director Gábor Zsigmond Papp's shimmering documentaries on the Good Life of the 1960s and 1970s. Báron writes:

These harmless-seeming film clips are an exact imprint of the Kádár-era compromise. They don't lie to us in a coarse, shameless way—they just don't tell the whole truth. They show how, in spite of everything, it was possible to live here. That this place was pleasant and livable again. *There was no democracy, nor would there be.* Once again, however, the stores, cafés, clubs, cabarets, and nightspots were open. Everyone could buy a television (the lightning-quick spread of television at the beginning of the 1960s effectively *contributed to the de-politicization of the society*: people sat at home and gawked at dance-music festivals and ice-skating championships). The selection of goods increased.[30]

Seen in this way, abundance starts to look like the price of silence, and vice versa. Krisztina Fehérváry, in her examinations of the centrality of pro-consumption policy to the "normal" nature of postsocialist Hungarian life, confirms such judgments of "the Kádár Compromise," noting that expanded opportunities for consumers were critical to the restoration of the "normal" in post-1956 Hungary as well and explicitly describing the new policy as a "bargain" intended to recover some degree of legitimacy.[31] "Attempting to appease a hostile populace," she writes, "the government prioritized improving standards of living by increasing production of consumer goods and housing *in exchange for political acquiescence*."[32] Mark Pittaway, one of the most careful and sensitive observers of these aspects of life in Hungary after socialism, likewise finds strong evidence that the "ability to deliver the goods, to offer the promise of a socialist consumerism" was a key element of what he argues were critical (and to a surprising extent overlooked) processes of "*bottom-up negotiation* of legitimation in Central and Eastern European societies" in the socialist period.[33]

The Hungarian case, with its clear shift to palliative pro-consumer policies in the wake of the failed 1956 revolution, offers perhaps the most obvious suggestion of a quid pro quo and the clearest example of the kind of contractual relationship that has been suggested. Whether the deal that Hungarians (and others) arguably made was a *good* one, of course, depends on a set of judgments that take us quickly beyond the historiographical historical and into the normative world of the moral and the political, and then further on into the still volatile arena of postcommunist wrong righting and score settling, with the multiple competing memory projects that play into those new political conflicts in subtle and not-so-subtle ways. But in any case, there is now a growing collection of contemporary East European social critics who, like György Báron, view in retrospect the rise of a potent mass consumer culture as a central element in the tragedy of the socialist venture.[34] And so the nature of the communist-era social contract has become (as contemporary moral questions often do) a guiding concern in the interpretation of the communist past, with a perhaps inevitable spillover into the professional historiography of state socialism and of Eastern Europe and the Soviet Union more generally.

WHAT'S THE DEAL? QUESTIONING THE TERMS OF THE COMMUNIST-ERA SOCIAL CONTRACT

Against the common proposition of a cynical, calculated effort to dampen the desire for democratic participation, we should consider another possibility: that the pro-consumption policies of the postwar period may have reflected a rather more genuine desire to raise living standards broadly across the society, to the ultimate benefit of the working class and the peasantry. Instead of some deliberate buy off, the authorities' moves could thus appear from this altered perspective as a more earnest, even innocuous effort to give working people their just rewards. Often enough, communist leaders described the diversion of resources away from the capital-intensive buildup of heavy industry and toward consumption aims in precisely such terms. It is in this spirit, for example, that we find Yugoslavia's Josip Broz Tito insisting that "the generation which is alive right now and which is building a new society with its efforts must enjoy the fruits of its labor, not just some distant, future generations."[35] And though the leaders of the Soviet Union, working against the backdrop of Stalinist ideology's familiar assurances of a "radiant future," could never manage to fully deliver on that shiny talk either in the short term or for any "distant, future generations," it may be appropriate to treat even their promises in this light as well: a better life, understood first and foremost in material and therefore reliably Marxist terms, was to be the payment for the long sacrifices of building socialism.

In other words, we need to recognize that as the productive capacities of the socialist societies grew in the aftermath of World War II, there was an eminently natural logical and ideological connection to the pursuit of consumer abundance, even if it turned out that the game had to be played on the rather unfavorable terms that the economic "miracle" of the postwar West had already established. The effort to generate real consumer satisfaction may accordingly support a somewhat contrarian and surprising reading as a principled extension of Marxist doctrine to new circumstances.

In the end, the indisputable excesses (and, yes, crimes) of the communist regimes may have made it a bit too tempting to dismiss as cynical and transitory what was arguably a genuine and enduring desire to honor labor. It is, in any case, undeniable that raising living standards for the broad masses was among the highest priorities for Marxian socialism from its very beginnings: a bedrock commitment of communist political activity. Our conceptualization of postwar socialist consumption, and of the course and consequences of the long effort at building and rebuilding that commenced after 1945, therefore ought to acknowledge the dangers of such a trivializing reading. Moving instead toward a different understanding of the new consumerist policies as "just rewards" would, of course, demand that we take the nearly always disquieting tack of accepting the communist leaders more or less at their word. And there is no doubt something worrisome about an approach that may assume too easily the good intentions behind their actions and the transparency of their statements.

Yet even in the absence of any deeper, darker, Mephistophelean purposes on the part of the communist authorities, this different rendering of history, grounded as it is in the idea of rewards earned by worker-citizens for their contributions to the socialist project and their role as the basis of the socialist state, would still leave us with a social contract, a deal with the masses. It becomes, however, a rather different kind of contract. Reimagining the arrangement in this way would no longer yield any simple Faustian bargain: no souls are being sold. Moreover, the parties' exchanges are negotiated on quite different terms—most notably, with no public quiescence as a quid pro quo—while "performance on the contract," to use the legal terminology for the actions required for the parties to satisfy their agreed-upon expectations, ends up being accomplished in a very different sequence, with citizens performing their obligations first (and basically delivering all that was required of them simply by virtue of their being citizens) in advance of the state's provision of increased material abundance. In such a reading, not only were the various regimes' decisions to allocate and reallocate benefits to their worker-consumers fully justified by the distributional imperatives of socialism, but the rewards in question would have been precisely that: rewards. This interpretation, in other words, posits something more like straightforward recompense for worthy work in the cause of socialism that had *already* been done, offered by the communists not as an advance payment to buy obedience but instead after the fact, in fulfillment of a principled pact with their peoples that reflected the fundamental goals and values of the socialist mission.

Framing the relationship in this way, as was repeatedly done in the public rhetoric of East European socialism, has the important analytical effect of ending this particular state-society transaction with the *delivery* of the consumer goodies: although there may well be the unstated promise of future rewards for future hard work, the contractual arrangement is not explicitly conceived of as one that entails later obligations from the populace (and much less as one that implicitly requires a future acquiescence in antidemocratic subjugation).

If it may be fairly understood in such terms, the consumer-oriented shift of the later postwar period thus begins to look less like some radical (desperate?) bargaining maneuver or a drastic, forced revision of the terms of a preexisting arrangement between state and citizens and more like a move toward accelerating the delivery schedule on an obligation that socialist governments had envisioned from the start.

At this point a word of caution is in order, however. Leaving aside the important question of the communists' intent in developing consumer-friendly policies, there is much to be lost by understanding the relationship at issue as one in which the benefits enjoyed by worker-consumers were, first and foremost, the material manifestations of an essentially unilateral move on the part of state and party officials, bestowed, as it were, on more or less passive, unchallenging, and powerless recipients. The evidence suggests otherwise: these may have been *just* (merited) rewards, but they were not just (merely) *rewards*. My observation on this point is not meant to stoke the smoldering debates, too often underproductive, about the wide dispersal of historical agency and the overrigidity of the state-society distinction. For Marxist-Leninist societies, at least, there is truly no serious danger of making "the state" disappear. Under socialism, governments maintained barriers against citizen participation that were quite real and considerably less fluid and permeable than the lines of division in liberal democracies, where a sharp state-society distinction makes (perhaps) less sense or does so less reliably. Indeed, in the communist context, the very category *citizen* may require a rethinking that sets it apart in fundamental ways from the terms and practices of the West. Moreover, communist rule limited the agency of ordinary citizens in ways so important and so real that to place too much emphasis on their state-resisting power and creative initiative runs the risk of insulting their experience of oppression (as, in fact, some of those who have lived through communism take offense today when they encounter this tendency in progressive Western historiography).

That much said, a more careful reading of the interplay between the desires of consumers and the aims of policy makers does suggest that, in many cases, worker-consumers proved to be very engaged participants in a complex, ongoing, and surprisingly *interactive* social negotiation over the further development of communist policy. However we are to best understand the exchange between state and society, it was certainly not what would be called in legal parlance a "contract of adhesion," that is, a take-it-or-leave-it deal that is essentially forced on one, much weaker contracting party. (Think here of the standard credit card or rental car agreement, which is not subject to any meaningful negotiation regarding its specific terms. The only alternative is to forsake the transaction altogether and walk away, and walking away was typically not an option for citizens of state-socialist countries.) The evidence from Hungary, Yugoslavia, Czechoslovakia, and the GDR, the cases I have examined in detail, suggests that ordinary consumers actually had plenty to say on the subject of their present and future well-being, and representatives of the state and party often took their interests and the expression of their attitudes seriously, especially during and after the 1960s. (The precise periodization of the shift varies, understandably, with the internal political and economic dynamics of a given society.)

In the end, then, it does make a good deal of sense to conceive of the interchange over consumption policy in transactional or even specifically contractual terms. Of course, the notion of the social contract has always been a metaphor, one that captures reality in ways that are either less or more concrete and accurate depending on the circumstances of the societies and regimes in question. Yet even the peculiar conditions of socialist governance may not stretch the metaphor too far. There were obvious limits to the negotiating room permitted in the Marxist-Leninist version of *le contrat social*. Whether the communists would govern was not subject to dispute. But *how* they would do so does appear to have been on the table.

Sociologists and political scientists were once especially keen to this insight, grounded in the theoretical as it is. It is from this perspective, for example, that we find Stephen White in 1986 taking the existence of some sort of essential bargain for legitimacy—variously termed a "social contract," a "social compact," or a "social compromise"—as a reliable, given feature of the encounters between all of the state-socialist regimes and their citizens.[36] In this social-scientific formulation, the communists' "social compact" is said to entail "the surrender of a wide range of political liberties, such as competitive elections and an independent press, in return for a range of socioeconomic benefits, such as comprehensive social security, full employment, stable prices, easygoing industrial discipline, and steadily increasing living standards."[37] At that particular historical juncture in the mid-1980s, of course, the persistence of authoritarian regimes of all stripes, not just communist, was a major academic concern, and a big legitimacy literature reflected those worries. For the state-socialist variants of authoritarianism, at least, the answers usually seemed to lie in the realm of the material.

Following the collapse of communism and the apparent triumph of liberalism, political scientists hastened on from red threats to greener pastures, with the body of scholarship on the legitimacy of European communist regimes, and even many of its underlying questions, tending to wither away. Among historians, the drop-off in interest in such issues was even more noticeable. Burdened with suspect Cold War associations, an explicit concern for regime legitimacy and how it was maintained is no longer a principal theme in the professional historiography of Eastern Europe, if indeed it ever occupied such a privileged place. (In recent years, however, there are some signs of an interesting revival, including interpretations that might refocus our inquiry away from the past's more pure concern with "high" politics.[38] Similarly, the resurgence of authoritarianism in Russia, Hungary, and Poland—and new worries about illiberal leaders and publics in Western Europe and the United States—may spark fresh interest in the tools used by authoritarian leaders to gain and keep power.) Inattention to such problems of legitimacy has been compounded of late by a marked shift in historiographical focus to the social, the cultural, and the everyday, a trend in which I have been a happy and (for the most part) unapologetic participant. But something of the old ways does need to be preserved here: the metaphorical (or not-so-metaphorical) contracts and the ways in which they were made and performed were, I believe, critically important, as they mattered not just for high politics but for the realm of everyday life as well. Consumption, both as a subject of policy and as a subject of lived experience, was where party leadership met citizen expectations—where the contractual arrangement lived or died. And it is here that the highest value of a new historiographical initiative, one that takes the concept of the social contract seriously, might lie.

DELIVERING THE GOODS: COMING TO TERMS WITH COMMUNISM'S DIFFICULT DEALS

The state-society bargain under communism was a hard one—hard on its participants and hard to pin down. For the communists, it was difficult to accept, difficult to construct, difficult to negotiate, and difficult to fulfill. And for their peoples, it proved difficult, too, albeit for different reasons.

First, there is good cause to believe that for many of the regimes involved, the idea of a reorientation of priorities to the consumer sector proved very hard to swallow. Many party leaders were fairly content with older inclinations toward the subordination of consumption, and we must also acknowledge the extent to which socialist culture propagated, with some notable successes, a set of alternative, more traditionally socialist ideas about consumption that focused on the collective rather than the individual, on the public rather than the private, on the virtues of time rather than the virtues of acquisition, and on experiences rather than things.[39] On this particular count, much of the most probative evidence is likely still to be examined, in the party archives of the various socialist states. Particularly regarding the troublesome issue of the communists' state of mind in opting for a consumerist direction—a diabolical ploy or just rewards?—it has been and may well remain difficult to establish any conclusive answer. A "smoking gun" may never be forthcoming. But the archives and other sources do reveal, over and over again, an abiding perception of the need to raise living standards, diversify consumer offerings, spur sales, and meet public demand. In addition, a good deal is already known about the high-level debates over economic policy, and some of the texture of the internal conflict over a perceived imperative for a social compact can be gleaned from that. As Mark Landsman observes, in the GDR "an unresolved tension persisted between... voices arguing for ever-greater productivity in heavy industry and strict modesty in individual consumption, and those calling for a richer, more-developed set of consumption possibilities. Between the poles of austerity and relative generosity, consumption policy swung back and forth, depending on the amount of pressure at any given moment to address consumer dissatisfaction."[40] The Poles, the Hungarians, and the Czechoslovaks were clearly subject to the same sorts of pressures, and when the option for some "new" economic system arrived, it typically came only after much debate, and it had to be defended with much after-the-fact propagandizing. Even the Yugoslavs, who gained tremendous international prestige (along with trading partners, military aid, and foreign credit) as a result of their break with Soviet-style economic orthodoxy, had difficulty relinquishing top-down guidance of the economy. In fact, tensions between the planning impulse and the market mechanism persisted even after the country's more dramatic self-management reforms of 1965, and the market never really won out completely. There, as elsewhere in Eastern Europe, the economy remained subject to the "soft budget constraints" that János Kornai has identified as a critical source of weakness in the socialist system. In other words, unprofitable enterprises could almost always be assured that they would not face the prospect of bankruptcy or otherwise be forced to bring their costs in line with their revenues.[41] That flexibility made the expensive option for increased consumption somewhat easier to countenance and to put into practice, but substantial resistance remained.

The social bargain was a hard one in another sense as well: the "contract" itself proved very difficult to design. Even after the decision in favor of a more (or more or less) consumer-oriented course, communists faced very serious problems in determining just what was to be offered. Compounding these economies' all-too-apparent difficulties in achieving output goals in *any* production sector, the isolation of government, party, and enterprise leaders from reliable channels of data about consumer desire tended to deprive the authorities of essential knowledge about the basic terms of the exchange. The continued reliance on top-down economic planning, even after the introduction of some market-oriented reforms, made matters more difficult still. This failure of information threatened to thwart any state-society accord from the outset.

There were efforts to cure these defects, to be sure. In particular, the economic elites of many East European states sought to varying extents to adopt and adapt the theories and practices of the new discipline of marketing, which contemplated not just the perfection of consumer-targeted advertising messages to stimulate sales but also—and more importantly for our purposes here—a complementary process of continuous market research designed to establish just what it was that consumers desired at any given moment. (The *marketing concept*, as developed in the postwar United States and Western Europe, envisions the sales relationship not as one of trying to market what the producer makes but rather trying to make what the consumer wants.[42]) Socialist economic specialists followed the evolution of marketing with interest and worked to elaborate their own variants, but despite significant developments in many locales, the discipline always remained embattled because of its undeniably capitalist provenance and foundations.[43] And to the extent that market research or other, less exact indicators of consumer preference showed an inclination toward tastes and standards that were identifiably Western, the effort to meet those desires by acknowledging them in the deal with citizens ran into sometimes staunch resistance from party leaders and cultural critics, who opposed what they perceived as a drift toward corrupt, capitalist consumerism.

Cultural transfers from outside the socialist sphere, something in its consequences akin to what lawyers refer to as third-party interference with contractual relations, also made the state-society transaction difficult to establish and settle. In the realm of the ideological, Soviet and East European communism had staked out a claim to be, as Victoria de Grazia observes, "the leading alternative to the hegemony of American consumer culture for practically the entire period from 1945 to its disintegration in the late 1980s."[44] Here there actually was serious resistance to capitalism's "irresistible empire," but the demonstration effects arising from East Europeans' observations of Western consumerist values and Western consumer standards proved so influential that they repeatedly intruded into the Marxist version of an alternative social compact, shifting the terms of the state-society bargain over consumer welfare in ways that made the communists' position much less tenable.

There was a third fundamental problem as well: to the extent that the authorities hoped to negotiate an enduring compact with worker-consumers, the modalities of communist governance deprived them of reliable means of doing so. Here again, the leadership faced a hard bargain: they had few good ways of knowing that the deal they proposed would be understood, accepted, and honored in practice. Admittedly, the liberal governments of Western capitalism have themselves faced a number of somewhat similar problems due to the imperfect information flows; the aggregation, dilution, and masking of citizen preferences; and other procedural defects inherent in representative democracy. But those governments were not "on the line" to nearly the same extent as their communist counterparts; they had not made the state itself directly responsible for delivering individual consumer satisfaction in the same way.

The difference between systems was critical. Democratic governance allows citizens to send fairly direct cues to state actors about the nature and terms of the social contract and about the state's performance in living up to its side of the bargain. In contrast, the methods of communist rule, the strictures of the state-socialist media, and the weakness of nongovernmental civil society left comparatively little scope for the transmission of such messages. There were, of course, a number of channels in which citizens' attitudes could flow and be observed—letters and complaints to party and state representatives, for example, or surveys of public opinion, which became a critical tool across the region. But often these methods communicated a sense of societal values and interests only very imperfectly, and communist leaders sometimes proved deaf to discontent. As a result, dissatisfaction could and did bubble over unpleasantly, even violently, from time to time. Such unrest did, of course, carry a real informational value of its own, and it no doubt had a certain salutary clarifying and focusing effect on policy makers. These episodes were particularly in evidence in the earlier decades of the postwar period, and they are typically understood, rightly I believe, to have been an essential inducement to the socialist state's offer of a new social contract grounded in living standards. If anything, though, they only strengthen the more general conclusion that a communist version of the social contract proved extraordinarily difficult to negotiate.

Finally, and most importantly, the bargain was a hard one for communist states to fulfill. The vital point is this: even the most prosperous societies of socialist Europe ultimately failed to meet the terms imposed by consumers. Structural flaws in the functioning of the socialist economies hampered the effort from the start, but even when there were early and genuinely impressive successes in raising living standards, these proved insufficient. The problem was exacerbated by the governments' efforts to celebrate those successes and promote a culture of consumption in the media, in advertising, and in other sectors of what became, in remarkably short order, a socialist "culture industry" with real similarities to the media machines so derided by the Frankfurt School and other critics of Western capitalism. Socialist consumers, it turned out, were quickly trained to expect more: a constantly expanding array of goods, services, and experiences, all to be supplied in constantly increasing quantity and quality. For the socialist economic system, even with the modest efficiency gains that may have resulted from the imposition of tentative market mechanisms, this abundance proved impossible to deliver over the long term. The problem, in brief, was that the deal with the populace was never fixed, finite, and reliable. Consumers demanded, in essence, a constant renegotiation of the social compact and an ever-higher price for their cooperation. Sated only for a time, they would not "lie quiet" indefinitely. Meanwhile, those of a more oppositional or dissident bent remained unsatisfied with the very notion of any compact based on consumption, calling instead for civic and political rights and citing the need "to proceed from the breakdown of the tacit consensus to open negotiations."[45]

All this emphasis on the many difficulties facing the state may run the risk of presenting socialist consumers, somewhat paradoxically, as the privileged parties to the transaction. But in important ways, they faced a hard bargain, too. I am not suggesting, however, that the exchange has to be understood as an exacting one in the ways implied by the harshest versions of the social-contract thesis. It is not at all clear, at least at this point in the development of the historiography of socialism, that we must see a bitter, dejected abandonment of citizenship as the unavoidable cost of comparative tranquility in the last two decades of European communism (with a very untranquil, politicized Polish citizenry as the most glaring exception to any such general pattern). Rather, the trade was a hard one in other, more subtle ways. Insofar as the communist authorities sought quiescence and the continued surrender of democratic-liberal prerogatives of citizen participation, they were loath to do so openly. Instead, state and party messages about social-contractual expectations and demands had to be communicated obliquely, through coded bureaucratese and the promotion of lifestyles linked to the pleasures of consumption. This indirectness left citizens (and leaves historians) with little in the way of specific details about just what the state was demanding from its contractual partners. Ordinary East Europeans also wrestled with other problems in acquiring the basic information needed to construct and ratify the compact. From what they saw in their grocery shops and department stores, they could judge well enough what the state had managed to deliver thus far. Promises about the future were another matter entirely. Communist production schedules were notoriously unreliable, to say nothing of the ever-present but ever-shifting one-year and

Five-Year Plans. Past failures to make good on prior commitments to improve living standards and even to surpass the West left a good deal of justified skepticism among consumers.

The bargain was hard for consumers in another important way as well. Accepting the premise of a social compact centered on consumer satisfaction leaves us with the difficult question of how ordinary socialist citizens could induce the state to perform on the contract, that is, to deliver on its side of the agreement. Are we to think of worker-consumers, acting either individually or more often through their unions, as trying to maximize their leverage and their potential returns under the terms of a continually renegotiated deal? If so, their interests might have been best served by the constant maintenance of a state of discontent just short of unrest and by the loudest possible airing of that discontent consistent with their own political, social, and physical security. (Perhaps surprisingly, socialist consumers were given fairly wide latitude to grumble openly about their government's failures to deliver in material terms.[46]) Such a perspective would suggest that communist leaders, noting high levels of endemic dissatisfaction, would have had an abiding incentive to compensate their consuming publics to the greatest extent possible. Or should we, in contrast, see worker-consumers as willing to maintain their quiescence as long as some basic minimum threshold of material necessity was maintained? Again, the *terms* of these putative social contracts remain ill defined: they were unclear at the time for states and for citizens, and they remain unclear for historians. We therefore need to consider whether socialist populations edged toward the unruly only when living standards became intolerable or whether their individual and collective demands amounted to a more conscious, aggressive, and activist strategy that pressed the state to deliver returns in excess of what would have been the bare contractual minimum. The latter formulation confers much more historical agency on the ordinary members of communist societies, a point that has its appeal to some present-day observers. But it may or may not be the more accurate conceptualization. So just how demanding were these consumer-bargainers? Even with many important new contributions to the field, that question lies open to future research.

There are other issues at stake as well and significant problems inherent in the adoption of interpretative schemata rooted in contractual concepts. Most importantly, we need to worry not just about whether the communists' pro-consumption reorientation was a calculated move against civic engagement in matters political but, just as importantly, about whether it had such effects, as the social-contract theory typically supposes. Can we fairly conclude that the satisfaction of material desires *supplanted* a more robust sense of political citizenship, as suggested by Slavenka Drakulić's finding of a consumerist "contract with the regime" built on the premise "career, money, but no politics, please"?[47] And if so, on what evidentiary basis? Problems of proof will be big problems indeed.

These questions of interpretation are especially delicate in the context of Marxist-Leninist governance. For the liberal democracies, the terrain is decidedly different: one can argue persuasively that there was no inevitable zero-sum trade-off between the pursuit of consumption and the exercise of citizenship, at least as notions of citizenship are habitually framed in liberal-democratic terms, that is, as comparatively circumscribed matters of political-legal rights. It has been easy enough, of course, to claim that a delusory, egoistic engagement with the pleasures of consumption has turned citizens of the capitalist West away from a genuine, substantive engagement with the world of the political, thereby vitiating the liberal-democratic concept of citizenship and leaving those hallowed political-legal rights as merely empty, hollowed-out shells. Yet the two domains have not been understood as hopelessly opposed in the way that the idea of a state-society trade-off, "diabolical" or otherwise, makes them out to be in the case of communism. Lizabeth Cohen is thus able to make a cogent case for the construction of the United States following World War II as a "Consumers' Republic," a fusion of market values and civic values "that entrusted the private mass consumption marketplace, supported by government resources, with delivering not only economic prosperity but also loftier social and political ambitions for a more equal, free, and democratic nation."[48] The melding of consumer identity with citizenship is, for Cohen, subject to shifts, changes, and tensions, and it is not without its problems, but her account leaves open the possibility that the two may be conjoined without the total eclipse of citizenship. The liberal democratic Consumers' Republic remains a republic—a res publica, a public matter, a thing of the people.

Citizenship meant something else under state socialism, even if what it meant is still not entirely clear. A few things are certain, though. The so-called people's republics were not real republics, and they had at best a very tortuous relationship with their citizens. In many if not most of the states of socialist Europe, the terms *citizenship* and *citizen* smacked of the bourgeois and were not favored categories of analysis in public discourse and political culture. Marxism-Leninism may or may not have been, as some have alleged, the demon spawn of the Enlightenment, but whatever the lineage, the revolutionary tradition's exaltation of *citoyenneté* was clearly a trait that failed to pass to that particular generation.

And yet the social contract theory of the Enlightenment may be more useful to the communist context than it appears initially. The latter-day historiographical propensity to insist on the "negotiated" quality of virtually every social interaction is now in danger of becoming a cliché, but for the cases at hand it may prove quite helpful. By reinforcing a sense of the limited, contingent, and—dare we say it?—contractual nature of even authoritarian communist governance, this sort of interpretative approach may go some way toward restoring "the people" to the people's republics. Of course, we need to be sensitive to the ways in which transactional theories in general and the notion of a social compact in particular may work to obscure rather than to illuminate. Still, there is a great deal to be said for this line of analysis. Seen in this way, the process of belonging in state-socialist societies becomes, if not precisely Ernest Renan's "everyday plebiscite" of national identification, then at least something very much like an everyday bargain: the repeated ratification of an elusive but nevertheless meaningful social contract, an expression of consent to the terms of governance if not to the identity of the governors themselves, and an acceptance of, or at least acquiescence in, the new and more limited identity of citizen that the socialist systems had sought to cultivate.

NOTES

The research for this article was supported by the International Research and Exchanges Board and the American Council of Learned Societies and by a grant from the National Council for Eurasian and East European Research, funds which that were made available by the U.S. Department of State under Title VIII 8 (The Soviet-East European Research and Training Act of 1983, as amended).

1. "U.S. Policies toward Yugoslavia," 1. This unsigned confidential memorandum was dated July 15, 1965, date declassified April 27, 2001, available through the Declassified Documents Reference System, a Gale Database (galenet.galegroup.com), with the document title "Paper Regarding U.S. Policy toward Yugoslavia" (emphasis added).

2. Ibid. On the promotion of consumption as a "weapon" against communist orthodoxy, see also the similar opinions of Johnson-era politicians and government advisers discussed in Neuburger, "Kebabche," 58.

3. It should be noted, of course, that socialist and other left-wing dissections of liberal democratic capitalist society have frequently asserted that the liberal economic "freedom" accorded to businesses in the consumer marketplace have resulted in precisely such losses in democratic engagement and public concern for politics, with citizens "bought off" by consumer abundance and the promise of expanding material satisfaction. Such critiques were typical of Cold War–era

socialist analysis, but they proved popular in the West as well, and they have survived the collapse of communism.

4. Liehm, "New Social Contract," 174. See also Liehm, "Intellectuals."

5. Liehm, "New Social Contract," 178.

6. Havel, "Power of the Powerless," 20. Another influential analysis of the dynamics of "post-totalitarian" governance, with repeated emphasis on the potential for public resistance, is Goldfarb, *Beyond Glasnost*.

7. See Patterson, *Bought and Sold*, 316–19; see also 225–51.

8. Drakulić, *Balkan Express*, 131–32.

9. Yugoslavia thus may present a significant counterexample to both the essentially fictive quality of production enterprises as economic subjects and the lack of autonomous nonstate political subjects that Jadwiga Staniszkis diagnosed as characteristic of state socialism. See Staniszkis, *Ontology of Socialism*.

10. Drakulić, *Balkan Express*, 132–33.

11. Ibid., 135 (emphasis added).

12. Ibid.

13. On China's "market social contract," see Tang and Parish, *Chinese Urban Life*.

14. See, for example, Crowley, "Warsaw's Shops," 25–47.

15. For example, Neuburger, "Kebabche," esp. 60–65; Neuburger, *Balkan Smoke*, chaps. 6–7.

16. Dimitrov, "What the Party Wanted," 280.

17. See, for example, Ost, "Polish Labor," 36–38; Verdery, "Theorizing Socialism."

18. Ost, "Polish Labor," 38. Ost concludes that the Gomułka-era social contract had been breached: "When it was broken by one side, as the government did with its cutbacks and retrenchments in 1969–1970, then the other side reevaluated it, too." Ibid.

19. Dunham, *In Stalin's Time*, esp. 41–58 (on possessions) and 87–109 (on status).

20. Millar, "Little Deal," 700. Provocatively, Lewis H. Siegelbaum's reading of the "deal" represented by the Soviet government's faltering efforts to accommodate demand for automobiles reverses the familiar formulations, suggesting that it was the communist regime that sold its soul and betrayed its values. "Faust enters into the bargain," he writes, "because in mass-producing cars and allocating most of them to the 'population,' the Soviet state virtually guaranteed that millions of its citizens would become entangled in webs of essentially private—in the double sense of invisibility to the state and as particularistic as opposed to collective activity—relations that were ideologically alien and often in violation of Soviet laws." Siegelbaum, "Cars," 97.

21. See the extensive analysis in Cook, *Soviet Social Contract*, 2–5. Cook notes that despite the popularity of the social-contract approach to the state-society power balance, Sovietologists developed a variety of alternative explanations.

22. See, for example, Merkel, *Utopie und Bedürfnis*; Merkel, "Consumer Culture."

23. See Patterson, "Making Markets Marxist?"; see notes at 285–88; Patterson, "Risky Business."

24. Landsman, *Dictatorship and Demand*, 215.

25. Landsman, *Dictatorship and Demand*, 215 (emphasis added). Landsman concludes that even Honecker's predecessor, Walter Ulbricht, had bowed to some extent to the "politically dangerous" imperatives of consumer demand. Ibid.

26. Judt, *Postwar*, 580 (emphasis added).

27. Ibid., 581.

28. Abrams, "Reklama ou Propagace?" 110.

29. See Bren, *Greengrocer and His TV*, 86.

30. Báron, "Neonfényes Budapest," n.p. (emphasis added).

31. Fehérváry, *Politics in Color*, 79.

32. Fehérváry, "American Kitchens," 384 (emphasis added).

33. Pittaway, "Home Front," (emphasis added); see also Pittaway, *Eastern Europe*.

34. These and other nostalgic memories of a communist Good Life have inspired a number of barbed antisocialist counterhistories. For an attempt to remind Hungarians of the repressive apparatus obscured by the beckoning storefronts, see, for example, Simon and Szerencsés, *Azok a Kádári "Szép" Napok*.

35. Tito, quoted in Šetinc, *Smo Potrošniška Družba*, 64.

36. White, "Economic Performance," 463, citing as examples of the three conceptions, respectively, of Kusin, *From Dubcek*, 179; Pravda, "Industrial Workers," 226–27, 250–52; and Fehér, Heller, and Márkus, *Dictatorship over Needs*, 104, 277–79. The idea that economic benefits may themselves confer legitimacy, White notes, takes the theory of legitimation well beyond the bases established in Max Weber's classic formulation: "rational-legal"/procedural, "traditional," and "charismatic." White, 462–64, citing Weber, *Economy and Society*, 212–99.

37. White, "Economic Performance," 468. White further observed that there was "every reason, at least on the face of it, to expect this economic slowdown [of the late 1970s and early 1980s] to have serious consequences for the social compact or for the . . . politico-economic equation upon which, it has been argued, the regimes' legitimacy has been based" (ibid.). But he concluded that communist authorities could likely still find adequate ways of adapting and building legitimacy through other techniques—largely by reaching out in other (still fundamentally nondemocratic) ways to incorporate broader social groups into party activities and the spheres of party concern.

38. Notable here is Ramet, *Three Yugoslavias*.

39. On this point, I acknowledge a number of the merits of Alexei Yurchak's challenge, made at the conference that inspired this volume, to socialist consumption-studies scholarship that has largely conformed to the terms of consumer "progress" established by Western developments. The more traditional socialist alternative values were strong, as Yurchak suggests, and they were popular in many quarters. But at least in the most prosperous socialist societies in the years of late-stage, "mature" socialism, the evidence of a widespread perceived need to respond to (and if possible surpass) capitalist-derived standards of the Good Life is also compelling.

40. Landsman, *Dictatorship and Demand*, 11–12.

41. See Kornai, *Socialist System*.

42. See the classic text, Kotler, *Marketing Management*. Kotler's text enjoyed a surprising currency in East European advertising and marketing circles.

43. Patterson, "Bad Science"; Patterson, "Prague Spring." "Market research," as opposed to marketing per se, fared somewhat better, even in more orthodox states such as Czechoslovakia and the GDR.

44. Grazia, *Irresistible Empire*, 11.

45. See, for example, Kis, Kőszeg, and Solt, "New Social Contract." Kis is credited in the original as the author of the section calling for a new social contract. These contributions suggest in turn a broader left-oriented attack on consumerism that confronted both its capitalist and socialist iterations. Seen most notably in the West through the work of the Frankfurt School critics, these Marxist-humanist perspectives evidenced deep dissatisfaction with what they diagnosed, in both systems, as elite impulses toward the authoritarian manipulation of culture. For an examination of how leftist critiques of this sort played out forcefully in Yugoslavia, see Patterson, *Bought and Sold*, 225–51.

46. This was true even in some of the more repressive communist states. See, for example, Berdahl, *Where the World Ended*, 60–66. Paul Betts recognizes the widespread use of *Eingaben* (complaints to authorities) in the GDR as the basis of an "elaborate institutionalized 'culture of complaint.'" Betts, "Building Socialism at Home," 123, citing Staadt, *Eingaben*, 9–13.

47. See Drakulić, *Balkan Express*, 132–33, 135.

48. Cohen, *Consumers' Republic*, 13.

REFERENCES

Abrams, Bradley. "Reklama ou propagace? Les vicissitudes de la publicité socialiste en Tchécoslovaquie Communiste." In *Vie quotidienne et pouvoirs sous le communisme: Consommer à l'Est*, edited by Nadège Ragaru and Antonela Capelle-Pogăcean, 109–41. Paris: Karthala, 2010.

Báron, György. "Neonfényes Budapest." *Élet és Irodalom* 47, no. 32 (August 8, 2003). http://www.es.hu.
Berdahl, Daphne. *Where the World Ended: Re-unification and Identity in the German Borderland*. Berkeley: University of California Press, 1999.
Betts, Paul. "Building Socialism at Home: The Case of East German Interiors." In *Socialist Modern: East German Everyday Culture and Politics*, edited by Katherine Pence and Paul Betts, 96–132. Ann Arbor: University of Michigan Press, 2008.
Bren, Paulina. *The Greengrocer and His TV: The Culture of Communism after the 1968 Prague Spring*. Ithaca, NY: Cornell University Press, 2010.
Cohen, Lizabeth. *A Consumers' Republic: The Politics of Mass Consumption in Postwar America*. New York: Vintage Books, 2003.
Cook, Linda J. *The Soviet Social Contract and Why It Failed: Welfare Policy and Workers' Politics from Brezhnev to Yeltsin*. Cambridge, MA: Harvard University Press, 1993.
Crowley, David. "Warsaw's Shops, Stalinism, and the Thaw." In *Style and Socialism: Modernity and Material Culture in Post-War Eastern Europe*, edited by Susan E. Reid and David Crowley, 25–47. Oxford: Berg, 2000.
Grazia, Victoria de. *Irresistible Empire: America's Advance through 20th-Century Europe*. Cambridge, MA: Belknap Press of Harvard University Press, 2005.
Dimitrov, Martin K. "What the Party Wanted to Know: Citizen Complaints as a 'Barometer of Public Opinion' in Communist Bulgaria." *East European Politics and Societies* 28, no. 2 (May 2014): 271–95.
Drakulić, Slavenka. *The Balkan Express: Fragments from the Other Side of War*. New York: Harper Perennial, 1993.
Dunham, Vera S. *In Stalin's Time: Middleclass Values in Soviet Fiction*. Cambridge: Cambridge University Press, 1976.
Fehér, Ferenc, Ágnes Heller, and György Márkus. *Dictatorship over Needs*. Oxford: Blackwell, 1983.
Fehérváry, Krisztina. "American Kitchens, Luxury Bathrooms, and the Search for a 'Normal' Life in Postsocialist Hungary." *Ethnos* 67, no. 3 (2002): 369–400.
———. *Politics in Color and Concrete: Socialist Materialities and the Middle Class in Hungary*. Bloomington: Indiana University Press, 2013.
Goethe, Johann Wolfgang von. *Faust, Acts I and II Complete*. Translated by A. S. [Tony] Kline. Accessed October 31, 2018. www.poetryintranslation.com/PITBR/German/FaustIScenesIVtoVI.htm.
Goldfarb, Jeffrey C. *Beyond Glasnost: The Post-Totalitarian Mind*. Chicago: University of Chicago Press, 1989.
Havel, Václav. "The Power of the Powerless." Translated by Paul Wilson. In Václav Havel, *The Power of the Powerless: Citizens against the State in*

Central-Eastern Europe, 2nd ed., edited by John Keane, 10–59. London: Routledge, 2009.

Judt, Tony. *Postwar: A History of Europe since 1945*. New York: Penguin, 2005.

Kis, János, Ferenc Kőszeg, and Ottilia Solt. "A New Social Contract." Translated by Radio Free Europe. In *From Stalinism to Pluralism: A Documentary History of Eastern Europe since 1945*, 2nd ed., edited by Gale Stokes, 233–36. New York: Oxford University Press, 1996. [Originally published as part of Kis, Kőszeg, and Solt, "Társadalmi szerződés."]

———. "Társadalmi szerződés." Special issue, *Beszélő*, no. 20 (1987). http://beszelo.c3.hu/cikkek/valsagban-cselekedni.

Kornai, János. *The Socialist System: The Political Economy of Communism*. Princeton, NJ: Princeton University Press, 1992.

Kotler, Philip J. *Marketing Management: Analysis, Planning, and Control*. Englewood Cliffs, NJ: Prentice-Hall, 1967.

Kusin, Vladimir. *From Dubcek to Charter 77*. Edinburgh: Q Press, 1978.

Landsman, Mark. *Dictatorship and Demand: The Politics of Consumerism in East Germany*. Cambridge, MA: Harvard University Press, 2005.

Liehm, Antonin J. "The Intellectuals on the New Social Contract." *Telos* 23 (Spring 1975): 156–64.

———. "The New Social Contract and the Parallel Polity." In *Dissent in Eastern Europe*, edited by Jane Leftwich Curry, 173–81. New York: Praeger, 1983.

Merkel, Ina. "Consumer Culture in the GDR; or, How the Struggle for Antimodernity Was Lost on the Battleground of Consumer Culture." In *Getting and Spending: European and American Consumer Societies in the Twentieth Century*, edited by Susan Strasser, Charles McGovern, and Matthias Judt, 281–99. Cambridge: Cambridge University Press, 1998.

———. *Utopie und Bedürfnis: die Geschichte der Konsumkultur in der DDR*. Cologne, Germany: Böhlau, 1999.

Millar, James R. "The Little Deal: Brezhnev's Contribution to Acquisitive Socialism." *Slavic Review* 44, no. 4 (Winter 1985): 694–706.

Neuburger, Mary. *Balkan Smoke: Tobacco and the Making of Modern Bulgaria*. Ithaca, NY: Cornell University Press, 2012.

———. "Kebabche, Caviar or Hot Dogs? Consuming the Cold War at the Plovdiv Fair 1947–72." *Journal of Contemporary History* 47, no. 1 (January 2012): 48–68.

Ost, David. "Polish Labor before and after Solidarity." *International Labor and Working-Class History*, no. 50 (Fall 1996): 29–43.

Patterson, Patrick Hyder. "The Bad Science and the Black Arts: The Reception of Marketing in Socialist Europe." In *The Rise of Marketing and Market Research*, edited by Hartmut Berghoff, Philip Scranton, and Uwe Spiekermann, 269–93. New York: Palgrave Macmillan, 2012.

———. *Bought and Sold: Living and Losing the Good Life in Socialist Yugoslavia.* Ithaca, NY: Cornell University Press, 2011.

———. "Making Markets Marxist? The East European Grocery Store from Rationing to Rationality to Rationalizations." In *Food Chains: From Farmyard to Shopping Cart*, edited by Warren Belasco and Roger Horowitz, 196–216. Philadelphia: University of Pennsylvania Press, 2009.

———. "The Prague Spring and the Big Chill: The Marketing Moment in Communist Czechoslovakia." *Journal of Historical Research in Marketing* 8, no. 1 (2016): 120–40.

———. "Risky Business: What Was Really Being Sold in the Department Stores of Socialist Eastern Europe?" In *Communism Unwrapped: Consumption in Cold War Eastern Europe*, edited by Paulina Bren and Mary Neuburger, 116–39. New York: Oxford University Press, 2012.

Pittaway, Mark. *Eastern Europe 1939–2000.* London: Hodder Arnold, 2004.

———. "A Home Front in the Cold War: Hungary, 1948–1989." Accessed October 31, 2018. http://www.history.ac.uk/ihr/Focus/cold/articles/pittaway.html.

Pravda, Alex. "Industrial Workers: Patterns of Dissent, Opposition and Accommodation." In *Opposition in Eastern Europe*, edited by Rudolf L. Tőkés, 209–62. London: Macmillan, 1979.

Ramet, Sabrina. *The Three Yugoslavias: State-Building and Legitimation, 1918–2005.* Washington, DC: Woodrow Wilson Center; Bloomington: Indiana University Press, 2006.

Siegelbaum, Lewis H. "Cars, Cars, and More Cars: The Faustian Bargain of the Brezhnev Era." In *Borders of Socialism: Private Spheres of Soviet Russia*, edited by Lewis H. Siegelbaum, 83–103. New York: Palgrave Macmillan, 2006.

Simon, István, and Károly Szerencsés. *Azok a Kádári "Szép" Napok: Dokumentumok a Hetvenes Évek Történetéből.* Budapest: Kairosz, 2004.

Staadt, Joachim. *Eingaben: Die Institutionalisierte Meckerkultur in der DDR.* Berlin: Freie Universität Berlin, 1996.

Staniszkis, Jadwiga. *The Ontology of Socialism.* Oxford: Clarendon; New York: Oxford University Press, 1992.

Šetinc, Franc. *Smo Potrošniška Družba.* Ljubljana, Slovenia: Zveza Delavskih Univerz Slovenije/Dopisna Delavska Univerza Univerzum, 1980.

Tang, Wenfang, and William L. Parish. *Chinese Urban Life under Reform: The Changing Social Contract.* Cambridge: Cambridge University Press, 2000.

"U.S. Policies toward Yugoslavia" [alternative title: "Paper Regarding U.S. Policy toward Yugoslavia"]. Unsigned confidential memorandum, July 15, 1965. Declassified Documents Reference System, Gale Databases.

Verdery, Katherine. "Theorizing Socialism: A Prologue to the 'Transition.'" *American Ethnologist* 18, no. 3 (August 1991): 419–39.

White, Stephen. "Economic Performance and Communist Legitimacy." *World Politics* 38, no. 3 (April 1986): 462–82.

Weber, Max. *Economy and Society.* Edited by Guenther Roth and Claus Wittich. Berkeley: University of California Press, 1978.

AUTHOR BIO

PATRICK HYDER PATTERSON is Associate Professor of History at the University of California, San Diego. He is author of *Bought and Sold: Living and Losing the Good Life in Socialist Yugoslavia* (2011). His research centers on the history of twentieth-century Eastern Europe and the Balkans, with major emphases on everyday life and consumer culture and on the interplay of Islam, Christianity, and secular society.

FOUR

CONCEPTUALIZING CONSUMPTION IN THE POLISH PEOPLE'S REPUBLIC

BRIAN PORTER-SZŰCS

The study of everyday life under communism has already blurred the once sharp dichotomies of the Cold War.[1] The distinction between a capitalist world of hedonistic consumption and an ascetic socialism of self-sacrifice and personal abnegation is now widely recognized as too simplistic, even when considering the Stalinist era (not to mention later). Nonetheless, there remains a general sense that consumerism was an unintended development in the communist bloc, a capitalist virus that the state planners had hoped to inoculate their populations against. Even as we learn more about consumer culture in the Soviet bloc, we all too often assume that "shortage economies" were the necessary outcome of existing socialism. Images of people standing in long lines for toilet paper remain a metaphor not only for the struggles of daily life in the four decades after World War II but for communism in the abstract. In some ways this is appropriate, but it is important to recognize that the economists of the communist world appreciated the importance—indeed, the centrality—of personal consumption. In fact, from the very earliest postwar years, the economists of the Polish People's Republic (Polska Rzeczpospolita Ludowa, or PRL) listed consumer abundance among their primary objectives, even as they recognized that Poland was a long, long way from achieving this goal. The proliferation of consumer goods was not an unanticipated side effect of socialist modernization; nor did it stem from bread-and-circuses concessions aimed at pacifying a restless population. In contrast to some of the other contributors to this volume, I do not see the increased production of consumer goods in the 1960s and (even more) the 1970s as a quest for legitimacy, as an economic means to a political end. Even if it did serve that function, I have found no evidence that any of the leading policy makers or professional economists perceived consumer production in such an instrumental way. Quite the contrary: they saw the provision of such goods as a crucial marker of socialist success. But *how* these men and women (mostly men) positioned consumption within their broader world views highlighted some important distinctions from their capitalist peers. To be more precise, there were sharp ideological differences between mainstream communist economists and mainstream capitalist economists in the 1950s and 1960s, but these distinctions began to blur in surprising ways in the 1970s. Unlike most of their Western counterparts immediately after World War II, but very much *like* those who rose to prominence a generation later, the economists of the PRL had a fundamentally supply-side world view that could only accommodate rational economic actors.

Focusing on this aspect of communist economics not only helps us better understand the people's republics but also offers a new perspective on why those states failed. It globalizes the story of communist Eastern Europe and suggests a possible unified framework for studying the shifts in economic thought during the second half of the twentieth century. We are accustomed to thinking of the period from 1945 to 1989 as a conflict between capitalism and socialism, and obviously that dichotomy was important. But cutting across it was another contest, one that we usually perceive only *within* capitalism: the debate between supply-side and demand-side perspectives, between Friedman and Keynes.

The sociologist Johanna Bockman has pointed out that a common set of assumptions based on neoclassical economics (with its emphasis on Pareto optimality) allowed economists East and West to share a common, mostly mathematical language.[2] Whether in communist planning bureaus or in Wall Street investment firms, economists have been trained since the early twentieth century to model economic life as a balanced equation in which efficiency and rationality are maximized if prices (however established) serve to bring production and consumption—supply and demand—into a state of equilibrium. Whether this balance is attained through the invisible hand of the market or the heavy hand of state planning is a separate issue as far as the theoretical modeling is concerned. Bockman's goal is to rehabilitate the contribution of Eastern-bloc economists to the development of neoclassical theory and debunk the tendency to collapse the broad range of neoclassical approaches into a single neoliberal box. Modern economic methods and theories, she shows, could be applied to market socialism just as well as laissez-faire capitalism. The eventual triumph of neoliberalism at the end of the twentieth century entailed the marginalization and willful forgetting of many antiliberal but still neoclassical arguments.

The shared ground of neoclassicism, however, was nonetheless a site for bitter arguments, even though these were sliced in ways that are not immediately visible through the Cold War fog. Recognizing the common assumptions and methods that united economists East and West allows us to see the global nature of the academic and ideological debates of the twentieth century, and that in turn frees us to reposition the key players in those conflicts. In the immediate post–World War II era, most economic policy makers (and probably most academic economists) in the United States and Western Europe accepted two fundamental premises: (1) that the "animal spirits" of consumer demand (to appropriate Keynes' phrase) fueled the engine of economic growth and (2) that the goal of economic policy was to maximize the living standards of the greatest number *precisely in order to harness that power*.[3] Challenging these ideas were those who believed (1) that economic behavior, like all human behavior, could be understood in terms of a universalistic rationality; and (2) that the goal of economic policy should be to concentrate decision-making authority in the hands of those best equipped to perceive and understand these economic laws, and work within them to maximize aggregate growth. In the former camp would be a range of left-liberal and social-democratic thinkers and policy makers in Western Europe and the United States; in the latter were their communist contemporaries in the Soviet bloc *and* (starting in the 1970s) in the economics departments of most US universities. To be more precise, the communists were committed to the general maximizing and equalizing of material well-being but within structures of power characterized by Leninist principles of "democratic centralism." They advocated the egalitarian distribution of wealth but the hierarchical and inegalitarian distribution of policy-making authority. Moreover, East European economists were accustomed to planning for consumption and for *needs*, but not for the "irrationality" (as they saw it) of consumer *demand*. Thus, they were flummoxed by the idiosyncratic and unplanned—indeed, unplannable—culture of consumption that arose throughout the Soviet bloc in the 1960s and 1970s but well equipped to appreciate the supply-side consensus that took hold within their discipline. In the late 1970s and 1980s, many of those East Europeans met their US counterparts thanks to academic exchange programs that brought Soviet-bloc economists to study at US universities. Those students did not have much in common with demand-side Keynesians, but they learned a lot from the supply-siders.[4]

Economists enjoyed a place of honor within the communist state, even at a time when the other social sciences lost funding or got squeezed into silence by censorship. Building on a foundation of internally famous economists from the prewar era like Oskar Lange, the newly expanded higher education system in the PRL began immediately to train people for the thousands of jobs in the rapidly growing state planning apparatus. Most firms employed economists in administrative positions, and these people were considered members of the intelligentsia.[5] Marxist economics became a topic in secondary school education, requiring even more university classes and postgraduate training programs for teachers. In other words, the category of *economist* was quite expansive in the PRL, and the ideas, assumptions, priorities, and rhetorical practices of these economists penetrated far beyond the academy.

If we go back to the Stalinist era, we find Polish economic textbooks predictably filled with quotations from Lenin and Stalin and with the tendentious prose that is familiar from that time. But the very fact that these writings were so clichéd helps us identify the ideological truisms that constituted the foundational assumptions of policy makers. For example, consider this passage from a 1954 textbook by Józef Zawadzki: "Joseph Stalin formulated the basic characteristics and requirements of the fundamental economic laws of socialism in this way: to ensure the maximum satisfaction of the ever-increasing material and cultural needs of the entire society, by means of uninterrupted growth and the improvement of socialist production based on the most advanced technology. An economic law of socialism formulated in this way... demonstrates its deeply humanist character. The goal of production is the person and his/her needs, it is the satisfaction of his/her material and cultural needs."[6] Similar phraseology can be found in just about every lecture on political economy, every official pronouncement, every textbook. In fact, that specific catchphrase—"guaranteeing the maximum satisfaction of the ever-increasing material and cultural needs of the entire society" (zapewnienie maksymalnego zaspokojenia stale rosnących materialnych i kulturalnych potrzeb całego społeczeństwa)—was repeated like a mantra. Another widely used economics textbook (by Włodzimierz Brus) affirmed that "in contrast to the capitalist system, in which production serves to ensure profits... the goal of socialist production is the maximum satisfaction of the ever-increasing material and cultural needs of society.... A socialist society cannot exist and grow if social production does not serve the person, with the ever-fuller satisfaction of his needs.... Production can never, in any system, be separated from consumption."[7] Similarly, in a public lecture he gave shortly after the war, Brus said that "growth in consumption in all spheres, growth in the wellbeing and the culture of the laboring person, is a fundamental goal of the socialist national economy."[8] Most accounts of economic policy during the Stalinist years emphasize the commitment to industrial expansion at the expense of consumer production, which is certainly appropriate.[9] But we misunderstand the goals and the mind-set of the people formulating these policies if we imagine them as puritanical zealots focusing only on how many tons of steel could be produced.[10] They shared a conviction that Poland had to rebuild as quickly as possible and that a rapid transition from an agrarian to an industrial society was of the utmost importance, but this was invariably cast as a means to an end. In a 1954 lecture to PZPR (Polska Zjednoczona Partia Robotnicza, the Polish United Workers' Party) activists, Brus emphasized this pressing need: "One of the most important economic tasks during the transitional period is a distribution of national production so as (on the one hand) to achieve growth in the population's consumption, and (on the other hand) to ensure the needs of accumulation, guarantee the ongoing growth and improvement of production, all of which is in turn an essential condition for the growth in consumption."[11] Or to quote Zawadzki once again: "Raising the living standards of the working class demands the socialist industrialization of the country. A country that does not want to fall into economic dependency on the capitalist world . . . cannot develop industry serving the direct satisfaction of the needs of society without simultaneously building industries that produce the means for that production. Socialist industrialization is thus the necessary means of raising the living standards of the working class."[12]

This mentality fit smoothly within the overarching worldview of Stalinism, with its fear of dependency and its emphasis on the autarky of the socialist bloc. But the foundation of this view went deeper than its Stalinist accoutrements. Brus stressed the need to sacrifice in the name of resisting "American imperialism," but he assured his readers that socialism was distinguished from capitalism precisely by its ability to realize the needs of the consumer. "The goal of capitalist production is profit," he wrote, "attained by means of the exploitation of the working class, which leads directly to a decrease in the consumption capacity, and thus to a decrease in consumption among the masses." Socialism, in contrast, "not only gives the people freedom, but simultaneously creates the conditions for a prosperous life."[13] After 1956 the Sisyphean quest for self-sufficiency would weaken considerably, and in many spheres it would be abandoned altogether. But it is more important to notice what did *not* change: the desire to provide consumer goods to individuals. Włodzimierz Brus and Kazimierz Łaski, writing in 1962, urged a slower pace and a more balanced economic strategy but did not alter their earlier objectives:

> Prolonging the time for accomplishing the process of acceleration is essential in order to weaken the contradiction between the growth of investment and current consumption. . . . By no means (aside from specific instances of an external nature) should one blindly aspire to decrease as much as possible the period in which the capacity of the labor force is underutilized (even if

that would be optimal in an abstract sense). Instead, one must aspire to the optimal harmonization of the interests of growth and future consumption with the needs of current consumption.... The strategy for growth during this time period must emphasize the utilization of all means to shorten the time of incomplete absorption of the labor force without weakening current consumption.[14]

"Underutilization of the labor force" refers to what would be called "unemployment" in the capitalist world. During the Stalinist era this problem was given a high priority both because of the demands of postwar reconstruction and because universal employment was one of the PRL's most obvious benefits. But creating all those jobs meant investing in the construction of new firms, and that in turn required that some profits be retained and not distributed in the form of wages.[15] For example, a 1968 text by Janusz Górski, written for officials in the PZPR's Department of Propaganda, acknowledged that wages had not increased as quickly as desired, and he recognized that this was an important failure. He explained that the need for "accumulation" (reserving resources for investment and growth) meant that an inadequate sum had remained for wages, but he offered arguments that could be used to persuade workers that this was all in their long-term best interest. He also noted that wages and consumption *had* in fact increased in the aggregate, because so many previously unemployed or low-wage workers had been brought into the mainstream of economic life. Górski admitted that such improvements were too abstract for many individual workers who were just a little bit higher up on the income scale, because their pay had indeed stagnated. But such people should be reassured, he wrote, that "the socialist system of production is dedicated to a goal different than every previous system of production.... That goal has become the aspiration to achieve the highest possible and always increasing satisfaction of the needs of the working people."[16]

By the 1970s most Polish economists realized that the PRL had not provided the abundance that had been promised two decades earlier, but the greater emphasis they gave to consumer production did not entail a reorientation of socialist goals. Stanisław Markowski, in a book from 1972 written for officials in the state-run trade-union apparatus, acknowledged that "mistakes had been made" in this area, "consisting of an inadequate recognition of the consumption needs of the population." Alluding to the infamous (and ultimately failed) attempt to raise prices in 1970, Markowski criticized the misguided "effort to balance the emerging economic disproportions exclusively by way of limiting the possibilities of improved consumption." Of course, he also cautioned that demands for consumer goods would always have to be balanced against the need

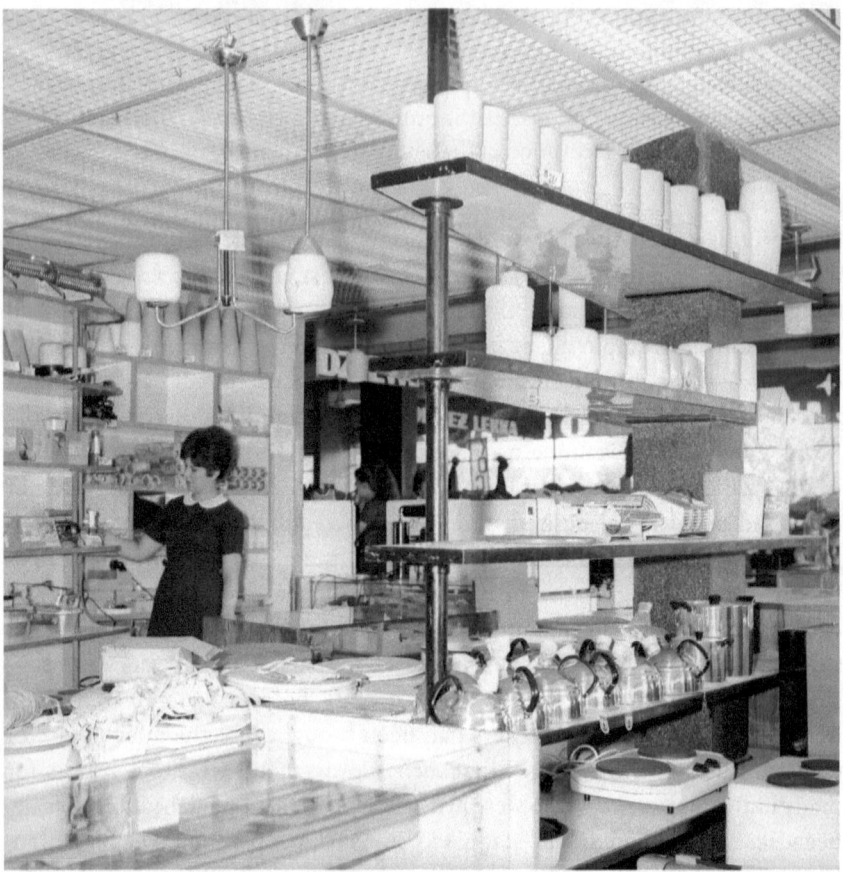

Fig. 4.1. Warsaw shop, 1967. National Digital Archive of Poland (Narodowe Archiwum Cyfrowe).

to amass reserves for future investment, but he lamented that too much stress had been placed on the latter. In fact, he wrote that in the 1960s there had been a tendency to lose sight of the primary goal of socialism ("the ever increasing satisfaction of the needs of society") and to instead expand "production for the sake of production."[17] There was no longer the need for such a breakneck pace of industrial expansion, Markowski argued. Instead it was time to focus on more careful steps toward greater efficiency and productivity. Historians have too often taken presentations such as Markowski's at face value, describing a fundamental shift in the 1970s toward the production of consumer goods (not just in Poland but throughout the communist bloc).[18] What is truly striking about this shift, however, is that comparatively little actually shifted (see table 4.1).

Table 4.1. Share of profit devoted to accumulation and consumption.

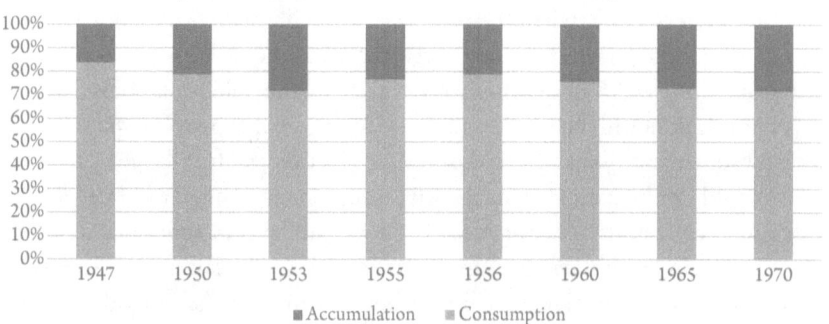

To be sure, accumulation had increased in the early 1950s and then again in the late 1960s, but emphasizing that point distracts us from the fact that the ebb and flow of this figure remained in the single digits, with about a quarter (give or take a couple percentage points) of all profits being directed to the satisfaction of consumer needs throughout the communist era.[19]

These differences were not trivial, but neither were they large enough to lead to major changes in living standards. And they certainly did not reflect a fundamental change in values or goals. The economists and policy makers of the 1970s constructed a straw horse in their polemics with their predecessors, such as when Markowski wrote that "consumption must not be treated—as it has often been treated in the past—as a burden, which got in the way of directing the national economy." In fact, he continued, "the loftier the culture of consumption, the more rational the consumption, the more efficient the production."[20] Compare this to the words of Józef Zawadzki from 1954: "Growing needs create demand for socialist production, and growing production permits a better and more comprehensive satisfaction of the needs of the population. At the same time, with the growth of production and aggregate supply, the real income of the population and its consumption capacity also rises. For a socialist system, the domestic market has a decisive significance. It follows that socialist industry requires for its development the expansion of a domestic market and of aggregate demand for manufactured goods."[21] Just as the goals remained the same, so did the key vocabulary.

Contained in that passage by Zawadzki is the core tension within the worldview of the PRL's policy makers and economists: the slippage between the terms *need* (*potrzeba*) and *demand* (*popyt*). While the word *demand* was discussed with increasing frequency over the course of the communist era, it tended to slide back toward the more comfortable concept of need. Markowski wrapped all this up in a nice tautology: "We can speak of the maximum satisfaction of needs only when the purchaser can obtain on the market the collection of goods that best corresponds to his individual needs as well as his purchasing power."[22] Underpinning virtually all the debates and discussions of economic policy in the PRL was a desire to assess what people *required*—not only for sustenance but also for personal satisfaction and fulfillment. This concept should not be caricatured: the PRL's economists understood need to be a dynamic concept that changed with the overall level of economic development and included material requirements as well as entertainment, recreation, sports, intellectual engagement, and other "cultural needs." The idea of *consumer production* was used narrowly to refer to things that would be purchased by individuals (in other words, household goods or services that involved out-of-pocket expenses).[23] But the category of *consumption* could also refer to needs in a way that encompassed spending on things like schools, concert halls, cinemas, vacation resorts, and so on. In 1955 Włodzimierz Brus emphasized what he called "social forms of satisfying needs," including "social insurance, paid leave, family allocations, education, culture, healthcare, maternal care and childcare, vacations, construction of housing and of community facilities, etc."[24] More than a decade later, Janusz Górski similarly wrote that "within the framework of socialist consumption we will give an ever-growing preference to rational relaxation, which will be expressed in the construction of vacation centers (both long-term and for Sunday getaways), urban recreation centers (beaches, swimming pools, parks), restaurant chains, etc."[25]

Jumping out from Górski's quotation is the word "rational," pointing to the fact that the PRL's economists were every bit as enamored with the utility-maximizing *Homo economicus* as are many economists today. This creature did not really change in his incarnation as *Homo sovieticus*; the only difference was that the object of efficiency maximization shifted from the firm to "society." In both cases this notional human was first and foremost (supposed to be) a *rational* being.[26] Górski jumped from adjective to adverb in his enthusiasm for rationality: he characterized the primary goal of economic policy as "the satisfaction of the immediate, rational needs of the individual" and argued that policy should be formulated "to rationally satisfy the needs of the individual." In fact, communist authors argued that capitalism was weak precisely because it was incapable of expressing genuine economic rationality. As Górski put it, capitalism "leads to the creation of an irrational structure of production, from society's point of view." Because the pursuit of profit led to activities that undermined the pursuit of what was "rationally" optimal, from the broadest perspective, capitalism was doomed to fail. In contrast, this text continued, in a socialist system "economic activity is subordinated to genuine social needs.... We want economic activity to be conducted in the most rational manner."[27] Stanisław Markowski directed a similar logic toward the policy choices faced within the socialist system. Though increased consumption must always be the goal of a socialist state, he wrote in 1972, if pay was allowed to rise too quickly, it could "weaken the interest of the workers in increasing the efficiency of their labor," and, more important, "some of the consumption could assume an irrational nature."[28]

For all the references to "humanism" in Polish economic texts, the concept of social justice on which this version of socialism was based had a firm grounding in rationality—which makes sense if we recognize that the humans in this humanism were conceived as rational beings who would respond consistently and predictably to economic stimuli. Among the many myths about communism is the assertion that it was a system without incentives. Although the ultimate threats of unemployment and homelessness were taken off the table, there were still plenty of incentives for both line workers and managers. Górski defended the (comparatively modest) inequalities within socialism by arguing that "the existing differences in income are based on the criterion of the utility of the individual for society, and therefore they constitute an incentive for raising the workers' qualifications and the efficiency of their labor."[29] Brus, writing in 1955, even defended consumer production in these terms: "If the economic policy of the state doesn't go in the direction of exploiting the existing possibilities for satisfying the needs of the working people, this would bring about a weakening of the incentives to work, and a divergence in the ratio between the amount of products manufactured and the purchasing power of the society—and as a consequence the impossibility of permanent growth in production, the employment of all those able to work, etc."[30]

The Keynesian idea that high wages could actually generate growth by increasing demand was either dismissed out of hand or (more commonly) not even recognized as a possibility. In a 1963 lecture at the Warsaw Center for Party Propaganda, Kazimierz Łaski contrasted Keynesianism with "a socialist economy characterized by a shift in emphasis (when dealing with growth) from the factors of demand to the factors of supply." He derided his British counterpart for caring only about employment and production and for believing "that the purpose and utility [of investment] is unimportant."[31] Demand-side approaches could appear in other guises as well. Janusz Górski condemned what he labeled "market socialism," which he identified with Dubcek's Czechoslovakia and Tito's Yugoslavia. Such an approach, he argued, promised "a better fit between the structure of supply and the structure of demand" but would in fact only introduce irrationality and "anarchy" back into the economy.[32] As Brus and Łaski put it in their 1962 textbook, "Socialism brings Alice out of the Wonderland in which the existing material productive capacity and the unemployed labor force remains unutilized because of some supernatural lack of adequate aggregate demand." If this sounds like supply-side economics, that is no coincidence—but not simply because of East-West exchange among professional economists or because they all shared a common neoclassical mind-set. More specifically, their interpretation of Marxism was focused on supply, with demand having no independent causal force.

This supply-side approach was quite explicit, and it was present from the very early postwar years. Brus and Łaski argued that "a realistic model of growth for a socialist economy takes as a point of departure not the problem of aggregate effective demand, but the problem of the size of disposable factors for growth, and thus it accentuates above all the supply side [*strona podaży*] as the factor limiting the size and the tempo of the growth of production."[33] In a public lecture from the late 1940s, Brus was already denouncing capitalism for basing production on demand, which in his opinion led to the "anarchy" of overproduction. He saw the quest for profit at the root of this economic chaos and promised that socialism would replace this with "creative cooperation and noble competition, free from the exploitation of the creators."[34] Discussions of monetary policy were cast in similar terms. Zdzisław Federowicz argued in 1959 that socialism utilized fiscal measures to ensure that "the size of the production of the means of consumption determine the level of pay," in contrast to a capitalist approach that allowed pay to rise and fall based on some arbitrary measure of the value of the labor performed. Federowicz posited steadily rising wages as a basic goal but believed that the only way to achieve this was to increase production. With more goods on the market, he believed, it would be possible to give workers more money to buy them.[35]

This supply-side orientation entailed more than just a repudiation of consumer demand as an engine for growth; even more important was an aversion to irrational *desire*. Górski wrote that "particular emphasis should be placed on creating the conditions for the development of the social being, educated and cultivated, integrated with society.... Our model of consumption consciously rejects the subordination of the individual to the domination of objects, the desire to uncritically collect new goods, when the collecting becomes the goal and the goods cease to be what they ought to be—that is, only the means to make life easier, the means to enable the free development of the individual."[36] Passages like this can be quoted to illustrate a supposed communist asceticism, but note that Górski was more precisely condemning irrational *desire*, not consumption as such. Indeed, he followed all the other authors I've discussed so far by insisting that socialism would eventually provide all the creature comforts of modernity. But it would do so *rationally*.

For this reason, communist economists give virtually no attention to the development of mechanisms aimed at translating consumer desires into production mandates. Even in the late 1980s, as economists were scrambling to come up with reforms that would save Poland from total collapse, they took it as a given that determining consumer desires was irrelevant; if anything, their reforms were aimed at *suppressing* desires in order to bring them into balance with current levels of production. In 1987 Jerzy Borowiecki wrote an essay for the party's Ideological Education Department in which he presented the axiom that "a growth in employment can be attained either thanks to a growth in the working-age population, or thanks to the professional activation of part of the population [not currently working].... The tempo of growth depends on the tempo of investment." In other words, the possibility that new consumer desires (new demands) could lead to new jobs was not even under consideration.[37] During the open discussion at an academic conference from 1983, one audience member said, "I differentiate demand from need; this has a fundamental significance. The role of the plan is to realize... social preferences, [but] such preferences are tied up not so much with demand, or not only with demand, but particularly with a system of needs."[38] Another participant at that conference argued that the main cause of the economic crisis was that "additional demand... has drained the market," so the solution could only be raising prices until that demand was suppressed.[39] Yet another laid out the problem starkly: "Market disequilibrium can be liquidated in two logically equivalent ways: either by increasing production and the supply of market goods, or by reducing effective consumer demand. Reestablishing equilibrium by increasing production and supply would of course be the most desired and the most attractive socially. The deficiency of supply related to demand, however, currently equals 25–30 percent of the population's expenses. In this situation, combating that deficiency with an annual growth in per capita GNP of 2 percent would be like shooting a tank with a bow and arrow. Therefore, we are left with reducing effective demand."[40] Such arguments were not evidence of the encroachment of neoliberal capitalist thinking at the twilight of the communist era. Quite the contrary: they were deeply embedded in the intellectual history of economic thought in the PRL. For example, Kazimierz Łaski made this point in the aforementioned lecture on Keynesianism from 1963, in which he argued (with what would turn out to be unjustified optimism) that inadequate demand was inconceivable in a socialist economy, because irrational desire had been replaced by rational need: "This is why attention in the analysis of growth in a socialist economy is directed mainly towards supply—towards the growth in the means of production—and not towards demand. A socialist economy develops therefore with the goal of increasing the abundance of goods for the satisfaction of social needs; this goal defines the mobilization and utilization of the means of growth and delineates the tempo of growth. . . . The phenomenon of limiting production because of insufficient demand does not arise."[41] In his 1974 research described in a paper titled "The Socio-Economic Aspects of Individual Consumption in Poland," presented internally at the PZPR's Higher School for Social Science, Ryszard Zabrzewski criticized what he considered an overly simplistic understanding of the old slogan of "maximizing the satisfaction of the material and cultural needs of the entire society." This could not be "reduced only to the needs of consumption," he argued, because "the subjective imaginings of consumers about their needs are often incompatible with the recommendations of science." For example, desire can lead to alcoholism, drug addiction, and bad eating habits, so a socialist economy could not commit itself to satisfying desires masquerading as needs. Worse still, Zabrzewski wrote, were demands created by "psychological and social factors, among which a critical role is played by fashion and other irrational motivations. . . . This is a problem that is very hard to resolve correctly." The difficulty came mainly from Zabrzewski's recognition that *need* was a difficult term to define, because different societies satisfied fundamental human needs for things like clothing and food in different ways. This was entirely appropriate, he thought, but such variety had to be accommodated in a way that did not surrender to irrationality. The solution, he argued, was to "prioritize the satisfaction of those needs of the individual that are in accord with social needs." This in turn, he believed, would create a new sort of demand. For example, "the development of culture and education, which has taken place here mainly thanks to social consumption funds [*społeczne funduszy spożycia*], has caused an acceleration in the growth of needs of a loftier kind, and as a consequence has awakened and cultivated a demand for books, magazines, cultural entertainment, etc. Probably, had these experiences not been financed by social consumption funds, the tempo and extent of the aforementioned growth would have been a lot less."[42] Keynesian capitalists did indeed delight in the spread of luxury goods and conspicuous consumption to the so-called middle class and reveled in the Mad Men hucksterism of the American 1960s. Łaski wasn't exaggerating when he claimed that the primary objective of that type of capitalism was to expand consumption as much as possible, regardless of the utility of whatever got produced or consumed.[43] But just as East Europeans began to develop a taste for *that* kind of capitalism, the winds blowing from the West shifted. Supply-side capitalism abandoned the promise of universal hedonism for jeremiads about "austerity." Where once US foreign policy sought to cultivate foreign *markets*, there arose a quest to find foreign low-cost *producers*. In this incarnation, the economists of the capitalist world merged almost seamlessly with their socialist counterparts. All the latter had to do was drop the word *socialism*, which most were willing to do without compunction by the 1980s.

A fascinating figure exemplifying this transition is Kazimierz Poznański, an economist trained at the University of Warsaw who left Poland after the declaration of martial law in 1981. After a series of temporary positions at several prestigious US universities (including Cornell and Northwestern), he settled into a tenured post at the University of Washington. He has served as a consultant for the World Bank, the US Congress, and the United Nations, and he even returned to Poland for a stint as vice minister of finance from 1994 to 1996. He was an opponent of the PRL, and after 1989 he became an equally harsh critic of what he considered the failure of the Third Republic to fully cleanse the system of its socialist remnants. But the basis for his criticism eloquently demonstrates the contact points between supply-side socialism and supply-side capitalism.

Poznański's basic analysis was set out in an English-language book from 1996 called *Poland's Protracted Transition*, which offered a sweeping argument about why communism failed. Perhaps surprisingly, he believed that the main weakness of socialism was not the inability to improve rates of consumption for ordinary Poles but precisely its attempt to do so. Because the PZPR under Gierek was so weak, he argued, it was unable to prevent strikes and to hold down wages so that throughout the 1970s "wages were allowed to outstrip yearly productivity increases, causing diversion of exportables to the domestic market." Gierek's infamous foreign loans from the early years of the decade could have benefited the country, Poznański wrote, had labor costs and living standards been suppressed and an export-oriented economy created. He saw at least two missed opportunities for the PZPR leadership: Gierek's 1976 austerity plan and Jaruzelski's declaration of martial law in 1981. Poznański approved of both moves in strictly economic terms but was frustrated when each got overturned as weak leadership surrendered to labor demands. Instead of continuing to "trim consumption" in the 1980s, the PZPR eventually allowed wages to increase so that "the export capacities created under Gierek were soon allowed to deteriorate." Only with the reforms of the Mazowiecki/Balcerowicz government after 1989 did a "reduction in real wages and their relative stability since greatly help to energize exports."[44]

At the root of Poznański's world view is a desire for a privately managed economy, not because of any philosophical commitment to liberty but because "under conditions of privacy—personal freedom and property—individuals perform best, i.e., are most economical." The goal of any economic system must be to allow this "natural condition" of rational economic behavior to prevail. Socialism was unable to establish such rationality because workers were too concerned about "protecting their newly acquired higher standard of living" and because the communist party had lost its ability to control such a critical economic variable as wages. As a counterexample, Poznański pointed to Romania, where (he believed) the Romanian bureaucracy was never shaken to the point of losing its ability to manage the economy. Romania's state machinery was, therefore, "in a position to force enterprises to export more while using fewer imports." To be sure, the standard of living in Romania plummeted, but this was acceptable to Poznański because it was a "historically more backward" country in the first place.[45]

In sum, the strength of any economic system can be measured (according to Poznański's vision) in terms of the power of its "coordination mechanisms" and the stability of its "property structures." By this standard, he appreciated Stalinism because "as long as people were terrorized or indoctrinated by the official ideology of sacrifice, the political center—the single leader or narrow party circle—had sufficient means to enforce proper economic behavior by state enterprises with respect to assets entrusted to them." But this system eroded in the 1970s, and to the detriment of the economy as a whole, "the workers were the winners." Once wages began growing faster than productivity, he wrote, "workers' motivation suffers" and "the economy's ability to divert resources to capital stock expansion may be eroded."[46]

Poznański's vision might seem the polar opposite of socialism, and certainly the ethical foundations differ profoundly. Instead of the desire to improve living standards, he offers a means to maximize productivity and enable what he considers "natural" economical behavior. But despite these differences, there is a common core to both world views. In each case, we see an attempt to replace the chaos of demand-driven growth, with its reliance on unchecked "irrational" desires, with a system of control capable of suppressing wages when necessary in order to maximize the accumulation of surplus capital. The Stalinists could do this because of the state's oppressive apparatus and (perhaps even more important) because the postwar reconstruction effort was able to elicit self-sacrifice among many Poles. In any case, neither violent force nor the suppression of desire could last more than a few years, and the communist economists could never figure out what to put in its place. They just continued to echo Brus's promise that "together with the improving means of production (a result of increases in labor efficiency and in the qualifications of the workers), incomes must increase proportionally."⁴⁷ Unleashing the Keynesian "animal spirits" was never an option—not because there was anything wrong with consumption but because such a policy would place *desire* as the motive force behind determining that consumption. This, in turn, would be "chaotic," "irrational," and "uneconomical."

Only with the transformations of 1989 could accumulation resume, and only then could the Polish *Homo economicus* be born. Stepping back, we can see that this did indeed mark the defeat of socialist economics, but not at the hands of its initial Cold War opponent. Instead, in a development that appears disconcertingly Hegelian, the thesis of demand-side Keynesian capitalism confronted the antithesis of supply-side socialism, and *both* were swept away by the synthesis of supply-side capitalism. This victorious formation combined the rational economic actor of the socialist theorists with the property regime of the capitalist theorists. But the promise made (in different forms) by both of those old foes—"the maximum satisfaction of the ever-increasing material and cultural needs of the entire society"—was jettisoned once and for all.

NOTES

1. Two seminal works launched the attempt to think globally about Eastern Europe in the Cold War: Brown, "Gridded Lives," 17–48; and Lampland, *Object of Labor*. For an excellent overview of the recent scholarship in this field, see the introduction to Bren and Neuburger, *Communism Unwrapped*, 3–19. Some of the key works that have used the study of everyday life to blur Cold War boundaries include: Bren, *Greengrocer and His TV*; Crowley and Reid, *Pleasures in Socialism*; Crowley and Reid, *Style and Socialism*; Crowley and Reid, *Socialist Spaces*; Fehérváry, "Goods and States"; Fehérváry, *Politics in Color*; Fidelis, *Women, Communism and Industrialization*; Ghodsee, *Red Riviera*; Gille, *Cult of Waste*; Giustino, Plum, and Vari, *Socialist Escapes*; Lebow, *Unfinished Utopia*; Mazurek, "Moralities of Consumption"; Neuburger, *Balkan Smoke*; and Stitziel, *Fashioning Socialism*.

2. Bockman, *Markets*, 7. For more on the emergence and ultimate hegemony of neoclassical economics, see Fine and Milonakis, *Political Economy to Economics*; Morgan, *What Is Neoclassical Economics?*; Gram and Walsh, *Classical and Neoclassical Theories*.

3. Keynes used the term to refer more narrowly to the choices made by investors, but it has since been broadened by proponents of behavioral economics. See Keynes, *General Theory of Employment*, 161–62. Compare with Akerlof and Shiller, *Animal Spirits*.

4. This argument indirectly challenges the claim of Kacper Pobłocki that a demand-side socialism emerged in the 1960s, at least regarding urban

development policies. It may be, however, that we are merely using this concept differently. See Pobłocki, "'Knife in the Water,'" 69.

5. For an example of the inclusion of all those with economics degrees as "intelligentsia" (including those employed in positions we might label *accounting*), see Surmaczyński, *Kryzys lat 80 w świadomości inteligentów*.

6. Zawadzki, *O przedmiocie ekonomii politycznej*, 96.

7. Brus, *O podstawowym prawie ekonomicznym*, 3, 5.

8. Brus, *Pogadanki z zakresu ekonomii politycznej socjalizmu*, 41. This text was italicized in the original.

9. For example, see Berend, *Central and Eastern Europe*, 78–82; or the strikingly revisionist work Allen, *Farm to Factory*.

10. For example, Crowley and Reid write that "in the period of Stalinization in the People's Republics before 1956, the desire to consume was often represented as a vice that must be kept in check." Crowley and Reid, *Style and Socialism*, 9.

11. Brus, *Podstawowe cechy okresu przejściowego od kapitalizmu do socjalizmu*, 23. This is a bound transcript of a lecture.

12. Zawadzki, *O przedmiocie ekonomii politycznej*, 99.

13. Brus, *O podstawowym prawie ekonomicznym*, 6, 10, 35.

14. Brus and Łaski, *Węzłowe problemy teorii wzrostu w socjalizmie*, 15.

15. The PRL's economists used the word *profit* (*zysk*) for socialist firms as well as capitalist firms. The difference was that profits under socialism would never be confiscated in the form of "surplus value" that disappeared into the pockets of owners. In contrast to surplus value, socialism created what Brus called "supplemental production," utilized by society for investing in future growth. See Brus, *Pogadanki*, 62–64.

16. Górski, *Istota i cele gospodarki socjalistycznej*, 5–6, 13, 20.

17. Markowski, *Spożycie w Polsce Ludowej*, 3–4, 11.

18. For example, Crowley and Reid describe how "the rhetoric of austerity associated with Stalinism increasingly gave way to the promise of materialism." Crowley and Reid, *Style and Socialism*, 11. Similarly Stokes perceives an attempt to use consumer goods to buy social peace in the 1970s. Stokes, *Walls Came Tumbling Down*, 20.

19. This chart is based on data from Markowski, *Spożycie w Polsce Ludowej*, 13. As I will discuss below, the concept of "consumer need" could be an expansive one, but in this case Markowski was focusing on a narrower range of household consumption items.

20. Markowski, *Spożycie w Polsce Ludowej*, 12–13.

21. Zawadzki, *O przedmiocie ekonomii politycznej*, 102.

22. Markowski, *Spożycie w Polsce Ludowej*, 63.

23. For example, in many planning office documents, the category of "culture, education, training, sport, tourism, and relaxation" was used to refer to individual expenditures within household budgets, not state spending that subsidized such things. See, for example, Deniszczuk, "Wzorzec konsumpcji"; and Kowalczyk, "Prognoza struktury."

24. Brus, *O podstawowym prawie ekonomicznym*, 29.

25. Górski, *Istota i cele gospodarki socjalistycznej*, 39, 40.

26. On the idea of "rational consumption" in socialism, see Crowley and Reid, *Style and Socialism*, 10.

27. Górski, *Istota i cele gospodarki socjalistycznej*, 20–21, 40.

28. Markowski, *Spożycie w Polsce Ludowej*, 25.

29. Górski, *Istota i cele gospodarki socjalistycznej*, 31.

30. Brus, *O podstawowym prawie ekonomicznym*, 9.

31. Łaski, *Główne czynniki określające tempo wzrostu gospodarczego*, 3, 9–10. This was a transcript of a lecture Łaski gave at the Stołeczny Ośrodek Propagandy Partyjnej.

32. Górski, *Istota i cele gospodarki socjalistycznej*, 28.

33. Brus and Łaski, *Węzłowe problemy teorii wzrostu w socjalizmie*, 4.

34. Brus, *Pogadanki*, 27, 35–36.

35. Federowicz, *Zagadnienia równowagi monetarnej w gospodarce socjalistycznej*, 8, 17, 199.

36. Górski, *Istota i cele gospodarki socjalistycznej*, 40.

37. Borowiecki, "Czynniki rozwoju gospodarski socjalistycznej," 19.

38. A transcript of the discussion was included in Woźniak, *Reforma systemu funkcjonowania gospodarki w Polsce w świetle teorii ekonomii*, 65.

39. Sztyber, "Aktualny system cen w Polsce," 115–24.

40. Herer and Sadowski, "Czy rozumiemy własną gospodarkę," 88.

41. Łaski, *Główne czynniki określające tempo wzrostu gospodarczego*, 11.

42. Zabrzewski, *Społeczno-ekonomiczne aspekty konsumpcji indywidualnej w Polsce*, 5–9, 14–16, 57.

43. Keynes himself famously argued that the most important task was to get people employed, even if they only produced goods of little or no real utility. This is the context for his famous example of hiring someone to dig holes in the ground for no purpose (which he equated with mining for gold). Keynes, *General Theory of Employment*, 130.

44. Poznański, *Poland's Protracted Transition*, xxiv–xxvi. For more on the ways in which the 1989–90 reforms undermined democracy, see Bockman, *Markets*, 193; Ost, *Defeat of Solidarity*; Shields, "East Was Won"; and Shields, "Too Much Shock."

45. Poznański, *Poland's Protracted Transition*, xxxii, 16–17, 125–26.

46. Ibid., 59, 262, 266.
47. Brus, *O podstawowym prawie ekonomicznym*, 17.

REFERENCES

Akerlof, George, and Robert Shiller. *Animal Spirits: How Human Psychology Drives the Economy, and Why It Matters for Global Capitalism*. Princeton, NJ: Princeton University Press, 2009.

Allen, Robert. *Farm to Factory: A Reinterpretation of the Soviet Industrial Revolution*. Princeton, NJ: Princeton University Press, 2003.

Berend, Ivan T. *Central and Eastern Europe, 1944–1993: Detour from the Periphery to the Periphery*. Cambridge: Cambridge University Press, 1996.

Bockman, Johanna. *Markets in the Name of Socialism: The Left-Wing Origins of Neoliberalism*. Stanford, CA: Stanford University Press, 2011.

Borowiecki, Jerzy. "Czynniki rozwoju gospodarki socjalistycznej." In *Podstawowe problemy gospodarki socjalistycznej: materiał pomocniczy dla zespołów kształcenia ideologicznego*, edited by Jerzy Borowiecki, Mieczysław Socha, and Ryszard Zabrzewski, 17–33. Warsaw: Biblioteka Lektora i Wykładowcy, Wydział Ideologiczny KC PZPR, 1987.

Bren, Paulina. *The Greengrocer and His TV: The Culture of Communism after the 1968 Prague Spring*. Ithaca, NY: Cornell University Press, 2010.

Bren, Paulina, and Mary Neuburger, eds. *Communism Unwrapped: Consumption in Cold War Eastern Europe*. New York: Oxford University Press, 2012.

Brown, Kate. "Gridded Lives: Why Kazakhstan and Montana are Nearly the Same Place." *American Historical Review* 106, no. 1 (2001): 17–48.

Brus, Włodzimierz. *Pogadanki z zakresu ekonomii politycznej socjalizmu*. Warsaw: Książka i Wiedza, 1949.

———. *Podstawowe cechy okresu przejściowego od kapitalizmu do socjalizmu*. Warsaw: Centralny Ośrodek Szkolenia Partyjnego PZPR, 1954.

———. *O podstawowym prawie ekonomicznym socjalizmu i jego działaniu w Polsce Ludowej*. Warsaw: Książka i Wiedza, 1955.

Brus, Włodzimierz, and Kazimierz Łaski. *Węzłowe problemy teorii wzrostu w socjalizmie*. Warsaw: Szkoła Główna Planowania i Statystyki / Uniwersytet Warszawski, 1962.

Crowley, David, and Susan Reid, eds. *Pleasures in Socialism: Leisure and Luxury in the Eastern Bloc*. Evanston, IL: Northwestern University Press, 2010.

———, eds. *Socialist Spaces: Sites of Everyday Life in the Eastern Bloc*. Oxford: Berg, 2002.

———, eds. *Style and Socialism: Modernity and Material Culture in Post-War Eastern Europe*. Oxford: Berg, 2000.

Deniszczuk, Lycyna. "Wzorzec konsumpcji społecznie niezbędniej (minimum społeczne) w pięciolatce 1976–1980 i 1981–1985," 1979, Archiwum Akt Nowych, teka 1.10/79.
Federowicz, Zdzisław. *Zagadnienia równowagi monetarnej w gospodarce socjalistycznej*. Warsaw: Państwowe Wydawnictwo Naukowe, 1959.
Fehérváry, Krisztina. "Goods and States: The Political Logic of State-Socialist Material Culture." *Comparative Studies in Society and History* 52, no. 2 (2009): 426–59.
——— . *Politics in Color and Concrete: Socialist Materialities and the Middle Class in Hungary*. Bloomington: Indiana University Press, 2013.
Fidelis, Malgorzata. *Women, Communism and Industrialization in Postwar Poland*. Cambridge: Cambridge University Press, 2010.
Fine, Ben, and Dimitris Milonakis. *From Political Economy to Economics: Method, the Social, and the Historical in the Evolution of Economic Theory*. New York: Routledge, 2009.
Ghodsee, Kristen. *The Red Riviera: Gender, Tourism and Postsocialism on the Black Sea*. Durham, NC: Duke University Press, 2005.
Gille, Zsuzsa. *From the Cult of Waste to the Trash Heap of History: The Politics of Waste in Socialist and Postsocialist Hungary*. Bloomington: Indiana University Press, 2007.
Giustino, Cathleen M., Catherine J. Plum, and Alexander Vari. *Socialist Escapes: Breaking Away from Ideology and Everyday Routine in Eastern Europe, 1945–1989*. New York: Berghahn Books, 2013.
Górski, Janusz. *Istota i cele gospodarki socjalistycznej*. Warsaw: Wydział Propagandy i Agitacji KC PZPR, 1968.
Gram, Harvey, and Vivian Walsh. *Classical and Neoclassical Theories of General Equilibrium: Historical Origins and Mathematical Structure*. New York: Oxford University Press, 1979.
Keynes, John Maynard. *The General Theory of Employment, Interest, and Money*. London: Macmillan, 1936.
Kowalczyk, Jerzy. "Prognoza struktury spożycia dóbr materialnych i usług niematerialnych na roki 1985," September 1979, Archiwum Akt Nowych, teka 1.10/79.
Lampland, Martha. *The Object of Labor: Commodification in Socialist Hungary*. Chicago: University of Chicago Press, 1995.
Lebow, Katherine. *Unfinished Utopia: Nowa Huta, Stalinism, and Polish Society, 1949–1956*. Ithaca, NY: Cornell University Press, 2013.
Łaski, Kazimierz. *Główne czynniki określające tempo wzrostu gospodarczego*. Warsaw: Wydział Propagandy i Agitacji KW PZPR, 1963.
Markowski, Stanisław. *Spożycie w Polsce Ludowej*. Warsaw: Centralna Rada Związków Zawodowych, 1972.

Mazurek, Małgorzata. "Moralities of Consumption in Poland across the Short Twentieth Century." *Annales: Histoire et Sciences Sociales* 68, no. 2 (June 2013): 393–418.

Morgan, Jamie, ed. *What Is Neoclassical Economics? Debating the Origins, Meaning and Significance.* New York: Routledge, 2016.

Neuburger, Mary. *Balkan Smoke: Tobacco and the Making of Modern Bulgaria.* Ithaca, NY: Cornell University Press, 2012.

Ost, David. *The Defeat of Solidarity: Anger and Politics in Postcommunist Europe.* Ithaca, NY: Cornell University Press, 2005.

Pobłocki, Kacper. "'Knife in the Water': The Struggle over Collective Consumption in Urbanizing Poland." In *Communism Unwrapped: Consumption in Cold War Eastern Europe,* edited by Paulina Bren and Mary Neuburger, 68–86. New York: Oxford University Press, 2012.

Poznański, Kazimierz Z. *Poland's Protracted Transition: Institutional Change and Economic Growth, 1970–1994.* Cambridge: Cambridge University Press, 1996.

Shields, Stuart. "How the East Was Won: Transnational Social Forces and the Neoliberalization of Poland's Post-Communist Transition." *Global Society* 22, no. 4 (2008): 445–68.

———. "Too Much Shock, Not Enough Therapy: Transnational Capital and the Social Implications of Poland's Ongoing Transition to a Market." *Competition and Change* 11, no. 2 (June 2007): 155–78.

Stitziel, Judd. *Fashioning Socialism: Clothing, Politics, and Consumer Culture in East Germany.* Oxford: Berg, 2005.

Stokes, Gale. *The Walls Came Tumbling Down: The Collapse of Communism in Eastern Europe.* New York: Oxford University Press, 1993.

Surmaczyński, Marian. *Kryzys Lat 80 w świadomości inteligentów.* Wrocław: Wydawnictwo Uniwersytetu Wrocławskiego, 1997.

Woźniak, Michał, ed. *Reforma systemu funkcjonowania gospodarki w Polsce w świetle teorii ekonomii: materiały z konferencji z ekonomii politycznej dla młodych nauczycieli akademickich (26–29 września 1983 r.).* Krakow: Akademia Ekonomiczna w Krakowie, 1984.

Zabrzewski, Ryszard. *Społeczno-ekonomiczne aspekty konsumpcji indywidualnej w Polsce.* Warsaw: Wyższa Szkoła Nauk Społecznych przy KC PZPR, Zakład Ekonomii Politycznej, 1974.

Zawadzki, Józef. *O przedmiocie ekonomii politycznej i o charakterze praw ekonomicznych.* Warsaw: Książka i Wiedza, 1954.

AUTHOR BIO

BRIAN PORTER-SZŰCS is Arthur F. Thurnau Professor of History at the University of Michigan–Ann Arbor, where he has taught since 1994. He is author of *Poland*

and the Modern World: Beyond Martyrdom (2014), *Faith and Fatherland: Catholicism, Modernity, and Poland* (2010), and *When Nationalism Began to Hate: Imagining Modern Politics in 19th Century Poland* (2000), which was translated into Polish (2011). Together with Bruce Berglund, he coedited *Christianity and Modernity in East-Central Europe* (2010).

FIVE

ORANGES AND THE NEW BLACK

Importing, Provisioning, and Consuming Tropical Fruits and Coffee in the GDR, 1971–89

ANNE DIETRICH

In the fall of 1977 the Socialist Unity Party of Germany (SED) assembled its members for the inauguration of the Parteilehrjahr 1977–78 in Dresden.[1] Seemingly routine propagandistic business, it became apparent that this year's event marked a shift toward a more pragmatic line of argument. In his opening speech, General Secretary Erich Honecker addressed the growing discontent over the formation of dichotomous retail structures, which, by separating what were understood to be bare necessities from luxuries, seemingly widened the gap between consumers with economic, social, and symbolic capital and those without. The latter were relegated to a local sphere of consumption whose access was limited to those with higher salaries or access to West German marks. This new division of the East German retail sector was perceived by many to stand in stark contrast to the socialist ideals of an egalitarian society. At the meeting, Honecker explained why it was economically necessary for the state to establish luxury stores, such as Intershop, Delikat, or Exquisit, which offered food and fashion articles that were not available at the ordinary Konsum or HO shops.

In his speech, Honecker also referred to the current supply shortfalls in coffee, which had shaken the German Democratic Republic (GDR) since the spring of 1977.[2] Honecker explained that this shortfall forced the GDR to spend approximately 300 million US dollars on the importation of raw coffee alone.[3] The unavailability of coffee highlighted increasing social distinctions and led to growing discontent in East German consumer society.

Only three months later, the arrival of grass-green, seemingly unripe Cuban oranges caused panic within the Politburo. Officials of the Ministry of Trade and Supply knew what was coming: "It is to be expected that, in the case of a sale of these Cuban oranges, the population will argue about their price and quality."[4] An official statement was prepared in advance, anticipating trouble with critical customers in stores. The panic over unripe oranges demonstrates the power of consumer demand as a metric for the successes and failures of state socialism and the vagaries of global socialist markets.

Consequently, "trivial" consumer products became the center of discussion at party events and Politburo meetings. But why did the provision of coffee and tropical fruits become such a political issue, and what does it tell us about the symbolic meaning carried by these commodities? Oranges were not the only tropical fruits understood as matters of real political sensitivity in the GDR. After the fall of the wall, bananas became a key symbol of the reunification. West German jokes in response to the East Germans' panic buying of bananas after the opening of the border gave the fruit a new connotation.[5] Some West German politicians mocked the East Germans' "banana patriotism," arguing that their consumerism and the promise of capitalist abundance led them to vote for the liberal-conservative Christian Democratic Union (CDU) instead of the center-left Social Democratic Party of Germany (SPD) in the first free elections in 1990.[6]

This chapter analyzes the provision of coffee and tropical fruits, including oranges and other citrus fruits, in the GDR during the 1970s and 1980s. These commodity groups were deeply significant for East German consumer society during those decades, as they stood at the intersection of luxury and basic necessities, and reflected the level of living standards within a global and Cold War context. Socialist regimes relied on popular support to maintain a stable political system. This support was gained by the promise of a new consumer policy, which promised to not only secure the provision of basic supplies but also to allow for "modest consumerism."[7] Oranges and coffee were an important metric measuring the successes and failures of socialism in East Germany. Due to recurrent supply shortfalls—shortfalls that presumably did not happen in the West—coffee and tropical fruits were scarce goods in most Eastern European consumer societies. As such, tropical fruits and coffee vacillated between being understood as everyday and luxury items in the East German imagination. They were considered scarce but necessary goods with a high symbolic value, whose acquisition required a great deal of time and effort.

As the 1970s and 1980s witnessed growing consumer sovereignty—as building socialism transitioned to developed socialism in Eastern European societies—socialist leadership, particularly in the GDR, could no longer ignore its citizens' demands for coffee, oranges, and bananas. This also included increasing the importation of semiluxury food and tropical fruits, items that had been in short supply for the previous decades. Ministerial documents demonstrate the importance the state placed in satisfying the consumer: the SED government spent much energy to observe customers' behavior in order to react immediately to warning signals of growing discontent among the population. Coffee and oranges were matters of state importance. The provision of rare coffee and tropical fruits, especially during political and seasonal holidays, served as a sop for conditioning East German consumers.

This chapter focuses on practices employed by institutions and ordinary citizens to overcome, or at least cope with, the scarcity of coffee and tropical fruits in the GDR. In analyzing these practices, I apply Michel de Certeau's conceptual differentiation between the strategies of powerful institutions and the tactics of everyday people.[8] De Certeau interprets institutions as "producers" of spaces and systems, in which individuals act as "consumers" by using the tactics of an antidiscipline to subvert the spatial order that has been produced by the institutions.[9] Within this structure, everyday life is understood as an intrusion: prowling through the territory of others.[10] Consumers in Eastern European societies had to adapt to the market under socialism, whose conditions forced them to develop certain purchasing techniques. These everyday coping strategies employed by East German consumers cannot be interpreted as unidirectional or channeling consumers toward a path predetermined by the socialist government. Instead, East German citizens proved quite creative and flexible when it came to adjusting to the inadequacies of a "shortage economy."[11] Furthermore, they were demanding.

The SED leadership, in turn, was aware of exactly these inadequacies and not only accepted insubordinate consumer behavior but actively sought for alternative trade strategies to solve the problem of securing supplies of coffee and tropical fruits—all against the backdrop of economic decline and a shortage of hard currency. Thus, the relationship between the "powerful" SED regime and "weak" consumers during the Honecker era was indeed one of interdependency—one in which the valences were often switched.

Consumers' voices and performances served as a barometer of public opinion in the "participatory dictatorship."[12] This was understood by all as both an opportunity and a threat. The SED's inability to satisfy consumer desire was a driving force, if not the sole factor, for both the viability of and loss of confidence in state socialism. The government's strategy of creating alternative exchange systems failed on an international level, since its long-term outcome could not assure mutual benefit for all trade parties. On an individual level, those same practices—bartering for scarce goods—seemed to work better, precisely because all those involved benefitted. Those without commodities and connections, those excluded from the second economy, had to rely on other coping strategies and on the state to meet their needs. Rising, if modest, consumerism was an important part of the social contract between the citizen and the state in the so-called welfare dictatorship.[13] As such, consumer perception is an important means to understand the complex relationship between the political elite and the general population in Eastern European societies. An analysis of Eastern European societies, focusing on the synergies of institutional strategies and individual tactics, has the potential to challenge the much-discussed framework of the public-private dichotomy and the state-society paradigm that has been used in many previous studies on the subject.

In the following sections, I focus on the development and role of coping strategies on the part of the state to meet the demands of East German consumers for coffee and oranges on the level of international trade relations (using the examples of citrus fruits imported from Cuba and coffee imported from Ethiopia) and on the level of everyday practices on the part of East German consumers. While quotidian techniques have been discussed frequently in recent publications on East European and East German consumer cultures, the analysis of interactions between state authorities and citizens are understudied.[14] Investigating buying behavior and customer petitions offered insight into consumers' minds (for the historian and the state); these investigations also helped the regime orient relationships and design requirements with foreign and domestic trade partners to improve the supply of consumer goods. Officials in the Ministry of Trade and Supply and the Ministry of Foreign Trade developed their own strategies to react to consumer demands and cope with scarcity, in a manner that was similar to the often-described tactics of consumers. To explain the specific circumstances under which these strategies were adopted, I start with a brief overview of the political and economic situation in the GDR in the 1970s and 1980s with emphasis on the supply of coffee and tropical fruits.

A NEW CONSUMER POLICY IN THE EASTERN BLOC: BORROWED PLEASURES?

In a keynote speech given at the Eighth Party Congress in June 1971, Erich Honecker declared that the "main task" of the Five-Year Plan (1971–75) was "raising the people's material and cultural living standards."[15] Honecker's new program for social policy aimed at satisfying workers' material demands as an incentive for increasing labor productivity. As such, it contrasted sharply with the policies of his predecessor Walter Ulbricht, which subordinated consumer interests to the requirements of heavy industry during the 1950s and 1960s. This new consumer policy, so-called consumer socialism, was not unique to East Germany.[16] In the beginning of the 1970s, as socialist party leaders across the region faced shrinking popular support, it was implemented all over Eastern Europe. Initiated by unrest in Poland in December 1970, which was directly linked to the announcement of price increases for basic consumer goods, the shift in Eastern European policies are best interpreted as a means to consolidate power by means of an interior appeasement policy.[17] Even more striking, and uniquely problematic, for East German leadership was the permanent comparison with the Federal Republic of Germany, especially as it related to questions of standard of living. Honecker's concept detailing the "unity of economic and social policy," outlined in 1975, was essentially a social security system combined with modest consumerism, which included the increasing importation of luxury items. The resulting high state expenses burdened the national economy with debts—a major problem for the GDR and for the Eastern bloc as a whole.

As early as 1972, Honecker's consumer policy aimed to secure the regular supplies of bananas. The Council of Ministers expected the future import volume of bananas to rise steadily between 1972 and 1974: the ministers intended to import an annual volume of 91 kilotons valued at 35.8 million in the hard currency Valutamark.[18] They justified their decision by noting that West German per capita consumption of bananas was nearly ten times higher than in the GDR.[19] While bananas had become an everyday food product in the Federal Republic of Germany (FRG), they were still scarce in the GDR. In order to facilitate the importation of bananas, the leadership of the GDR instituted a set of new programs, including new trade agreements and plans to improve storage and transportation technology. To reduce costs, GDR leadership instructed foreign-trade officials to turn away from intermediaries and buy bananas directly from the governments of banana-producing countries. Once the bananas arrived in the GDR, they were to be treated in special banana ovens to catalyze the ripening process and avoid frost damage.[20] In the end, none of these measures was implemented. The importation of Western technology for heating the bananas proved to be too cost intensive. Cost issues proved to be a constantly recurring problem.

In East Germany and across Eastern Europe, price increases were considered taboo after the uprisings in Poland in 1970. Frightened by the anger displayed by Polish consumers, Honecker argued against any proposal to raise prices in the GDR. Yet consumer demand required that extra money be found to finance just that demand promised by the new social policy. The result—government-controlled, artificially low prices for basic requirements—led to modest prosperity for many GDR citizens, but it had the worrisome effect of creating new demands that the state found difficult to meet. To absorb rising purchasing power, SED leaders decided on an expansion of the Delikat and Exquisit retail chains. While Exquisit shops offered high-priced clothes, Delikat stores focused on regional specialties and luxury foods. One commodity of striking importance, which could be specially purchased at the Delikat gourmet food store, was high-quality coffee. Expressed as a percentage, GDR citizens bought less than 1 percent of the coffee they consumed at those specialty stores in 1978, but this percentage rose to nearly 5 percent over the course of the 1980s.[21] This is probably a consequence of the falling quality standards of East German coffee available at nonspecialty stores.[22] A similar development held true for the consumption of *Westkaffee*, which could be purchased at Intershops by those citizens that possessed hard currency, but mostly it arrived as a present from West German relatives or acquaintances by mail.

Consumption in the GDR was not as egalitarian as the state claimed. Real distinctions marked consumption patterns and pointed to social class. Drinking "good" coffee and eating "proper" oranges are textbook examples of East German social distinction. While the supply of basic consumer goods was steady enough by the beginning of the 1970s, coffee and tropical fruits became a measure for the "good life." As Daphne Berdahl has pointed out, "Pierre Bourdieu's theories of distinction and forms of capital" are quite useful for "conceptualizing social differentiation under socialism."[23] Social capital in East Germany was mostly made up of connections and networks, which were the integral parts of the country's informal economy. The concept of the so-called *Beziehungen* (connections to people in the capitalist West) was "extremely important in the GDR, as in other socialist societies, where social connections were the principle means of obtaining scarce consumer goods and services."[24] Those unlucky consumers of coffee without access to hard currency or supporting social capital had to put up with the East German brands Kosta, Rondo, and Mona or the ground coffees Mocca-Fix Gold and Mocca-Fix Silber introduced in 1973. In general the quality of these blends were understood as satisfactory by most East Germans until the end of the 1970s, when Latin American coffee varieties were replaced by lower-quality beans from Africa and Asia.

Before the coffee crisis in 1977–78, coffee had been an everyday, if expensive and sometimes scarce, beverage in the GDR.[25] By definition, coffee was a luxury good, which meant it was sold at artificially raised prices. Coffee was one of the most expensive commodities in the GDR, with prices ranging from sixty to eighty East German marks per kilogram. (As a result it was usually sold in small, 125-gram packages.)[26] While workers and employees could generally afford a

Fig. 5.1. Kosta coffee package, ca. 1972. In the collection of the Stadtgeschichtliches Museum Leipzig (inventory number V/248/2006), 2017.

regular cup of coffee, those without wage incomes often could not. It is hardly surprising, then, that it was the poor pensioners who complained most when the cheapest brand, Kosta (see fig. 5.1), was withdrawn from the market in 1977.[27]

The elimination of Kosta was not the only measure that GDR coffee consumers had to bear in 1977. The year 1977 marked a watershed event for the coffee supply situation in the GDR. It started with crop failure in Brazil, which caused global coffee scarcity and soaring prices on the world market.[28] This hit the national economy of the GDR harder than Western capitalist countries, because its fixed-price guarantee—an implicit contract between the state and citizens about the cost of goods—eliminated any possibility to pass the rising prices on to consumers. To make matters worse, prices for oil and other raw materials also increased rapidly over the course of the 1970s.[29] Further, the debt crisis of the Eastern bloc eliminated the possibility of borrowing on Western credit to offset higher state expenses.[30] Honecker's social policy was stretched to its limits. As a result, the party leaders decided on an austerity policy, which included the reduction of coffee, cocoa, and tropical fruits imports.[31] In these circumstances Alexander Schalck-Golodkowski, the leader of the Commercial Coordination Division (Bereich Kommerzielle Koordinierung, or KoKo), worked to develop a plan providing for the future provision of coffee.[32] In addition to the elimination of Kosta, Schalck-Golodkowski's plan included another suggestion, which would cause popular indignation: the introduction of the so-called Kaffee-Mix, consisting of 51 percent roasted coffee beans and 49 percent coffee substitutes (mostly rye). Consumer reaction was swift: shortly after its market launch, customers boycotted stores and restaurants selling Kaffee-Mix and wrote letter after letter of complaint.[33] Among other things, the new coffee product was highly criticized because of its terrible taste, its bad smell, and its disproportionate price. GDR citizens had come to expect a certain lifestyle, including the consumption of real coffee; substitutes were no longer accepted. Even considerable price reductions could not convince them to buy it.

The so-called coffee crisis of 1977 was just a forerunner of worse things to come. Consumer discontent reached its climax at the end of the 1980s when severe shortfalls in vegetables and fruits exasperated the GDR citizens in 1988–89. Within a decade per capita consumption of tropical fruits had dropped by close to 35 percent.[34] In 1978 the government had imported 106,823 tons of oranges and tangerines and 104,353 tons of bananas—by 1988 it only imported 91,687 tons of oranges and tangerines and 46,775 tons of bananas.[35] In sum, the tropical fruits imported in 1988 accounted for 138,462 tons. There was no money, no coffee, no tropical fruits. The East German government and its citizens were caught in a "scarcity trap" and were forced to juggle their limited resources. It was a time of privation.[36] I describe below which strategies and practices they used to cope with this.

COPING WITH SCARCITY 1: BARTER AGREEMENTS BETWEEN THE SECOND AND THE THIRD WORLD

The East German government felt this privation and worked hard, if at times at cross-purposes and ineffectually, to meet the expectations of East German consumers in times of scarcity. This section deals with alternative trade relations initiated by the GDR government during Honecker's term of office. In the 1970s and 1980s the GDR concluded barter agreements with many countries of the third world, including Cuba, Ethiopia, Angola, Mozambique, Vietnam, Laos, and the Philippines. A key attraction to these agreements to both the GDR and its partners was that they allowed for the acquisition of raw materials or products without the use of foreign currency. Below I focus on two case studies. First, I explore the GDR's decision to import coffee from Ethiopia, emphasizing the conflicts that arose from both the imbalanced trade transactions on an international level and from consumer discontent in the GDR with the resulting lower coffee quality. Second, I analyze the GDR's obligation to take Cuban citrus fruit deliveries within the Council for Mutual Economic Assistance's (COMECON) trade agreements.[37] This arrangement was greatly criticized by East German consumers, who much preferred the Mediterranean varieties they were used to. Global socialist solidarity, East German consumers found, could be bitter fruit. While the payment transactions between Cuba and the GDR fell within the scope of the International Bank for Economic Cooperation, applying the transfer ruble as an accounting unit, the GDR's trade agreement with Ethiopia was confidentially arranged between the two national governments and worked on the basis of a so-called clearing system, in which the exchanged commodities were accounted for in US dollars.

Socialist Blends: The Coffee Crisis of 1977

The coffee barter business between the GDR and Ethiopia was part of a bilateral trade agreement between the two countries signed in 1977. Initially, it was mutually beneficial; each trading party was requesting an exchange good the other could easily supply. While the GDR was seeking affordable raw coffee, Ethiopia's Derg regime under Mengistu Haile Mariam desperately needed weapons and other military equipment to fight not only a Somali invasion in the Ogaden region in the east of the country but also to quell domestic opposition.[38] The United States had stopped their deliveries of arms after Mengistu's coup d'état in February 1977, and the Provisional Military Administrative Council (PMAC) had to search for other military assistance, especially because Somalia and separatist groups in Eritrea were still supported by the USSR.[39] Facing the global spike in coffee prices in the second half of the 1970s, the GDR was willing to take over this task in return for Ethiopian coffee. A crop failure in Brazil in 1975 had caused a global coffee scarcity and soaring prices. This was a blessing for other coffee exporting countries, especially in Africa, but a curse for the coffee importing nations in Europe and North America. The change in coffee prices was dramatic: the GDR spent an average of 150 million Valutamark (VM) annually on coffee imports between 1972 and 1975; in 1977 it had to pay the record amount of 667.2 million VM for only 53,307 tons of raw coffee.[40] East Germans were paying more for less coffee. These figures explain the GDR's growing interest in alternative coffee trade relations.

Facing restive consumers, the 1977 Coffee Agreement between the GDR and Ethiopia was treated as a top priority, and high officials of both governments were directly involved in the negotiation processes. Immediately after the new PMAC leader had sent a letter to Erich Honecker, asking for East German support, the East German government sent Werner Lamberz as their representative for the onsite discussions in Addis Ababa. Lamberz, who was the secretary for agitation and propaganda at the Central Committee of the SED, had a history of skillful negotiation with leaders from the third world. He arrived in Ethiopia in February 1977.[41] Shortly afterward the first GDR weapon deliveries arrived.[42] When Lamberz returned to Addis Ababa in June 1977, he had another mission. Erich Honecker and Günter Mittag had briefed him beforehand to discuss the acquisition of Ethiopian coffee on a barter basis. As a result, a trade protocol was signed on June 16 by the East German Ministry of Foreign Trade and the Ethiopian Ministry of Commerce and Tourism.[43] The initial contract was about the import of 5,000 tons of raw coffee to be delivered annually by the state-owned Coffee Marketing Corporation.[44] In turn the GDR was supposed to send trucks and military goods, especially smaller weapons, munitions, steel helmets, and durable bread for the Ethiopian forces. (Ethiopian soldiers called this "Lamberz-bread.")[45] Demand on both sides was constant: the GDR needed more coffee, and Ethiopia, more military equipment. A new trade arrangement was signed one month later in Berlin, resulting in the delivery of 10,000 tons of Ethiopian coffee to the GDR in 1977.[46]

Ethiopia was not the only coffee producing country the GDR concluded barter agreements with. Angola delivered 5,500 tons of raw coffee in 1977 and 8,929 tons in 1978.[47] Honecker himself negotiated with President Marcos in the Philippines, who agreed to ship 5,000 tons of raw coffee in 1978.[48] Similar "special arrangements" followed with Vietnam and Laos. The "socialist blends" from Africa and Asia were intended to replace coffee from Brazil and Colombia. From August 1978 on, coffee imported under these new agreements was used for the low-priced GDR brand Rondo. Accordingly, the Ministry of District-led Industry and Foodstuffs Industry, in charge of implementing these new arrangements, had to lower its standards, as the coffee varieties from Africa and the Asian robusta coffees did not meet former quality requirements.[49] Nor did they meet East German consumers' taste: 14,000 complaints criticizing the new taste of Rondo were either sent to the authorities or handed to grocery store employees during the fourth quarter of 1977.[50] The consumers were upset, and officials were concerned.

Complaints were not limited to customers, and the coffee barter business between Ethiopia and the GDR lasted only until 1979. From the very beginning, the East German foreign trade firm AHB Genußmittel complained about the unwillingness of its Ethiopian partners to deliver raw coffee on time.[51] Coffee was Ethiopia's number one cash earner. In 1976 Ethiopia earned 300 million birr with the sale of nearly 70,000 tons of raw coffee to foreign markets.[52] In 1977 it earned 540 million, although it sold only 50,000 tons to capitalist countries.[53] The more coffee Ethiopia sold on the free market, the more it earned. The question of hard currency was a matter of contentious debates between the Ethiopian ministries and the National Bank of Ethiopia. Ethiopian officials also complained about the quality of the GDR products, especially about the trucks made in the GDR, which proved to be unsuitable for Ethiopian road conditions.[54] In the end, the Ethiopians were unwilling to maintain the barter arrangement. This did not mean that trade relations with East Germany were cut completely. The GDR continued to import coffee from Ethiopia, even though it had to pay in foreign currency from 1980 onward.[55]

The coffee barter trade with Ethiopia in 1977 and 1978 illustrates how the actions of the GDR's foreign-trade officials were shaped by transformations within socialist consumer societies at the end of the 1970s. To be precise, securing supplies and saving foreign currency through economic cooperation with socialist-leaning countries in the third world became their primary objective. Furthermore, this cooperation demonstrates that the GDR followed its own economic interests and did not act solely in the interest of the Soviet Union in Cold War Africa. In the beginning, the Ethiopian–East German barter trade was advantageous for both parties, but it failed in the end, since Ethiopia could find better deals elsewhere. While barter trade with Ethiopia lasted only two years, the exchange with Cuba was part of a long-term COMECON program.

Cuban Oranges: The Curse of the COMECON Citrus Program

In the winter of 1977–78, very shortly after the shock of the coffee crisis, GDR officials were confronted with another serious supply problem. Since the beginning of the 1960s, the GDR had imported small amounts of citrus fruits from Cuba. In accordance with the terms of COMECON's 1976 Comprehensive

Program for Socialist Economic Integration, Cuba was to specialize in the production of citrus fruits for consumption in the Soviet bloc.[56] As a result, Cuban orange exports grew in number, and the GDR became one of its main customers. In December 1977 the container ship *Theodor Storm* arrived at the port of Rostock loaded with green oranges of apparently doubtful quality. The Cubans denied the East German claims for compensation deliveries or discounts, as they did not recognize their green fruits as faulty goods.[57] They passed the color problem on to their trade partners, who had to find an answer to the question of how to sell oranges that were not as orange as the Mediterranean ones that East German consumers were used to. As a result of different local climate conditions, Cuban oranges tend to be rather greenish in color. After some partially successful experiments to color the Cuban oranges by means of artificial ripening processes, the Ministry of Trade and Supply came to the conclusion that selling these fruits would cause consumer debates about price and quality.[58] Therefore, officials decided "to withhold the 'grass green' oranges until they could be colored or used for other purposes, and to sell the rest before they rotted."[59] Since, in the long run, a distribution of the green Cuban oranges could not be prevented, the Ministry of Trade and Supply searched for ways to promote the sale of the Caribbean fruit.[60] An official statement for retail employees was prepared, containing the following information about the economic backgrounds and positive features of the tropical fruits imported from Cuba: "They [Cuban oranges] have a high juice content and a sweet and aromatic taste. As a result of the specific Cuban vegetation conditions, they do not develop a yellow color, which is so typical for oranges from other growing regions, such as the Mediterranean countries. Cuban oranges have therefore a green, yellowish-green and partially brown spotted skin. The green or greenish-yellow skin color does not interfere with the degree of ripeness. The fruits are ripe."[61] Furthermore, labels in grocery stores across East Germany informed consumers about the general good quality of Cuban oranges. Brochures and advertisements in regional newspapers and on local radio stations were to attract some further attention for Cuban citrus fruits (such as the advertising brochure for Cuban grapefruits in fig. 5.2).[62] This was to little avail. Despite their efforts, trade officials could not convince East Germans to give up the southern European navel oranges they were used to and consume a Caribbean substitute instead. Navel oranges had a symbolic meaning (one similar to that of bananas): they were a symbol of prosperity and were provided, especially during the Christmas season, as a political present at the end of the year.

Fig. 5.2. East German advertising brochure for Cuban grapefruits, ca. 1980. Published by the Czech news agency ČTK (Česká tisková kancelář). In the private collection of Uwe Hessel, Dresden, 2018.

Although never fully accepted by East Germans, the Cuban oranges became an integral part of the GDR's tropical fruit supply. At the end of the 1980s, consumers were still complaining about the, by this time infamous, Kuba-Orange, whose quality had proved to be insufficient indeed. These consumers were well informed about the economic and political background of this imported product—they blamed not only the SED government but also COMECON as an institution that forced better-developed member states, such as the GDR, to accept lower-quality standards from less-developed member states, such as Cuba, as a means of socialist economic integration.[63] One petitioner, for instance, asked if contracts were made to be kept forever and mentioned in that context the importation of "miserable, withered *Kuba-Orangen*, which are good enough only for GDR citizens."[64]

Although there were several socialist-leaning countries in the Global South, which offered tropical fruits on the basis of barter agreements, Cuba was the only one that profited from a COMECON membership. Therefore, it succeeded in selling its citrus fruits at preferential prices and also attracted funding from the Eastern bloc for the modernization of its domestic citrus industry.

COPING WITH SCARCITY 2: EVERYDAY PRACTICES OF GDR CITIZENS

In his book *The Practice of Everyday Life* Michel de Certeau describes and analyzes what he calls productive and consumptive activities: his distinction between the "strategies" of powerful institutions and "tactics" of everyday people puts the individual at a level of a "consumer" who reacts by use of tactics within a given environment, structured by the strategies of those in power.[65] He is particularly interested in minor practices of the "common man" to cope with given structures, conditions, and situations. In focusing on "oppositional practices of everyday life" de Certeau describes "ripping-off" practices as widespread "in the most normative institutions of modern times," which "flourish within bureaucratic or commercial administrations just as much as in factories."[66] Such subversive tactics infiltrate and subtly erode the structures created by the ruling institutions. Similarly, the German historian Ina Merkel emphasizes the importance of equally widespread coping strategies found in East German consumer practices.[67] These practices included informal, semi-legal, and illegal actions, such as thievery, possession of contraband, and black marketeering, to compensate for perceived deficiencies in the GDR's planned economy. Perhaps surprisingly, insubordinate behavior patterns were more or less accepted by the government, or, as de Certeau would frame it, the government "'look[ed] the other way' in order to know nothing of it."[68] Quite common was the hoarding of rare commodities. Like elsewhere in the Eastern bloc, recurring supply bottlenecks caused a specific culture of waiting. If available at all, high-demand goods were purchased in large numbers. Once consumers could stand waiting no longer or felt overlooked, many exercised their right to complain. Waiting patiently or addressing a petition often proved successful. In fact, these two consumption practices were built in to the system. Additionally, some East German citizens benefited from connections with relatives or acquaintances in West Germany, who provided them with access to coffee and tropical fruits.[69] Waiting, hoarding, and petition writing were each common practices all over the Eastern bloc.

Waiting and Hoarding

The socialist queue, caused by a lack of goods, service, or employees, was a characteristic feature of everyday life throughout East Germany. But mostly, the queue indicated the arrival of special commodities that people were willing to stand in line for (even if they sometimes did not know what they were actually waiting for).[70] Buying in socialism was always an activity linked more to the expenditure of time and energy rather than money.[71] As goods were seemingly always limited in number, waiting patiently did not necessarily guarantee the acquisition of the desired commodity. Consumers always had to fear coming away empty-handed. Thus, consumers in socialist societies, such as the GDR, acquired a specific habitus of waiting and observing that enabled them to react spontaneously at just the right moment.[72]

Prior to public holidays, the regime took special care to address its citizens' demand for luxury food. State functionaries also paid attention to the phenomenon of the waiting line itself, which was understood as "an element of street publicity."[73] GDR officials were aware of the potentially explosive political nature of lines, as spontaneous consumer revolts occurred sporadically. To secure the viability of the socialist system, consumer frustration had to be kept to a minimum.

But waiting in line was only one of many practices that demonstrated socialist consumers' unique relationship to scarce commodities. In contrast to consumers of the Western "affluent society,"[74] East Germans seemed to attach an outstanding symbolic value even to articles of daily use. Throwing away goods (with the idea that they could be easily replaced) was not an option. Therefore, the life-span of many durable goods in socialism was longer than that in the West. Furthermore, scarce and Western goods, everyday products in capitalism, became luxury products in socialism. Berdahl illustrates how these luxury products served as an ideal base for social distinction in socialist societies: "The tremendous symbolic value of such commodities was demonstrated in their display. Kitchens were decorated with neatly arranged packages of coffee and cocoa."[75]

They transported messages and were used in terms of "conspicuous consumption."[76] Once available, rare consumables were acquired in quantities seemingly larger than those actually needed. Thus, collecting and hoarding scarce commodities was a common practice.

Many consumers considered stockpiling a necessity. However, from the perspective of the state, hoarding, practiced on a large scale, held the potential to create additional supply shortfalls, as required goods were withdrawn from the economic cycle.[77] For that reason, trade officials kept track of bulk purchasing and took legal steps against contrabandists and black-market dealers. Stockpiling was condemned ideologically as nonsocialist behavior. But ironically, it was the GDR's economic system and the SED's policy itself that motivated its citizens to buy ahead. Often stockpiling was directly linked to political events, such as the construction of the Berlin Wall in 1961.[78] When coffee prices increased in Eastern Europe in the summer of 1977, a report was sent to the Council of Ministers informing them about panic buying.[79] When the most inexpensive coffee blend, Kosta, was withdrawn from sale, consumers' attention moved rapidly to the next-lowest-priced brand, Rondo, in large numbers, indicating stockpiling. Some districts reported that individual citizens often purchased four or more packages at once.[80] The same report stated that many female employees at the tile factory Boitzenburg in the district of Schwerin tended to leave their workplace when Rondo was on sale at the in-house grocery store.[81] It seemed as if consumers feared another reduction, which might explain why they bought coffee in such large quantities and at officially inappropriate occasions. The culture of waiting for and hoarding scarce goods pervaded all aspects of everyday life.

From time to time consumers grew sick and tired of waiting. Metaphorically speaking, they attempted to break through the waiting line. Bypassing the queue by illegal or semilegal means, such as bribery or under-the-counter sales, was often practiced, though officially taboo. In contrast, petitioning for consumer goods was not only permitted but also encouraged by the state, as it resonated with the socialist values of fair sharing, as I describe below.

Writing Letters of Complaint: Citizen Petitions

As historians have indicated, the GDR was characterized by a culture of complaint, which was not only embedded within everyday life but also established by law. This lasted from the very beginning of the GDR until its end.[82] Complaints, the so-called *Eingaben*, were therefore highly valued as a means of communication between the state and its citizens. The right to complain was institutionalized, having its legal basis in the GDR's 1949 Constitution.[83] In 1953 a petition act was passed that guaranteed the bureaucratic processing of these written complaints. (In 1962 the State Council of the GDR was placed directly in charge of processing the complaints.)[84] As a result, the state was uniquely attuned to and sought to manage the expression of public opinion. According to Paul Betts these complaints "served as barometers of common hopes and expectations, individual investment in the state, as well as a controlled and controllable outlet of everyday discontent."[85] As long as individuals decided to offer constructive criticism in a letter of complaint, they stuck to and reinforced common socialist values. Writing and processing a petition in that sense meant arriving at and maintaining a consensus between the authorities and the population.

And East Germans were more than willing to offer their criticism. They raised typical topics, such as housing issues, supply bottlenecks and poor standards in retailing, service conditions and workplace discrimination, travel requests, and environmental problems. It is estimated that nearly each household wrote at least one letter of complaint between 1949 and 1989, adding up to more than 70,000 annual petitions.[86] At the end of the 1980s this number was even higher—the State Council received over 134,000 petitions in 1988 alone. Over one million citizen complaints were sent nationwide in 1989.[87] Not only was the quantity of complaints changing; the tone was as well. Growing discontent with the supply situation led citizens to state their concerns in harsher and more demanding ways. Despite this shift in tone, there were recurring elements that most petitions from the 1950s until the 1980s had in common: the (honorific) form of address, the self-portrayal of the letter writer, the often overstated description of his or her problem, the invocation of the addressee's help and understanding, references to common norms and values, the reproduction of rumors concerning the current supply situation, quotes from party documents or politicians' speeches, claims and (idle) threats, and the valediction at the end of the letter.[88] All of these elements served to legitimate the writer's demand. These components can best be understood through some examples. The petitions below were written in 1977, 1988, and 1989, when the supply situation with coffee and tropical fruits became disastrous. They both reflect recurring points of criticism and support the conclusion that GDR citizens perceived themselves as self-confident consumers who demanded their portion of individual pleasure. Not all petitions were written from a position of strength: some letters employed a more desperate tone.

When coffee prices rose and coffee quality declined in 1977, numerous petitions were sent to the coffee-producing companies and government agencies.[89] Mostly, consumers complained about the poor quality of coffee blends. Some of them used quite objective arguments, as an example from a professional product tester illustrates:

> In consideration of the current coffee quality, I feel compelled to complain. On August 8, I bought a package of coffee at the specialty store Kaffeefreund as I usually do. I wanted to grind the coffee immediately—but this poor quality. No! ... When prices are rising on the world market, especially for coffee, tropical fruits, and crude oil, everyone knows that our GDR has difficulty guaranteeing a stable price, too. ... I justifiably reject quality to the disadvantage of the consumer. My socialist work collective [*Kollektiv der sozialistischen Arbeit*] holds the same opinion.[90]

In that case, the petition writer legitimated her complaint with her extraordinary competence; she was a technical inspector at the TKO (Technisches Kontrollorgan), the GDR's own product-testing institution. She demonstrated her understanding by referring to the broader global contexts. She also indicated her continuing support for the political system and that she had not lost confidence in the socialist project—yet. Her criticism was straightforward, and she demanded an "immediate examination": a quality control of the coffee she rejected.[91]

Other complaints were less constructive, while still adhering to the "essentials of political propaganda of the GDR," as the following example of a peasant laborer makes clear:[92] "Agricultural workers in our villages, but other workers as well, who are recently forced to drink substitutes instead of real coffee in the restaurants they used to visit, feel downgraded in their normal consumer demands and tend to think that the wish for a cup of coffee in an ordinary restaurant is a plea for luxury. It is an unsustainable situation. The rural population is most badly affected as it suffers mostly from an undersupply of restaurants. The memory remains that in past times real coffee was a luxury for rural workers indeed."[93] Officials distributed the newly introduced Kaffee-Mix primarily to inexpensive restaurants, which gave the impression that the coffee austerity policy of 1977 was directed against everyday people. Considering that the GDR called itself a "workers and peasants' state," this was generally interpreted as a contradiction in terms. As a result, the coffee crisis of 1977 had the effect of promoting a social distinction that manifested itself through varying degrees of consumer participation. Low-paid workers, poor pensioners, and members of the rural population were angry about being excluded from the pleasures of purchasing and consuming "high-class coffee," which was expensive and usually only available at specialty stores in the major cities.

While the 1970s witnessed primarily short-term supply crises, the end of the 1980s was characterized by a permanent shortage in consumer goods. This was especially the case with the provision of tropical fruits (which everyone agreed was insufficient). As the everyday lack of fruits and vegetables became evident, consumer protests reached their peak in 1988–89. Petition writers were not reluctant to compare their situation with those of consumers in Western capitalist societies: "Bananas, good oranges, peanuts etc. are not capitalist privileges. If small countries, such as Switzerland and Austria, can afford to offer a wide range of tropical fruits, it should be possible in our country, a fully industrialized country, as well. Old people like us, our children, and our grandchildren do not want to receive tropical fruits as charitable gifts from relatives in the FRG only; we want to buy them in our stores ourselves."[94] Another point of criticism was the threat of vitamin deficiency, especially in reference to healthy nutrition for children, and it was therefore frequently mentioned by many parents:

> In my opinion, a significant criterion for the evaluation of the living standard is to what extent the state is in the position to care for the healthy nutrition

> of its population.... I am a mother of two children (kindergarten and school age), and I deem it beneath me to feed my children chemical preparations, such as Sumavit-forte or Traverdin, to give them some vitamins. I am 30 years old and when I look back upon my childhood remembering what was offered to us at the fruit shops and the greengroceries I wonder if the contemporary supply situation might be for the purpose of the policy in the interests of the people. The provision of tropical fruits declined significantly. At the beginning of the 70s ... there were tangerines, oranges, bananas, and figs.[95]

The biopolitical issue addressed here was not unique to East Germany. Socialist concerns about a lack of vitamin C spread all over Eastern Europe. The availability of tropical fruits in winter was highly valued and a symbol of the failure of the socialist system. Parents demanding access to citrus fruits and domestic fruit and vegetables argued in line with the public opinion on health issues in socialism.

It is striking that petition writers at the end of the 1980s still referred to socialist goals and expectations, while their confidence in the "SED's paternalistic claims to provide for all" must have been seriously tested.[96] Although the broad consent between leadership and population was fading away, a common line of argument, of language and code, was maintained throughout. Applying James Scott's concept of "everyday forms of resistance" while describing the practice of writing letters of complaints, Paul Betts concludes, "These relatively modest *Eingaben* became powerful 'weapons of [the] weak' for those without power, privilege, or status, to the extent that people exploited the legal language, cultural codes, and narrative conventions to advance their claims."[97] There is no way of knowing for certain the extent to which they actually succeeded, as incomplete files often do not tell us the whole story. Nevertheless, we can conclude that petitions were used as legal means to exert pressure. They provided leverage "from below," which could only function in a society that was relying on the support of the majority of its citizens. The GDR was such a society and therefore heavily dependent on its consumer-citizens.

CONCLUSION

This chapter uses the provision of coffee and tropical fruits in the GDR during the Honecker era to outline the development of certain strategies of coping with the scarcity of these symbolically important commodities. The East German case shares many similarities with its socialist neighbors, with one important distinction. Within the Eastern bloc, East German consumers measured their standard of living against that of West Germany. This comparison was drawn not only on a synchronic level but also on a diachronic one. East and West German citizens shared a common tradition of consumption. Drinking coffee, for instance, was "firmly entrenched in German consumption habits and social patterns" prior to socialism.[98] Consumers in the GDR contrasted the past with the present and the supply situation in the GDR with the FRG repeatedly. Their demand for coffee, oranges, and bananas grew as the role of consumption spread in East European societies in the 1970s and 1980s.

Consumer practices, such as the writing of petitions and the hoarding of scarce goods, illustrate the growing discontent with a system that legitimated its existence through social welfare. I consider these everyday practices to be neither subservient reactions to party policy and shortage economy nor radical acts of oppositional resistance. Rather, they should be interpreted in terms of what James Scott has described as "petty acts of insubordination."[99] These invisible techniques of the masses seldom left traces in the archives: in the case of the GDR, they did, recorded in Stasi files or citizens' petitions, and they demonstrated the typical East German "Eigen-Sinn."[100] Considering the unsatisfactory supply situation with coffee and tropical fruits and the decline in quality of these commodities, one can witness, in real time, the regime's loss of legitimacy as certain petty acts became a manifestation of a "broken contract between the socialist consumer system and the consuming populace."[101] To understand East German consumers' initial hopes and final discontent, we need to see the bigger picture, which includes the study of foreign-trade relations, transnational comparisons, and global competition. Thus, focusing on institutional strategies and everyday practices that go beyond the national scope is a promising approach for the analysis and interpretation of East European consumer societies.

NOTES

1. The Parteilehrjahr was an annual course of ideological training for members of the SED party in the GDR. It started each year with a ceremonial mass gathering.
2. Honecker, *Reden und Aufsätze*, 492–93. Cf. Allison, "1977," 257–58; and Gries, *Produktkommunikation*, 182.
3. Honecker, *Reden und Aufsätze*, 493.
4. SAPMO-BArch, DY 30/16776: Information zum Import von Kubaorangen im IV./77 und im Jahre 1978, 6.
5. Berdahl, *Where the World Ended*, 164.
6. Karasek, "Mit Kanonen auf Bananen?" 57.
7. Allison, "More from Less," 102. Cf. Crowley and Reid, "Introduction," 11.

8. Certeau, *Practice of Everyday Life*, xi. For further theoretical discussion on the distinction between strategy and tactics, see Certeau, Jameson, and Lovitt, "On the Oppositional Practices," 5–10.

9. Certeau, *Practice of Everyday Life*, xii–xv.

10. Ibid., 91.

11. Kornai, *Economics of Shortage*. For a critical analysis of the terms *scarcity, shortage, lack,* and so on in relation to the GDR, see Merkel, *Utopie und Bedürfnis*, 10–12.

12. Fulbrook, *People's State*, 251–306.

13. For further discussion on welfare dictatorship, see Jarausch, "Care and Coercion," 67–69.

14. Berdahl, *Where the World Ended*; Betts, *Within Walls*; Merkel, *Utopie und Bedürfnis*; and Mühlberg, *Bürger, Bitten und Behörden*; Staadt, *Eingaben*.

15. Steiner, *Von Plan zu Plan*, 167.

16. The original term *Konsumsozialismus* was coined by the Politburo member Werner Krolikowski in 1980. See Malycha, *Die SED in der Ära Honecker*, 6; Fulbrook, *People's State*, 42–44; Judt, "Bananen," 1–3; Skyba, "Konsumpolitik in der DDR," 343–50.

17. Steiner, *Von Plan zu Plan*, 167.

18. BArch, DC 20-I/4/2654: Geheime Ministerratssache 402/72, 82–85. 1 VM was approximately 1 DM or 0.49 USD at that time.

19. BArch, DC 20-I/4/2654, 85.

20. BArch, DC 20-I/4/2654, 102–3.

21. Sigmund, *Genuss als Politikum*, 273.

22. Ibid.

23. Berdahl, *Where the World Ended*, 112.

24. Ibid., 115.

25. Katherine Pence has discussed how private snapshots captured moments of everyday coffee consumption in the 1950s and 1960s. Pence, "Grounds for Discontent?" 210–15.

26. Wünderich, "Die 'Kaffeekrise' von 1977," 247.

27. Sigmund, *Genuss als Politikum*, 241.

28. Döring, *"Es Geht um Unsere Existenz,"* 115; Topik, "World Coffee Market," 244.

29. This was due to the Yom Kippur War in 1973. Its impact on the Eastern bloc was delayed by the COMECON price policy, as prices were adjusted only every five years. Winrow, *Foreign Policy of the GDR*,160. Kotkin, "Kiss of Debt," 83.

30. Steiner, *Von Plan zu Plan*, 191–96.

31. Ibid., 189.

32. For further information on Alexander Schalck-Golodkowski and the Bereich Kommerzielle Koordinierung see Judt, *Der Bereich Kommerzielle Koordinierung*.

33. SAPMO-BArch, DY3023/1218: Coffee and Cocoa Provision, 206–14.
34. SAPMO-BArch, DY 30/9021: Warenfondsentwicklung bei importierten Südfrüchten, 0370. My own calculation on basis of the per capita consumption of bananas, oranges, and tangerines in 1978 is 12.57 kg and 8.34 kg in 1988.
35. SAPMO-BArch, DY 30/9021: Warenfondentwicklung bei importierten Südfrüchten, 0370.
36. For theoretical discussions of the phenomena of "tunneling" and "bandwidth tax," see Mullainathan and Shafir, *Scarcity*, 123. Although they discussed individuals' cognitive processes primarily, the mechanics at work can be observed on a societal level as well.
37. The Council for Mutual Economic Assistance (English abbreviation COMECON, CMEA, or CAME) was an economic organization of Eastern-bloc countries, equivalent to the European Economic Community. It was founded in 1949 by the Soviet Union, Bulgaria, Czechoslovakia, Hungary, Poland, and Romania to strengthen economic cooperation between the Soviet Union and socialist states in Central Europe. While the GDR became a full member in 1950, Cuba only joined in 1972.
38. Below I will use the terms PMAC and Derg synonymously when referring to the military regime that governed Ethiopia after 1974.
39. Westad, *Global Cold War*, 259–65.
40. 1 VM was approximatey 1 DM or 0.49 USD at that time. DY 3023/1218: Coffee and Cocoa Provision, 404. Cf. Döring, *"Es Geht um Unsere Existenz,"* 115; cf. Pence, "Grounds for Discontent?" 216. Staadt, *Eingaben*, 41; Wolle, *Die heile Welt der Diktatur*, 200.
41. Dagne, *Das Entwicklungspolitische Engagement*, 271–72.
42. Döring,*"Es Geht um Unsere Existenz,"* 115.
43. MoFA/GDR-DMG-6/15, n.p.
44. Ibid.
45. Döring, *"Es Geht um Unsere Existenz,"* 119.
46. MoFA/GDR-DMG-6/15, n.p.
47. SAPMO-BArch, DY3023/1218: Coffee and Cocoa Provision, 404.
48. Ibid.; Döring, *"Es Geht um Unsere Existenz,"* 61.
49. SAPMO-BArch, DY3023/1218: Coffee and Cocoa Provision, 477–79.
50. Staadt, *Eingaben*, 46.
51. SAPMO-BArch, DY 3023/1218, 493–504.
52. 1 ETB was approximately 0.48 USD at that time. "Ethiopia Gets 300m Birr"; "Official Comments on Coffee Price."
53. "Ethiopia Earns 540 Million Birr"; cf. SAPMO-BArch, DY 3023/1218, 494.
54. Dagne, *Das Entwicklungspolitische Engagement*, 63.
55. MoFA/GDR-DMG-6/15, n.p. Therefore, the GDR government focused on securing its coffee supply from Southeast Asian countries during the 1980s.

Vietnam was especially important in that context. After all, the East German development plan for the Vietnamese coffee economy proved to be successful in the end, albeit too late for the collapsing GDR, which could not profit any more from the program's first harvest in 1989. Sigmund, *Genuss als Politikum*, 267.

56. González, *Aspectos Económicos*, 36.

57. SAPMO-BArch, DY 30/16776: Information zum Import von Kubaorangen im IV./77 und im Jahre 1978.

58. SAPMO-BArch, DY 30/16776: Dokumentation zu Ergebnissen der Nachfärbung von Grünschaligen Kuba-Orangen in Ausgewählten VEB OGS (Test in der Zeit vom 23. bis 30. Dezember 1977); SAPMO-BArch, DY 30/16776: Information zum Import von Kubaorangen im IV./77 und im Jahre 1978. Allison, "1977," 258.

59. Allison, "1977," 258.

60. Information für die Mitarbeiter des Groß- und Einzelhandels zum Import von Orangen aus Kuba in SAPMO-BArch, DY 30/16776: Information zum Import von Kubaorangen im IV. Quartal 1977 und im Jahre 1978.

61. Information für die Mitarbeiter des Groß- und Einzelhandels zum Import von Orangen aus Kuba in SAPMO-BArch, DY 30/16776: Information zum Import von Kubaorangen im IV. Quartal 1977 und im Jahre 1978. (The last sentence was highlighted and underlined in accordance with the original document.)

62. SAPMO-BArch, DY 30/16776: Brief von Briksa an Weiß vom 9. Januar 1978.

63. Allison, "1977," 266.

64. SAPMO-BArch, DY 30/9021, 0091.

65. Certeau, *Practice of Everyday Life*, xi.

66. Certeau, Jameson, and Lovitt, "On the Oppositional Practices," 4.

67. Merkel, *Utopie und Bedürfnis*, 278.

68. Certeau, Jameson, and Lovitt, "On the Oppositional Practices," 3.

69. For further information about the provision of the so-called Westkaffee, see Dietrich, "Kaffee in der DDR," 245–47.

70. Merkel, *Utopie und Bedürfnis*, 278–79; Stitziel, "Shopping, Sewing, Networking, Complaining," 256.

71. Stitziel, "Shopping, Sewing, Networking, Complaining," 256.

72. Merkel, *Utopie und Bedürfnis*, 278. Merkel is using the terminology of Pierre Bourdieu. According to Bourdieu, the term *habitus* subsumes a certain mentality and specific behavioral patterns that are usually shared by people with a similar social, religious, educational, national, and so on background.

73. Ibid.

74. Baudrillard, *Consumer Society*; Galbraith, *Affluent Society*.

75. Berdahl, *Where the World Ended*, 124.

76. Veblen, *Theory of the Leisure Class*, 49.

77. Merkel, *Utopie und Bedürfnis*, 290.
78. Stitziel, "Shopping, Sewing, Networking, Complaining," 258.
79. SAPMO-BArch, DY 3023/1218, 318: Information zur Versorgung mit Röstkaffee.
80. Ibid.
81. Ibid.
82. Betts, *Within Walls*; Merkel, *"Wir sind doch nicht"*; Mühlberg, *Bürger, Bitten und Behörden*; Staadt, *Eingaben*.
83. Betts, *Within Walls*, 174.
84. Ibid.; and Mühlberg, *Bürger, Bitten und Behörden*, 275, 276.
85. Betts, *Within Walls*, 176.
86. Mühlberg, *Bürger, Bitten und Behörden*, 7.
87. Betts, *Within Walls*, 175.
88. I am referring here to certain components that Felix Mühlberg has identified, which were common to most East German petitions. Mühlberg, "Wenn die Faust," 178; and Mühlberg, *Bürger, Bitten und Behörden*, 198–245.
89. SAPMO-BArch, DY 3023/1218, 206–14.
90. SAPMO-BArch, DY 3023/1218, 206. My own translation.
91. Ibid.
92. Gries, *Produktkommunikation*, 183.
93. BArch-Potsdam, DL 1-26068, cited in Gries, *Produkte als Medien*, 266. My own translation.
94. SAPMO-BArch, DY 30/9021, 0365. My own translation.
95. Ibid. My own translation.
96. Merkel, "Luxury in Socialism," 53.
97. Betts, *Within Walls*, 191; Scott, *Weapons of the Weak*.
98. Pence, "Grounds for Discontent?" 198.
99. Scott, "Scott's Law," 43.
100. The term was first used by the German historian Alf Lüdtke; see Lüdtke, "Cash, Coffee-Breaks, Horseplay." For the use of this terminology when describing everyday life in the GDR, see Lindenberger, *Herrschaft und Eigen-Sinn*.
101. Pence, "Grounds for Discontent?" 203.

REFERENCES

Allison, Mark. "More from Less: Ideological Gambling with the Unity of Economic and Social Policy in Honecker's GDR." *Central European History* 45, no. 1 (2012): 102–27.

———. "1977: The GDR's Most Normal Year?" In *Power and Society in the GDR, 1961–1979: The "Normalisation of Rule"?* edited by Mary Fulbrook, 253–77. New York: Berghahn Books, 2013.

Baudrillard, Jean. *The Consumer Society: Myths and Structures*. 2nd ed. Thousand Oaks, CA: Sage, 2012.

Berdahl, Daphne. *Where the World Ended: Re-unification and Identity in the German Borderland*. Berkeley: University of California Press, 1999.

Betts, Paul. *Within Walls: Private Life in the German Democratic Republic*. Oxford: Oxford University Press, 2010.

Boyer, Christoph, and Peter Skyba. *Repression und Wohlstandsversprechen: Zur Stabilisierung von Parteiherrschaft in der DDR und der ČSSR*. Dresden, Germany: Sächsisches Druck- und Verlagshaus, 1999.

Certeau, Michel de. *The Practice of Everyday Life*. Berkeley: University of California Press, 1984.

Certeau, Michel de, Fredric Jameson, and Carl Lovitt. "On the Oppositional Practices of Everyday Life." *Social Text* no. 3 (Autumn 1980): 3–43.

Crowley, David, and Susan E. Reid. "Introduction: Pleasure in Socialism?" In *Pleasures in Socialism: Leisure and Luxury in the Eastern Bloc*, edited by David Crowley and Susan E. Reid, 3–51. Evanston, IL: Northwestern University Press, 2010.

Dagne, Haile Gabriel. *Das Entwicklungspolitische Engagement der DDR in Äthiopien. Eine Studie auf der Basis Äthiopischer Quellen*. Münster, Germany: Lit Verlag, 2004.

Dietrich, Anne. "Kaffee in der DDR: Ein Politikum Ersten Ranges." In *Kaffeewelten: Historische Perspektiven auf eine globale Ware im 20. Jahrhundert*, edited by Christiane Berth, Dorothee Wierling, and Volker Wünderich, 225–47. Göttingen, Germany: Vandenhoeck & Ruprecht, 2015.

Döring, Hans-Joachim. *"Es Geht um Unsere Existenz." Die Politik der DDR gegenüber der Dritten Welt am Beispiel von Mosambik und Äthiopien*. Berlin: Ch. Links Verlag, 1999.

Fulbrook, Mary. *The People's State*. New Haven, CT: Yale University Press, 2005.

Galbraith, John Kenneth. *The Affluent Society*. 40th anniversary edition. New York: Houghton Mifflin, 1998.

Gries, Rainer. *Produkte als Medien. Kulturgeschichte der Produktkommunikation in der Bundesrepublik und der DDR*. Leipzig, Germany: Leipziger Universitätsverlag, 2003.

———. *Produktkommunikation. Geschichte und Theorie*. Vienna: UTB, 2008.

Honecker, Erich. *Reden und Aufsätze. Band 5*. Berlin: Dietz Verlag, 1978.

Jarausch, Konrad H. "Care and Coercion: The GDR as Welfare Dictatorship." In *Dictatorship as Experience: Towards a Socio-cultural History of the GDR*, edited by Konrad H. Jarausch, 47–70. New York: Berghahn Books, 1999.

Judt, Matthias. "Bananen, gute Apfelsinen, Erdnüsse u.a. sind doch keine kapitalistischen Privilegien. Alltäglicher Mangel am Ende der 1980er Jahre in der DDR." *Bundeszentrale für politische Bildung*, December 7, 2013. Accessed September 25, 2019. http://www.bpb.de/163470.

———. *Der Bereich Kommerzielle Koordinierung: Das DDR-Wirtschaftsimperium des Alexander Schalck-Golodkowski—Mythos und Realität*. Berlin: Ch. Links Verlag, 2013.

Karasek, Hellmuth. "Mit Kanonen auf Bananen?" *Spiegel*, no. 13 (1990): 56–57.

Kornai, János. *Economics of Shortage*. Amsterdam: Elsevier, 1980.

Kotkin, Stephen. "The Kiss of Debt: The East Bloc Goes Borrowing." In *The Shock of the Global: The 1970s in Perspective*, edited by Niall Ferguson, Charles S. Maier, Erez Manela, and Daniel S. Sargent, 80–93. Cambridge, MA: Belknap Press of Harvard University Press, 2010.

Lindenberger, Thomas, ed. *Herrschaft und Eigen-Sinn in der Diktatur: Studien zur Gesellschaftsgeschichte der DDR*. Cologne, Germany: Böhlau, 1999.

Lüdtke, Alf. "Cash, Coffee-Breaks, Horseplay: *Eigensinn* and Politics among Factory Workers in Germany circa 1900." In *Confrontation, Class Consciousness, and the Labor Process: Studies in Proletarian Class Formation*, edited by Michael Hanagan and Charles Stephenson, 65–96. New York: Praeger, 1986.

Malycha, Andreas. *Die SED in der Ära Honecker. Machtstrukturen, Entscheidungsmechanismen und Konfliktfelder in der Staatspartei 1971 bis 1989*. Munich, Germany: De Gruyter Oldenbourg, 2014.

Merkel, Ina. "Luxury in Socialism: An Absurd Proposition?" In *Pleasures in Socialism: Leisure and Luxury in the Eastern Bloc*, edited by David Crowley and Susan E. Reid, 53–70. Evanston, IL: Northwestern University Press, 2010.

———. *Utopie und Bedürfnis. Die Geschichte der Konsumkultur in der DDR*. Cologne, Germany: Böhlau, 1999.

———."*Wir sind doch nicht die Meckerecke der Nation!*" *Briefe an das Fernsehen der DDR*. Berlin: Schwarzkopf & Schwarzkopf, 2000.

Mühlberg, Felix. *Bürger, Bitten und Behörden. Geschichte der Eingabe in der DDR*. Berlin: Dietz Verlag, 2004.

———. "Wenn die Faust auf den Tisch Schlägt... Eingaben als Strategie zur Bewältigung des Alltags." In *Wunderwirtschaft. DDR-Konsumkultur in den 60er Jahren*, edited by Neue Gesellschaft für Bildende Kunst e.V., 175–84. Cologne, Germany: Böhlau, 1996.

Mullainathan, Sendhil, and Eldar Shafir. *Scarcity: Why Having Too Little Means So Much*. New York: Henry Holt and Company, 2013.

Nova González, Armando. *Aspectos Económicos de los Cítricos en Cuba*. Havana: Editorial Científico-Tecnica, 1988.

Pence, Katherine. "Grounds for Discontent? Coffee from the Black Market to the Kaffeeklatsch in the GDR." In *Communism Unwrapped: Consumption in Cold War Eastern Europe*, edited by Paulina Bren and Mary Neuburger, 197–225. Oxford: Oxford University Press, 2012.

Scott, James C. "Scott's Law of Anarchist Calisthenics." *Powision* 6, no. 2 (November 2011): 43–47.

———. *Weapons of the Weak: Everyday Forms of Peasant Resistance.* New Haven, CT: Yale University Press, 1985.

Sigmund, Monika. *Genuss als Politikum: Kaffeekonsum in beiden Deutschen Staaten.* Berlin: De Gruyter Oldenbourg, 2015.

Skyba, Peter. "Konsumpolitik in der DDR 1971 bis 1989: Die Verbraucherpreise als Konfliktgegenstand." In *Geschichte des Konsums: Erträge der 20. Arbeitstagung der Gesellschaft für Sozial- und Wirtschaftsgeschichte 23–26 April 2003 in Greifswald*, edited by Rolf Walter, 343–66. Stuttgart, Germany: Franz Steiner Verlag, 2004.

Staadt, Jochen. *Eingaben. Die institutionalisierte Meckerkultur in der DDR. Goldbrokat, Kaffee-Mix, Büttenreden und andere Schwierigkeiten mit den Untertanen.* Berlin: Forschungsverbund SED-Staat, 1996.

Steiner, André. *Von Plan zu Plan. Eine Wirtschaftsgeschichte der DDR.* Bonn, Germany: Bundeszentrale für politische Bildung, 2007.

Stitziel, Judd. "Shopping, Sewing, Networking, Complaining: Consumer Culture and the Relationship between State and Society in the GDR." In *Socialist Modern: East German Everyday Culture and Politics*, edited by Katherine Pence and Paul Betts, 253–86. Ann Arbor: University of Michigan Press, 2008.

Topik, Steven. "The Integration of the World Coffee Market." In *The Global Coffee Economy in Africa, Asia, and Latin America, 1500–1989*, edited by William Gervase Clarence-Smith and Steven Topik, 21–49. Cambridge: Cambridge University Press, 2003.

Veblen, Thorstein. *The Theory of the Leisure Class.* Oxford: Oxford University Press, 2009.

Westad, Odd Arne. *The Global Cold War: Third World Interventions and the Making of Our Times.* Cambridge: Cambridge University Press, 2007.

Winrow, Gareth M. *The Foreign Policy of the GDR in Africa.* Cambridge: Cambridge University Press, 1990.

Wolle, Stefan. *Die Heile Welt der Diktatur. Alltag und Herrschaft in der DDR 1971–1989.* Bonn, Germany: Bundeszentrale für politische Bildung, 1999.

Wünderich, Volker. "Die 'Kaffeekrise' von 1977: Genussmittel und Verbraucherprotest in der DDR." *Historische Anthropologie: Kultur—Gesellschaft—Alltag*, no. 11 (2003): 240–61.

ARCHIVAL SOURCES

Federal Archives, Foundation Archives of Political Parties and Mass Organizations in the GDR (Stiftung Archiv der Parteien und Massenorganisationen der DDR im Bundesarchiv) (Berlin, Germany)

SAPMO-BArch, DC 20-I/4/2654
SAPMO-BArch, DC 20-I/4/2654
SAPMO-BArch, DC 20-I/4/2654
SAPMO-BArch, DL/2/1522
SAPMO-BArch, DL 2/ 6462a
SAPMO-BArch, DY 3023/1218
SAPMO-BArch, DY 30/9021
SAPMO-BArch, DY 30/16776

Ministry of Foreign Affairs Archive (Addis Ababa, Ethiopia)
  MoFA/GDR-DMG-6/15

Ethiopian National Archives and Library Agency (Addis Ababa, Ethiopia)
  "Ethiopia Gets 300m Birr From Export of Coffee." *Ethiopian Herald*, January 19, 1977.
  "Official Comments on Coffee Price." *Ethiopian Herald*, January 21, 1977.
  "Ethiopia Earns 540 Million Birr From Year's Export of Coffee." *Ethiopian Herald*, January 1, 1978.

AUTHOR BIO

ANNE DIETRICH is a PhD candidate at the University of Leipzig and a freelance curator. Her research focuses on the provision and consumption of coffee, sugar, and tropical fruits in the GDR, focusing on supply shortfalls and trade relations with socialist-leaning countries in the Global South. She has authored several articles on East German consumer culture and foreign-trade relations and curated a permanent exhibition in Leipzig's Arabian Coffee Tree Museum.

SIX

VCRs, MODERNITY, AND CONSUMER CULTURE IN LATE STATE SOCIALIST POLAND

PATRYK WASIAK

This chapter investigates the spread of videocassette recorders (VCRs) in late socialist Poland, a period of evolving consumer culture. During this period, consumers, government agencies, retailers, and cultural intermediaries invested the VCR with multiple and contested meanings. VCRs were understood as one of the most distinctive symbols of consumer desire, were read as a symbol of individual identity made possible through consumption, and stood as a symbol of contradictory and ideologically charged values: the consumer culture of the West and universal technological modernity. As such, analyzing the social life of VCRs in 1980s Poland well demonstrates the interdependencies and tensions between affluent consumption and socialist ideology, the politics of mass consumption and the modernization process writ large.

This chapter investigates the social life of VCRs from three different perspectives, each of which points to larger negotiations about the role of consumer desire in late socialist Poland. First, I outline the role of the VCR in identity construction, focusing on the manner in which individuals experienced the consumption of VCRs as a means of self-fashioning. VCRs were understood first and foremost as an expression of upward social mobility. Second, I investigate how the hard-currency chain stores, Pewex and Baltona, sought to meet, channel, and capitalize on this consumer desire by organizing and expanding new modes of distribution and retail in order to attract intended VCR owners. Finally, I explore the state-sponsored attempts to design, manufacture, and distribute Polish VCRs more broadly—a policy aimed at refashioning the cultural meanings of VCRs to those more closely related to official ideology and the promises of developed socialism. These policies sought to remove VCRs' symbolic connection to the West and to underplay the role of VCRs as status symbols by recoding the VCR as a universal artifact of high-technology modernity of the 1980s. The failure of the Polish electronics industry to independently manufacture "a synonym of modernity" is instructive, and demonstrates not only the incapacities of socialist high-tech industries but also articulates tensions over aims and means in the politics of mass consumption.

In their introduction to *Communism Unwrapped*, Paulina Bren and Mary Neuburger note how histories of consumer culture can contribute to better understandings of broader economic, social, and cultural processes in the Eastern bloc: "Consumption, we propose, offers a window into these still-shadowy interiors of everyday life and state-society negotiations in Cold War Eastern Europe. It also promises to illuminate the region's complicated engagement with the 'West'—a West both real and imagined."[1] Understanding the VCR as a key commodity within an evolving Polish consumer culture of the 1980s and closely investigating its cultural meanings can shed light on three key issues that emerged throughout socialist consumer cultures across Eastern Europe. First, it illuminates the impact of a consumer product on the "shadowy interior of everyday life" in late socialist Poland and points to new possibilities of consumption-based identity formation. Second, it highlights tensions between different groups that had an impact on shaping local consumer culture. This is seen most clearly in the expansion of the VCR trade by hard-currency chain stores and in attempts to manufacture and market a Polish VCR, two different and, at times, contradictory forms of reaction to the popularity of imported VCRs by the key actors within the state apparatus. Finally, unpacking the various and contesting cultural meanings of the VCR within a changing Polish society of the 1980s sheds light on the "complicated engagement with the West" and universal entanglement of discourses surrounding the consumer culture and modernity of the 1980s.

Media experts have estimated that the number of privately owned VCRs in Poland in 1988 ranged from five hundred thousand to seven hundred thousand.[2] This number is puzzling if we consider that, at that time, a VCR cost more than the yearly average salary of a Pole employed in a state enterprise. Where did these VCRs come from? What accounts for their symbolic importance? Since it was the only state socialist country where the VCR became a highly popular and relatively easily available commodity—one highly visible in the public sphere—late socialist Poland provides an interesting case, which illuminates the interaction between consumers and VCRs. Radio Free Europe often reported on the spread of VCRs in the Eastern bloc, and noted that Poland was the country in the region where the first mass "video revolution" took place.[3]

In Poland, the 1980s were spent trying to come to terms with the perils and possibilities of VCRs. Until the mid-1980s, only Poles who worked illegally abroad and "trade tourists" were able to buy and sell VCRs (brought from Western Europe or Asia) in Poland. Prior to the development of a Polish-manufactured VCR, these international networks alone were responsible for the spread of several hundred thousand VCRs.[4] For instance, there was a good chance that the Polish laborers depicted in the movie *Moonlighting* purchased not only staples but also a VCR (or some VCRs) before returning to Poland, to improve the quality of life and the social status of their families.[5] Seeking to tap into and domesticate this trade, from the mid-1980s on, both Polish hard-currency chain stores, Pewex and Baltona (exact counterparts of the East German Intershop, Czechoslovak Tuzex, and Soviet Beryozka stores), introduced imported VCRs as their flagship product. Pewex and Baltona secured direct trade contacts with Sony, Sanyo, and Matsushita (which was the owner of the Panasonic brand) to secure the steady flow of VCRs to their stores. At the same time, on government orders, domestic electronics manufacturers sought to manufacture a Polish VCR. The intention of this governmental program, generally referred as "polskie wideo," was to fill the demand for this commodity with, to use the official propaganda claim, "one hundred thousand Polish VCRs" affordable for employees of the state sector. This project was intended to prove that state socialist Poland was capable of independently carrying out research on and development and manufacturing of VCRs, the quintessential symbol of the new era of high-tech electronic goods in the global 1980s. Such an achievement was to be a tangible indicator of Poland's place among the ten most developed countries in the world. It also was an attempt to provide consumers with a high-tech commodity that could have only "use value," and thus deprive the VCR of its meaning as a status symbol.

As a result of the popularity of VCRs, Poland became arguably the biggest and fastest-growing pirate video market in Europe in the 1980s. Because of the relative ease of travel to the West, Poles were able to import not only VCRs in very large numbers but also an impressive amount of videocassettes. These cassettes tended to be action movies, horror films, and pornography. Why these genres? Polish movie critics in the 1980s argued that the popularity of such movies was the result of an orchestrated campaign by Western media industries aiming to stupefy the audience. The popularity of these genres was equally condemned by Western critics and became a source of much consternation and moral panic in the West as well.[6] However, those were simply the most popular genres distributed globally on videocassettes.[7] In the Polish case, another factor that contributed to the popularity of such movies was consumer desire for something new. As the owner and operator of a video store in the late 1980s in Wrocław told me, Poles were particularly interested in new movie content—content previously unseen on state television or cinemas. As he explained, his clients were particularly interested in watching violence, cruelty, and explicit sex because they were eager to see something novel.[8] Several hundred semilegal and illegal video stores across Poland offered a wide selection of the newest movies catering to those tastes. Watching American action movies became a highly fashionable leisure activity, further stimulating demand for VCRs. As a result, the VCR in late socialist Poland emerged as a contested symbol of pleasure: it stood as a symbol of affluent consumption, of the unwelcome (to some) emergence of a new class, and as a marker of those who thoughtlessly consumed the low-brow content offered by Western media industries.

I situate the case of Polish VCRs as a commodity within the interpretative framework of consumer culture studies, which provides a necessary tool set for understanding the interdependencies between ideologies, the policies of key social groups (such as manufacturers and retailers), and the role that commodities play in consumers' identity formation. The proliferation of the VCR in late socialist Poland is perhaps best understood as an instance of "making the consumer."[9] VCRs focus the question of "how and why the consumer developed as an identifiable subject" within a specific economic and social context.[10]

This chapter understands consumption as an act of identity formation and investigates how its practices became a contested field of public debate. The chapter is divided into three sections, each of which highlights the process by which a consumer is made. First, I investigate how consumers exercised agency in the formation of their consumption-based identities (and speak to the way in which this process was understood by social critics). Second, I show how trade organizations acknowledged the purchasing power of these consumers and developed new supply chains and retail systems to attract them. Finally, I investigate how movie critics, representatives of media and electronics industries, and economic planners developed the polskie wideo project, in an attempt to create a different type of consumer: one who would use the VCR according to their normative visions of what a Polish consumer-citizen should be and desire.

In this I borrow from Sharon Zukin and Jennifer Smith Maguire, who emphasize how studies of consumer culture successfully link analysis of the macro level of activities of key groups that manufacture and facilitate the flow of consumer goods with the micro-level consumers' identity formation: "New technologies, ideologies, and delivery systems create consumption spaces in an institutional framework shaped by key social groups, while individual men and women experience consumption as a project of forming, and expressing, identity."[11] Following Zukin and Maguire, this chapter stresses interdependencies between the ideology of technologically driven modernity, the policies of key social groups, and the newly forming identities of VCR users.

The source base for this chapter includes a series of twenty interviews with consumer electronics owners who were young adults in the 1980s; six interviews with video store owners and videocassette traders active in the late 1980s; and a range of relevant periodicals, documents of governmental agencies, audience surveys, advertisements, and other promotional materials. The chapter first outlines studies on consumer culture and modernity in postwar Europe, before exploring the emergence of consumption-based identities among VCR owners in Poland during the 1980s. The chapter then outlines contacts between multinational consumer electronics producers and Polish retailers, and programs designed to distribute imported VCRs through "modern" systems of salesmanship. Finally, the chapter explores the research and development on and manufacturing of affordable Polish VCRs due to a deliberate policy, which was intended both to demonstrate Poland's "catching up" to highly developed countries of the West and to limit the problematic use of VCRs as a status symbol.

POLITICS OF CONSUMPTION, MODERNITY, AND TECHNOLOGY IN EASTERN EUROPE

Much recent scholarship focuses on post-Stalinist attempts to build "socialist modernity" in Eastern Europe through manufacturing and the distribution of technological products. These products of industrial technology became embedded in the politics of mass consumption in Eastern Europe, viewed as symbols of progress, comfort, and a high standard of living brought about by postwar technological developments and state planning.[12] These products were understood within a framework of Cold War competition and attempts by state socialist systems to "catch up and overtake the West." For many, success and failure in this endeavor was measured and felt through and by the availability of home technologies—the imaginary "modern household" (where the East and West were compared) included such marvels as black-and-white TVs, automatic washing machines, radios, and electric ovens. Susan E. Reid and David Crowley explain the common agenda behind such policies as a series of questions: "What forms of dress, furniture and housing ... would provide a stimulating environment that could meet the needs of, and give shape to, modern, socialist life? What was appropriate style for socialist modernity?"[13]

Key social groups sought to provide answers: consumers wanted goods, which they understood as evidence of living in an advanced modern society and of their own arrival as advanced modern subjects. Increasingly these were understood as "rights." Policy makers, economic planners, and industrial managers attempted to meet these demands by securing the necessary material base for the advent of developed socialism (or to demonstrate its arrival) through the mass production of housing, industrial goods, and an expanding range of technological products. According to Marxist ideology, this technological and material base was required in order to reach the imaginary and promised socialist modernity.

As Reid and Crowley note, in the 1950s and 1960s "increasing emphasis was placed [by policy makers] on a technologically driven conception of modernity."[14] This is also true for the 1970s and 1980, when electronics-based high technologies dominated the visions of tomorrow's world. However, while the postwar modernity of the 1950s and 1960s in Eastern Europe is extensively discussed in the scholarship, we know little of the social lives of commodities that constituted the modernity of the global 1970s (audio cassette recorders and color TVs) and the global 1980s (home computers, CD players, boom boxes, camcorders, satellite dishes, cable television, microwave ovens, and, of course, VCRs).[15] There is a small volume of works that cover the media landscape in state socialism, but such studies primarily cover the television as a means of political communication.[16] Due to such studies, we know much about what happened in newsrooms and the offices of media policy makers, but we still know little of how TV sets and radios were actually used in the households of people in Eastern Europe and even less about the aforementioned home technologies that came after TV sets and radios.

In the 1960s, Polish economic planners and domestic electronics manufacturers generally succeeded in manufacturing and distributing large numbers of consumer technologies. However, despite heavy investments in providing for the availability of staples and industrial goods in domestic retail trade, the 1970s and 1980s had rather mixed results. For instance, attempts to mass-produce color televisions, a flagship product of Polish "consumer socialism," were a failure, resulting in few televisions produced at a tremendous financial cost. Similarly, attempts to mass-produce Polish VCRs, discussed in the last section, were an even more spectacular failure. However, as Raymond Stokes discusses in his work *Constructing Socialism*, the study of several failed "socialist technologies" (in this case, in the GDR) could potentially be as instructive as studies of successes.[17] In this vein, the mass spread of imported VCRs in Polish households demonstrates an astounding instance of an appropriation of foreign consumer technology and a failure of the state apparatus to influence local consumer culture by delivering a viable local alternative.

This dynamic—and the idea of consumption and electronic goods as a measure of development against the backdrop of Cold War competition—has a long history. It is worth noting that the first appearance of videotape recording technology, which was intended from the beginning to stand as a symbol of Western technological dominance over the Soviet Union, took place during the "kitchen debate," an event that had a significant impact on the manufacturing of consumer goods behind the Iron Curtain, held in Moscow in 1959.[18] Footage of the debate was recorded not with a movie camera but with Ampex, the first commercially released video recorder. During the debate, one member of the US delegation even brought up the ability to record movies on a magnetic tape as an example of US technological prowess and, by extension, Soviet backwardness.[19] Showing the capacities of the Ampex system during a high-profile political event demonstrates how a symbol of state-of-the-art media technology was embedded in the orchestrated US postwar policy of a technological "civilizing mission" from the early days of the Cold War.[20]

VCRs in late state socialist Poland were a reference point for Polish modernity (understood as a feature of both technological sophistication and of Western-style consumer culture) and served as a way for Poles to situate themselves within the global 1980s. Many social actors considered the VCR to be a technological marvel—a silver bullet that, when harnessed, would instantly bring modernity to Poland. While popularly understood as universal, the concept of modernity carried within itself heavy ideological baggage. First among these was the idea of consumption—typically imagined as a capitalist form—which, for obvious reasons, made state socialist planners rather nervous. Don Slater in *Consumer Culture and Modernity* shows how practices of consumption define "the modern West": "Consumer culture is in important respects *the* culture of the modern West—certainly central to the meaningful practice of everyday life in the modern world; and it is more generally bound up with central values, practices and institutions which define Western modernity, such as choice, individualism and market relations."[21] Modernity was understood differently in Polish media during the 1980s. For example, in 1986 the local Gdańsk newspaper *Głos Wybrzeża* enthusiastically outlined how the local Gminna Spółdzielnia (GS, Rural Cooperative), a state enterprise tasked with building and maintaining culture centers in rural areas, brought VCRs to such centers in the region: "Video is considered as a synonym of modernity. The GS in the region of Gdańsk doesn't shun modernity and progress."[22] In this specific context, the VCR was presented as a technological device situated in the context of modernity as understood as a socialist project of providing cultural uplift in rural areas. This VCR—which, as we may assume, was used under the supervision of the employees of the local center—was not used as an artifact of "Western modernity," one that promotes Western-style consumer culture, but within the correct context (socialist modernity), thus contributing to the process of modernization and a genuine cultural uplift. Modern technology was universal; the values—socialist and capitalist—were specific and coded morally and ideologically. This argument—that VCRs were to be seen as artifacts of a universal modernity—will be further relevant to the discussion about the project of polskie wideo.

VCRs, POLES, AND CONSUMER DESIRE

In this section I discuss the emergence of a new type of socialist (or not so socialist) person—"the VCR consumer"—and show how VCRs were appropriated as a significant status symbol. To paraphrase Trentmann's question, I address how and why the VCR consumer developed as an identifiable subject. To discuss this process, it is important to provide a concise background of the state policy toward consumption in late socialist Poland. A steady increase in consumer durables in Polish households began in the early 1970s. This coincided with the introduction of policies designed to promote "consumer socialism," aiming toward a significant rise in living standards, as measured by the numbers of industrial goods owned by households. Virtually all consumer durables available for Polish consumers were products of domestic state enterprises or imports from the USSR. State media extensively promoted mass manufacturing and the importation of consumer durables, such as the popular Soviet-made Rubin color TVs and refrigerators, as tangible indicators of the modernization of Poland and real demonstrations of the successful satisfaction of citizens' needs.[23] Consumption was a matter of state policy—and the state alone, at least officially, was responsible for meeting these metrics and the resulting consumer demand.

Until the early 1980s virtually all electric appliances available in Poland were manufactured or imported and sold through a state system of distribution. The VCR was the first appliance that emerged from outside of this system. It would be difficult to find any comparable instance of a commodity more central to informing and expressing identity than the VCR, which quickly stood at the center of a contested field of social action and public debates in late socialist Poland. The first privately owned VCRs appeared in Poland around 1980, brought by *gastarbeiters* working in Western Europe, mostly in West Germany, who brought with them collections of prerecorded movies as both entertainment and status symbols. At the same time, wealthy private entrepreneurs (*prywaciarze*) began appropriating VCRs as important status symbols. According to unofficial data collected by the economist Piotr Gaweł, who has published several well-researched economic analyses of the Polish video market, in 1981, the number of privately owned VCRs was around ten thousand.[24] In the early 1980s, private importers offered VCRs at *giełdy*, open-air markets held in the main cities on every weekend, where peddlers distributed durable goods and clothing (goods both "privately imported" from the West and those that had somehow "leaked" from domestic retail trade). Such sites were central to the flourishing of the informal economic sector in Poland in the 1980s. Those who were eager to buy VCRs sought them out at giełdy. A 1983 newsreel shown in Polish cinemas about the *giełda* in the Skra stadium in Warsaw depicts two individuals, one who offers an older Sony reel-to-reel video recorder, another with a sign that says, "I'll buy a VCR."[25] The newsreel editors apparently decided to include such vignettes to illustrate recent trends and fashions at Skra, the biggest *giełda* in Poland. Gaweł estimated that in 1984 there were nearly one hundred fifty thousand VCRs in Poland, and at that time a VCR available at a giełda was priced at a rough equivalent of two years' average annual salary for a state-enterprise employee.[26] These figures are perhaps a bit misleading and point to the presence of plural and overlapping Polish economies. In the 1980s, Poles could earn additional money in the informal economy: moonlighting, working for private companies, working illegally abroad as construction workers, and through work as an occasional or professional trade tourist. Thus, despite the seemingly prohibitive price, for a resourceful individual it was feasible to purchase a VCR. Here it is worth summarizing the specificity of the Polish video market of the 1980s. On the one hand, the VCR (or in Polish, *wideo*), became a household name—Poles had many opportunities to own and enjoy a VCR. On the other hand, due to its price, the VCR was still a "(not-so-)mass commodity."[27]

VCRs became widespread in 1984–85, and in response, new private video stores sprang up in the larger cities offering a great selection of pirated movies. Gaweł has argued that the year 1984 was a threshold for Polish *videomania*—by this time, a large number of affluent households already owned a VCR. Such availability engendered social pressure among consumers eager to emulate the lifestyle of the new income elite—the *gastarbeiters* and *prywaciarze*—by owning this commodity.[28] The symbolic power of a VCR was heightened by the fact that this commodity came from the West and could not be purchased through the state-owned retail trade. As Franciszek Skwierawski, the columnist of the popular media weekly *Ekran* (The Screen), noted in 1986, the popularity of

VCRs in Polish households was a remarkable phenomenon in a country where VCRs were neither manufactured nor offered in domestic retail trade for purchase with legitimate domestic currency.[29] The term videomania used by Gaweł became regularly used in the media discourse of the late 1980s to illustrate the mass fascination with VCRs and video movies, and subsequently VCR users were referred as *videomaniacy*—video maniacs.

Moreover, in public discourse the VCR became identified as a symbol of upward mobility and as a commodity owned by and marking a single social group—a social class officially unwelcome in socialist society. Possession of a VCR became embedded in occupational stereotypes. For instance, an owner of a video store in Józefów, a small town near Warsaw and recognized as a town of *prywaciarze*, claimed that his clientele included mostly local market gardeners (*badylarze*—private entrepreneurs who grew and sold flowers and vegetables) and owners of small manufacturing and service businesses (*rzemieślnicy*), who could afford a VCR.[30] In other words, the petit bourgeoisie. Officials, journalists, and social critics who influenced public discourse in the mid-1980s identified imported videos as "entertainment for *badylarze*" (*rozrywka badylarzy*), an occupational group considered the richest group of private entrepreneurs with the lowest cultural capital, because of its members' peasant backgrounds—in other words, philistines.[31] Despite the fact that VCRs were available for wider social strata—for instance, the representatives of the working class, who had many opportunities for profitable moonlighting—such media images of VCR owners remained constant until the end of state socialism.

According to the ideological principles of state socialism, an individual should achieve his or her position in socialist society not through acts of consumption but rather through participation in the system of production as a worker, as an office clerk, a teacher, or engineer. In his study of commercial culture in Yugoslavia, Patrick Hyder Patterson insightfully explains how, even in Yugoslavia, despite giving more weight to the manufacturing of consumer goods, there was no official acknowledgment that consumption practices were generative of social stratification or of identity:[32] "Socialist states were not supposed to generate 'consumer societies' where shoppers' desires supplanted genuine human needs and where the symbolic, expressive, cultural value of the goods and services purchased became a primary factor of individual and group identity."[33] This model held true for Poland as well (at least in theory). According to the vocabulary of economic planners and the researchers who carried out surveys on domestic trade and consumption, the production and distribution of consumer products were aimed to secure *genuine needs*—only commodities that had specific *use value* were to be distributed in the retail trade.

One of the main beliefs embedded in the politics of mass consumption in the Eastern bloc was that electrical goods distributed by the state were supposed to bring modernity, comfort, the rationalization of housework, and selected forms of leisure, which would necessarily provide cultural uplift for all. These goods had particular use value in the state socialist political project and reflected genuine needs: needs that were translated into expectations across a broad spectrum of Poles under late socialism. In Poland, state media presented the spread of VCRs as a controversial blessing, since it provided somewhat independent access to popular culture, which in most cases was seen as contrary to cultural uplift. Furthermore, since they were the exclusive preserve of economic elites, VCRs threatened to augment and highlight class distinctions in a supposedly classless society. Moreover, and most dangerously of all, VCRs were spreading as an object of pleasure and desire unwelcome in socialism: other consumers were trying to "emulate" the lifestyle of these elites by spending all their savings on VCRs.

The dissemination of a commodity affordable to only a small number of consumers belonging to a distinctive social group is best understood as an instance of the "singularization of a commodity." Krisztina Fehérváry, borrowing from Daniel Miller and Igor Kopytoff, points out that a singularized commodity is "inserted into a particular context and generally associated with a specific person or social group."[34] The trajectory of the spread of VCRs in Poland significantly differed from the trajectory of the spread of VCRs in the United States discussed by Joshua Greenberg. As he shows, in the 1980s the early adopters of VCRs were so called "videophiles," technologically savvy middle-aged men with working- or middle-class backgrounds, who were fascinated with the technical possibilities of image recording and eagerly tinkered with their VCRs.[35]

In the Poland of the 1980s, the experience of living in "existing socialism," which included the emergence of a small economic elite made up of private entrepreneurs—with limited opportunities to manifest their position in social hierarchy—framed the cultural meaning of VCRs, which came to be the most distinctive status symbol of this era. From 2013 to 2014, I conducted twenty in-depth, oral history interviews with the generation of young adults who came of age during the period of transition. Virtually all my informants mentioned that in the 1980s a VCR was the most distinctive status symbol, which could only be compared with the even more expensive and much less widespread satellite dish. Of course, a detached house or a Western car was also a status symbol, but their ownership was often the result of a high rank in the *nomenklatura* or the ownership of a large legitimate private business, rather than simply being a matter of (substantial) disposable income. It is worth noting that, in the popular view, being a member of the nomenklatura and/or running a large private business in a hostile bureaucratic environment required extensive connections within the local power structure. Moreover, a flashy Mercedes car could not trigger an "emulation effect," since it was completely unaffordable for a person with an average income. One had to be connected to even dream of such things. On the other hand, the VCR was a symbol of a more democratic form of upward social mobility, since it could be afforded through intensive saving, moonlighting, and occasional trade tourism.

The estimated seven hundred thousand VCR owners in 1988 is definitely larger than the number of prywaciarze, and such a massive spread of this commodity *could* be explained by the demonstration effect. Some sources suggest that a VCR was considered to be the top-priority purchase by those who had disposable income. In one of his tongue-in-cheek articles in *Pan* (Gentleman) monthly, the first magazine dedicated to affluent consumption (it sought to copy *Playboy*'s format), a columnist who regularly commented on the video market described VCRs as the primary object of consumer desire: "More and more frequently I meet people who suffer terribly because they still don't own a VCR.... They own clapped-out radios, vintage record players; however, they don't even consider replacing them with modern ones. All their dreams are focused on a VCR."[36] Remarkably, there is some truth in a comment in one of the newsreels on the popularity of VCRs from 1988, titled *Pod każdą strzechą* (Under Every Roof): "Sony, Hitachi, JVC, Panasonic ... they conquered Poland with an easiness that astounds Europe and doesn't fit into the notion of Polish sociologists about our society."[37] Despite the spread of VCRs and their presence in media discourse, large-scale research on consumption and statistical surveys from the 1980s completely ignored the practices of VCR consumption. It is remarkable that the Central Statistical Office (Główny Urząd Statystyczny, or GUS), which carefully collected data on consumer durables (for instance, meticulously collecting data on differences in ownership of monophonic and stereophonic audio systems), included VCRs in its surveys for the first time only in 1989. This omission is understandable if we consider that the GUS covered only patterns of consumption organized by state agencies, manufacturers, and trade organizations. According to this survey, 0.9 percent of Polish households owned a VCR at that time.[38]

Above I showed how the consumer of a VCR developed as an identifiable subject and how, in specific social and economic contexts, the VCR became a major status symbol. Its popularity as a status symbol and its massive spread in Polish society were influenced by the fact that, contrary to Western cars, it was affordable for those eager to emulate the individualized lifestyle of the consumer elite. The following section demonstrates how a form of social action—massive purchases of VCRs—became a contested field of public debate as an indicator of broader and unwelcome dynamics in socialist society.

VCRs, DOLLARS, AND NEW DISTRIBUTION SYSTEMS

Rising demand for VCRs led to the emergence of new retail practices—practices driven not by state political agendas but rather by the profit motive. I have shown how the purchase and ownership of VCRs was relevant to the emergence of the new figure of the consumer. Here I address how two powerful trade organizations modified their business strategies by acknowledging the existence of consumers interested in defining themselves and pursuing their consumer desire by buying VCRs. This section discusses the retail trade in VCRs and the opening of new distribution channels outside of the distribution system used by policy makers, as Polish society moved toward mass consumption. In this section I discuss how VCRs were sold through "modern methods," that is, through a Western-style salesmanship system based on international trade routes established by Polish hard-currency chain stores and Japanese multinationals.

Much of this work was done by the hard-currency chain stores Pewex and Baltona. These stores played a strategic role in the Polish economy, since their main goal was to collect badly needed hard currency from Polish citizens, who earned this money by working abroad or as remittances from relatives in the West. It is worth noting that this retail mode was constructed as an alternative space in the public discussion about consumption in the 1980s. In 1982 a group of activists established the first consumer protection organization: Consumers' Federation (Federacja Konsumentów, or FK), which was not directly embedded in any state apparatus.[39] The unofficial press organ of the FK was the *Veto* weekly (1982–95). As *Veto*'s subtitle "Every Consumer's Weekly" suggests, this magazine was dedicated to the problems of consumers dependent on the state mass-consumption distribution system. Reading *Veto* issues from the 1980s gives us a bleak picture of late socialist Poland: a world of everlasting lines, shortages, spoiled foodstuffs, and "ugly" and failure-prone industrial goods. According to *Veto* columnists and readers sending in their angry complaints, ordinary consumers hoped not to buy but rather "to get" (*dostać*) commodities that would not spoil or break down quickly. It is remarkable that, within these comments, there is virtually no mention of VCRs. VCRs existed only in an alternative retail system. While those who had to depend on mass distribution systems provided by government agencies were waiting in lines, those who had enough disposable income, particularly in hard currency, experienced rather different possibilities of consumption.

In the early 1980s, VCRs were available only for those who brought them privately from the West. The rising demand for VCRs led to ever more creative ways of supplying them to the consuming public. Increasingly, VCRs were imported from the West and redistributed on the domestic market through fairs and privately owned commissioner shops, which together became a highly profitable sector of the private economy. An owner of a video store in Wroclaw remembered the rise of the local VCR market:

> First, VCRs were owned by traders who were trading goods imported from the West and Turkey. It was about 1985; at that time the market for small-scale private trade had greatly expanded and there were more and more VCRs. Suddenly those people who were trading in washing powder and T-shirts realized that it would be profitable to import VCRs because of the steady rise of the demand. An acquaintance of mine traveled to West Germany once a week to bring back around one hundred VCRs; he sold all of them each week. He traveled directly to a manufacturing plant, where he managed to establish a direct "connection." As far as I remember it was a Blaupunkt plant. Because of this connection to the plant, he was able to get a discount price and he sold those VCRs instantly. Only later did VCRs come to be offered by Pewex and Baltona chain stores.[40]

This testimony illustrates an important trend in marketing in hard-currency chain stores, which researched and followed trends on the black market. Both economies—official and unofficial, one following the other—began importing commodities in massive numbers. From the mid-1980s on, a wide range of "made in Japan" consumer electronics became flagship products offered by the Pewex and Baltona chains. Pewex began selling VCRs in its stores in 1986, a fact made possible by signing agreements with a number of Japanese companies: Sony, Sanyo, and Matsushita. In so doing, these chain stores joined global trade routes. The marketing studies scholar Robert Collins, in his award-winning article "Sony in Poland," understands the establishment of trade contacts between Pewex and Sony as part of a much broader trend: the expansion of multinationals into East European "emerging markets."[41] Both Pewex and Baltona had a significant advantage, since they were exempt from high rates of turnover tax; as a result, they were able to competitively price consumer electronics. Potentially this could cause *gastarbeiters* returning to Poland to choose to purchase a domestically made VCR domestically rather than abroad (which would require them to pay a substantial customs duty). Moreover, both chain stores provided reliable warranty service, while an owner of an imported appliance was left to his or her own devices when electronics broke down.

VCRs bought in Pewex and Baltona had another advantage: Poland, as well as other Soviet-bloc countries, adopted the Soviet SECAM broadcasting system, while most West European countries adopted the PAL system.[42] This incompatibility became a significant problem in the 1980s when Poles started bringing PAL-only-equipped VCRs while their domestically or Soviet-made TV sets had only a SECAM decoder. VCRs purchased at Pewex and Baltona avoided this problem. (This was not the only solution: most Polish manufacturers in the mid-1980s equipped their TV sets with both PAL and SECAM decoders. There was also a garage industry of TV repairmen who installed PAL decoders into older TV sets.) But hard-currency chain stores provided VCRs equipped with both PAL and SECAM decoders, thus guaranteeing that their customers would not have to tinker with their TV sets.

Unfortunately, Pewex archives are not accessible to the public, and we can reconstruct market data only through columnists writing on the video market quoting numbers provided by Pewex representatives. From 1986 Pewex offered a selection of Sony, Sanyo, JVC, and Panasonic VCRs priced at between 450 and 500 USD. (The same models in West Germany were priced at 1,200–1,400 DM, the equivalent of 600–700 USD.) At this time, the monthly salary in the state sector was around 40–50 USD, so VCRs were affordable only to those who had worked abroad or engaged in trade tourism or some other form of moonlighting. In its first year selling VCRs and videocassettes, Pewex had a turnover of 80 million USD on those products alone—a significant percentage of its receipts.[43] In 1987 Pewex sold approximately eighty thousand VCRs. A columnist reporting on the company's offerings claimed that the demand for VCRs in Pewex much exceeded managers' expectations, leading to the organization of "intervention shipments" by cargo jet from Japan to Frankfurt. He also claimed that Pewex was fifth on the worldwide list of purchasers of Panasonic goods.[44] While I was unable to corroborate these data, interviews conducted by Robert Collins with Sony sales representatives show their astonishment with the high demand for Sony products on the Polish market.[45] In 1987 Pewex went even further and changed one of its stores in Krakow into a Sony trade salon, selling exclusively Sony products, most likely the first such site opened in Eastern Europe.[46]

Baltona had a different market strategy. While Pewex offered VCRs from respectable Japanese companies and contracted directly with their branches in Western Europe, Baltona offered appliances from the less expensive Hitachi brand. Baltona signed a trade agreement with a Polish private joint venture company with foreign investment (firma polonijna), ITI, which imported Hitachi electronics through its subsidiary, Contal Ltd., with headquarters in Ireland.[47]

Baltona and ITI opened their flagship electronics store in Warsaw's prestigious Grand Hotel. At the same time, ITI was also the first private distributor of video movies in Poland. Press reportage on the Baltona/ITI store outlines its wide offerings: color TVs, VCRs, video cameras, and a large selection of legally distributed video movies. This report well demonstrates the new approaches employed in the retailing of video-related products. These alternative retail models stood as a harbinger of retailers' Western-style approach to clients: "The market for consumer electronics is becoming more normal [*normalizuje się*] and offers a better selection of commodities for clients due to the increasing number of stores.... Customs in the Hitachi store significantly vary from those in other electronic stores [that is, state-owned stores with domestically manufactured products]. Clients are able to test hardware, carefully inspect and touch it. We can only hope that trade customs that are normal in the world will prevail ... or hopefully even became more widespread."[48] *Ekran*'s editor welcomed the emergence of such retail customs—customs clearly built on the model of a consumer's market—stating that they are "normal in the world," that is, in the West. In the quote above, we can see how Polish journalists in the 1980s situated the emerging retail practices put in place at hard-currency chain stores, welcoming the process of "normalization," that is, the embrace of business practices identified as intrinsic elements of market economy. For columnists of *Ekran, Pan,* and *Hi-Fi Audio Video,* the emergence of trading and distribution systems that had no counterpart in any other consumer goods sector was an indicator of the process of normalization, understood as the first steps toward joining "the modern West," in terms presented by Don Slater.[49]

These new marketing techniques were mirrored by the emergence of a new style of consumer guides. In the second half of the 1980s, a large number of guides about VCR purchase and use appeared in the two magazines *Ekran* and *Pan*. These guides did not share the official world view of consumption expressed in *Veto*'s pages. Articles about VCRs in *Ekran* and *Pan* resemble those in the popular British consumer magazine *Which?*. Within *Ekran* and *Pan*, there are no discussions of lines and shortages, only guides and pricing information for VCRs, rendered in hard currency as reflected in chain stores, fairs, and commissioner shops. These magazines understood the lack of knowledge about different formats and technical novelties to be the most substantial problems of potential owners of VCRs. There were no complaints about pricing, which mostly goes without saying since editors assumed that the readers interested in Western consumer electronics had enough disposable income to pursue their hobbies. Information on technical features dominated such guides. For instance, in early guides consumers were discouraged from buying VCRs in the

Betamax standard, since the VHS standard was about to become the market leader. Other articles covered the potential advantages of such technical novelties as VCRs with hi-fi sound recording and the improved S-VHS standard.

Pan guides on buying VCRs also spoke to a broader pattern: the emergence of individualized male lifestyles and identity expressed primarily through consumption and leisure. The cover of the first issue of *Pan* clearly states what the proper hobbies of red-blooded men of the 1980s were (or should have been): "Career, Cars, Video, Sport, Thrill, Sex."[50] Those slogans echo the values of the hyperindividualized lifestyle of the West in the 1980s. Don Johnson would approve. *Pan* understood private ownership of a VCR, and watching video movies, to be not only status symbols of a new economic elite but also an expression of an individualized lifestyle of young men capable of making careers as private entrepreneurs. As a prize for their entrepreneurial spirit, they were to reward themselves through the pursuit of their own individualized lifestyle: expressing their agency and identity by choosing their own movies without being dependent on the state television broadcaster, with its two channels.

The VCR market in Poland in the 1980s points to the early stages of socioeconomic change related to the collapse of state socialism in Eastern Europe. The VCR market was also avant-garde in one important aspect: advertising practices. Except for the unique case of Yugoslavia, the histories of advertising practices in state socialist countries are mostly uninvestigated by historians.[51] In Poland, some commercial advertisements appeared in the mass media in the 1980s. These were mostly locally made, crude advertisements with basic information about the commercial offers of private companies. VCRs brought about new forms of advertising—here too we can see the beginnings of broader trends. In 1989, *Hi-Fi Audio Video* published the first full-page advertisement for GoldStar (currently LG) VCRs. This advertisement was not designed locally, but rather it was a localized version of a global advertisement, published by a privately owned company that had established a partnership with the Korean electronics firm, which, as we will see below, already had previous trade contacts with Polish partners.[52]

This section has shown how a specific key social group—managers of hard-currency chain stores—acknowledged and sought to tap into both the consumer desire for VCRs and the new figure of the consumer. These consumers had enough disposable income that it seemed worthwhile to substantially expand the "video sections" of their stores. As Pewex and Baltona welcomed these new consumers, editors from several periodicals welcomed the emerging business practices designed to attract them on the part of both trade organizations. This mutually reinforcing trend within the video market was understood by both sides as normalization—meaning the adoption of practices characteristic to a market economy.

ONE HUNDRED THOUSAND POLISH VCRs

In the mid-1980s cultural critics and representatives of electronics and media industries regularly appealed for polskie wideo, a state-funded program for research on and the development and manufacturing of a Polish VCR affordable for average-income households. According to its supporters, these manufactured, affordable VCRs would be used by the working class for cultural uplift. For instance, in his economic analysis of the video market, Gaweł concluded that the incorporation of a VCR into a collective-consumption distribution system would cause the demise of the highly unwelcome "demonstration effect" and change the negative public understanding of this technology: "Only the availability of a VCR affordable for an average-income family can change the negative aura of pornography and Rambo which prevails in the public understanding of this medium."[53] For example, a columnist for the Życie Warszawy daily who covered plans for manufacturing Polish VCRs saw the wide distribution of Polish VCRs to working-class families, culture centers, and schools as a means to combat the current cultural meaning of a VCR as "an object of opulence and desire of those who yearn to embrace the capitalist model of individual consumption."[54] This quotation clearly shows the central problem as defined by economic experts and cultural critics. According to their opinions, the VCR in the Poland of the 1980s had become a symbol of individual consumption practices—it threatened to overturn traditional collectivist understandings of consumption. As demonstrated above, VCRs became appropriated as a status symbol for those eager to differentiate themselves from the rest of socialist society. Not everyone was pleased with this turn of events.

Daniel Miller points out one of the basic principles of the state socialist project of collective consumption: "Mass consumption is highly normative and is clearly concerned to avoid status competition at all costs."[55] Manufacturing Polish VCRs should be interpreted as an attempt to introduce a consumer product into such a normative sphere of consumption in a manner in which consumers would be unable to use it for status competition. Such appeals sought to bring VCRs into the sphere of collective consumption, governed by state agencies, thus limiting its cultural meaning as a status symbol and its role in articulating social inequalities in socialist society. The main assumption behind this project was that the domestic manufacturer would produce a large quantity of a single model of VCR with an affordable price, making the product available for employees of the state sector and, implicitly, the working class. This program was an instance of the policy of mass consumption mentioned by Miller: to make products that only have use value, thus avoiding transforming consumer products into tools of status competition.

Conversations about the research, development, and manufacturing of the Polish VCR were embedded in broader discussions about the domestic manufacturing of consumer durables. During the 1980s, despite the severe economic crisis, state agencies attempted to develop and introduce a range of innovative products. One *Veto* columnist argued that the state should make the manufacturing of technologically innovative durables that could successfully compete in the market with products imported from the West a matter of state politics: "There is a need to change the production structure, and to carry on manufacturing of other, innovative commodities. . . . It is impossible to control processes of consumption without introducing new commodities and technologies."[56] Here it is worth noting that the main agenda of the consumer movement in state socialism was to improve the efficiency of state agencies tasked with planning consumption and the manufacture of consumer goods. This voice traces one of the main arguments: that the state had to find ways to domestically produce more "modern" and technologically innovative products in order to provide Polish consumers with more affordable alternatives to prohibitively priced products imported from the West by trade tourists and hard-currency chain stores.

This was very much apparent in conversations on the domestic production of VCRs. The official communiqué for the Tenth Polish United Workers' Party (Polska Zjednoczona Partia Robotnicza, or PZPR) Gathering in 1986 included a statement on the necessity to carry on active support for manufacturing new media technologies under the slogan "Today we make tomorrow" (Jutro tworzy się dziś). According to the communiqué, the state would soon prescribe the "development of manufacturing of videocassettes and video hardware [which supposedly included VCRs and video cameras]" as one of the focal points of the centrally planned economy. The agenda behind such a policy was explained further: "We cannot lag behind when others move forward, when they spread new communication technologies such as video, cable and satellite television."[57]

In 1986 the government implemented a large-scale program in support of manufacturing VCRs and blank videocassettes and for the distribution of domestically produced movies on video.[58] Two state enterprises, Kasprzak Radio Works in Warsaw and Diora Radio Works in Dzierżoniów, were ordered to carry out the research and development of two different VCR models to be independently designed by engineers of both manufacturers.⁵⁹ Records of the discussion on manufacturing these VCRs in the Committee for Culture of the Central Committee PZPR suggest that the whole program was initiated by Kasprzak Radio Works, whose directorate declared its readiness and capacity to carry out such an enterprise.⁶⁰ The project of designing the Polish VCR was linked to the policy of developing a system for the distribution of Polish movies on videocassettes, which, when released, would supposedly be preferred by the Polish socialist audience over the low-brow fare offered by Western media industries. The early Polish VCR plan included a plan for manufacturing one hundred thousand VCRs, a number quoted in several media sources.⁶¹

This number was not met. Kasprzak was only able to manufacture a preliminary series of around five thousand VCRs. The state enterprise lacked the independent research-and-development foundation required to design VCRs from scratch, and decided to manufacture them by assembling VCR kits from the Korean company GoldStar, leading to the launch of the model branded Kasprzak GoldStar. Kasprzak further released a small number of its own VCR model, the MTV-100, which were presumably distributed exclusively to state institutions, such as schools and cultural centers. There is no indication of any attempts to continue the production of VCRs in Kasprzak. In 1990, when Kasprzak was slowly falling into bankruptcy, Teodozjusz Życzkowski, an engineer and a secretary of the workers' council in Kasprzak, complained about the decision to make a Polish VCR: "Now there are accusations that it was our sole decision. . . . But it was a strictly political decision made by policy makers and endorsed by KW [Voivodeship Committee in Warsaw—the regional PZPR branch] and KC [Central Committee] to provide comrades with a reason to boast. Which country could afford the manufacturing of such a device not in one but immediately in two plants at the same time, since at the same time Diora also started preparations to build their VCRs? We built only a few pieces and assembled some more."⁶² Sources suggest that in 1988 Diora alone was supposed to manufacture this one hundred thousand VCRs.⁶³ Analysis of most media sources suggests that manufacturing one hundred thousand VCRs was primarily a project governed by the principles of the politics of mass consumption discussed above. However, some sources, primarily information provided by Diora representatives, suggest that they hoped a Polish VCR would result in substantial profit, indicating that this decision was based on market research rather than simply being a decision made by policy makers in the Central Committee.⁶⁴ In an interview, the deputy director of Diora's research-and-development unit claimed that the decision to create a Polish VCR was primarily a commercial enterprise and that before starting its production, Diora carried out a detailed market survey showing an enormous demand, worth half a billion dollars, for a VCR that would belong to the "average European class" of this product.[65] This interview suggests that Diora's ultimate plan was to manufacture and market not one hundred thousand, but a rather more astounding three hundred and fifty thousand VCRs. The language of the press coverage on the Polish VCR reveals a unique mixture of the state socialist mass-consumption politics, focused on production quotas rather than products sold, and free market economic thought. In 1989 Diora became one of the first state enterprises to undergo privatization, and VCRs became Diora's flagship product, promising great prosperity to the company in the new free-market environment.[66] The transition was hard on Diora: in 1995, when the company finally released its first VCRs, the MVD-101 and MVD-200, the company achieved only 0.04 percent of the Polish VCR market share.[67] By that time the Polish consumer electronics market was already completely saturated by Western manufacturers, and Diora, which could not compete in terms of price or innovation, went into bankruptcy in the late 1990s.

In the early 1980s, after the fall of Gierek's rule, several elements of socialist consumer policy were criticized in the media as costly "Gierek extravaganzas" or as attempts to foster "elite consumption."[68] For instance, economists criticized the extensive investment in manufacturing color TV sets in the 1970s. They argued that these resources could have been used elsewhere to better contribute to raising the general standard of living. One joke claimed that the main aim of manufacturing color TVs was to show Poles what a ham, a premium good unavailable in stores at that time, looked like in color.[69] While the Polish press of the early and mid-1980s highlighted appeals for the Polish VCR, the manufacturing project, introduced in 1986, was met with a lukewarm reception in the media, due to the constant delays, the obvious inferiority of Kasprzak VCRs to Western VCRs, and the fact that the prices were much higher than promised.[70]

From the 1980s we can find several highly critical voices in the media that, similarly to the criticisms of color TVs, openly questioned the rationality of a high-cost program that had no clear benefits to either Polish consumers or the state economy. Remarkably, one of the economists from the government advisory body Komitet Polska 2000, an affiliate of the Polish Academy of Sciences, whose primary aim was to provide futurology-style "prognoses" for socialism through the year 2000, claimed, "I build my estimates [on the spread of VCRs] not on the activities of our industry that ran into a dead end and decided to invent the gunpowder on its own. I rather believe in importing cheap yet decent VCRs, for instance, from South Korea."[71] The focal point of this criticism was whether it was more reasonable to spend the money invested in manufacturing Polish VCRs on importing large numbers of "world-class" VCRs at a low profit margin (or even to commit to the extension of Pewex trade offerings).[72] This debate touches on one of the most significant dilemmas for policy makers when thinking about mass consumption in a centrally planned economy: Should the state pursue the development of the domestic production of technological modernity at all costs, or should it acknowledge the unfeasibility of such pursuit and import such products to satisfy consumers' growing desires?[73]

Scholars have explored several spectacular failures of the GDR's high-tech industries, such as the famous one-megabyte memory chip and attempts to introduce the massive manufacturing of consumer products made with plastics.[74] We can definitely identify polskie wideo as another case of a spectacular failure of the socialist consumer goods industries and centrally planned economies. Attempts to manufacture a Polish VCR were embedded in at least three different ideologies. Some sources suggest that these programs are best understood as an attempt to catch up with the global 1980s by independently making a product that was one of the resonant symbols of technological modernity. Polish attempts to manufacture affordable VCRs were also meant to combat the use of electric appliances as a means to express individual identity as a marker of affluent consumption. Finally, it seems clear that Diora managers viewed this project as a viable commercial enterprise driven by the profit motive. Here we can see VCRs as, to borrow from Reid and Crowley, an object of divergent aspirations of key social actors engaged in the planning of the collective consumption, design, and manufacture of consumer technologies.[75]

CONCLUSION

The emergence of the VCR as a commodity of mass desire in Poland during the 1980s sheds light on the interdependencies between consumer culture and modernity understood both in the context of the modern West and in the context of a supposedly universal technological modernity.[76] The VCR as an object of consumer desire was also an important means of expressing social identity. Meeting these demands led to the emergence of "modern methods" of salesmanship, often understood as "Western" and "normal." It also led to heartbreakingly failed attempts to manufacture domestic VCRs—VCRs intended to both meet the demand for "modern consumer products" and to serve as a flagship product of the socialist technological modernity of the 1980s. Each of these social actors—manufacturers, government agencies, state media, and social critics—endowed both the production and the consumption of VCRs with a variety of cultural meanings, all against the larger background of the struggle to "catch up and overtake the West" and resulting definitions of modernity and backwardness.

VCRs also point to the logic of consumer culture in late state socialism (the multiple delivery systems: private importation, hard-currency chain stores, and private showings of videos) as it intersected with two key ideologies: technological modernity and political guidelines of socialist mass consumption. The Polish case of the VCR stands as a nexus for a host of social actors—videomaniacy who saved money for VCRs, trade tourists, hard-currency chain stores, multinationals, the media, social critics, and economic planners—demonstrating how a single commodity can become an object inscribed with several contradictory cultural meanings. Close readings of these negotiations challenges the popular notion that the year 1989 was a definitive threshold for the history of consumer cultures in Eastern Europe.

State projects of manufacturing and distributing technologically innovative home appliances in previous decades in the Eastern bloc were generally initiated by policy makers. The case of VCRs is different, since the largest state-sponsored project of designing and making an industrial good in the Poland of the 1980s emerged as a form of feedback. Key social actors from the state apparatus were eager to preserve the most substantial elements of socialist-style consumer culture, limiting the possible use of consumer goods as status symbols. At the same time, the contested status of the VCR in Polish consumer culture was fueled by the meaning of "a synonym of modernity" inscribed in this artifact. Finally, VCRs demonstrate the entanglement of different imaginaries of modernity of late state socialism. What constituted modernity as understood in state socialist systems in the 1980s? Was it measured by whether or not the state was capable of manufacturing a high-tech electronics product—the fashionable worldwide hit of the decade? In this case Poland failed. Was it the fact that even small, rural culture centers owned such a product? Here the results were less clear. Or perhaps modernity should be measured by whether or not trade organizations could introduce new modern methods for selling this product, which came from global supply chains rather than from the assembly lines of domestic electronics manufacturers? Was modernity capitalist? Such questions demonstrate how fraught consumer culture could be in socialism (and potentially, in capitalism as well).

NOTES

Research for this paper was supported by the Polish National Science Centre grant 2016/23/D/HS3/03199. I would like to thank Zsuzsa Gille, Diana Mincytė, and Cristofer Scarboro for their comments, which helped me to improve my manuscript, and Cristofer Scarboro for his extensive editing help.

1. Bren and Neuburger, "Introduction," 5.

2. See Gaweł, "Rynek wideo w Polsce." The question of how many VCRs Poles owned was a regular topic of mass media debate in the late 1980s.

3. Radio Free Europe often reported on the spread of VCRs in the Eastern bloc. This term was originally used by the Radio Free Europe analysts to describe the mass popularity of video entertainment in Eastern Europe. See "Video Revolution in Eastern Europe." The term refers to the "revolutionary potential" of this new media technology and its supposed significant impact on social change; see Newman, *Video Revolutions*.

4. According to Mark Keck Szajbel, trade tourism across the Iron Curtain has not yet been investigated in the scholarly literature. See Keck-Szajbel, "Shop Around the Bloc."

5. Skolimowski, *Moonlighting*.

6. Critcher, *Moral Panics*, 64–80.

7. Greenberg, *From Betamax to Blockbuster*, 81–96; Wasser, *Veni, Vidi, Video*, 105–57.

8. Interview with J., July 2013, Wrocław.

9. Trentmann, "Knowing Consumers," 1–27.

10. Ibid., 14.

11. Zukin and Maguire, "Consumers and Consumption," 173.

12. Reid and Crowley, *Style and Socialism*; Reid and Crowley, *Socialist Spaces*; Siegelbaum, *Socialist Car*. See Zachmann, "Socialist Consumption Junction," for an in-depth reconstruction of negotiations of meanings of household appliances and the imaginary East German modernity.

13. Reid and Crowley, *Style and Socialism*, 3.

14. Ibid., 9.

15. For a discussion on the symbolic meanings of electronic products in the 1970s and 1980s, see Chandler, *Inventing the Electronic Century*. In the chapter "Consumer Electronics: Japan's Path to Global Conquest" (50–81), Chandler discusses how the commercialization of the VCR by Japanese manufacturers in the late 1970s and 1980s was embedded in the struggle between electronic potentates for dominance in terms of introducing innovative "modern products" in the high-technology field. Several works in the history of technology address the entanglement of technologies in the discourse of modernity and modernization. The most notable include Misa, "Compelling Tangle of Modernity"; and Morley, *Media, Modernity and Technology*.

16. Gumbert, *Envisioning Socialism*; Roth-Ey, "Finding a Home."

17. Stokes, *Constructing Socialism*, 3.

18. Oldenziel and Zachmann, *Cold War Kitchen*.

19. For the history of using the Ampex to record the "kitchen debate," see Abramson, *History of Television*, 88.

20. Adas, *Dominance by Design*.

21. Slater, *Consumer Culture and Modernity*, 8 (emphasis in the original).

22. "Wideo w geesie," 4.

23. This was a broader tendency in the whole Soviet bloc in the 1980s. For examples, see Chernyshova, *Soviet Consumer Culture*, 184–201.

24. Gaweł, "Rynek wideo w Polsce."

25. *W nowej roli*.

26. Gaweł, "Pierwsza runda dla Rocky'ego," 1.

27. I would like to thank Cristofer Scarboro for proposing this term, which grasps the cultural status of the VCR in Poland.

28. Gaweł, "Pierwsza runda," 1.

29. Skwierawski, "Telewizja traci monopol," 2.

30. Gaweł, "Pierwsza runda," 6..

31. Gołębiewska, "Bieg po wideo," 7.

32. Patterson, *Bought and Sold*.

33. Ibid., 1.

34. Fehérváry, "Goods and States," 436.

35. Greenberg, *From Betamax to Blockbuster*, 17–40. In the scarce scholarly literature on the spread of VCRs in US society, I have not found any clear historical evidence that the VCR became a distinctive and widely recognizable status symbol in the United States of the 1980s.

36. Radgowski, "Video i szafa," 7.

37. *Pod każdą strzechą*, 1.

38. *Mały Rocznik Statystyczny*, 174.

39. Mazurek and Hilton, "Consumerism, Solidarity and Communism."

40. Interview with J., Wrocław, July 2013.

41. Collins, "Sony in Poland." I would like to express my gratitude to Professor Collins for providing me a copy of his text.

42. The SECAM system was introduced in Eastern Europe in the 1960s as a result of the high politics around Cold War broadcasting; see Fickers, *"Politique de la Grandeur."*

43. Gaweł, "Rynek wideo w Polsce," 39.

44. Skwierawski, "Co kupić?" 30.

45. Collins, "Sony in Poland."

46. A press reportage about the opening and successful business operations of a Sony trade salon will be included in the source collection Wasiak, "Sony in Cracow."

47. "Kupić nie Kupić," 10.

48. Ibid.

49. Slater, *Consumer Culture and Modernity*, 8.
50. *Pan*, cover.
51. Cf. Patterson, *Bought and Sold*.
52. *Hi-Fi Audio Video*, no. 3, 1989, inside cover.
53. Gaweł, "Rynek wideo w Polsce," 51.
54. Siwik, "Gorący kartofel w gardle," 3.
55. Miller, "Vanguard Of History," 25.
56. Podwysocki, "Kukła na Targowisku,"5.
57. "Jutro Tworzy Się Dziś," 4.
58. See "Program rozwoju wideofilmów." Starr offers a brief outline of a similar project, that of the manufacturing of the Elektronika VM-12 VCR in the USSR. Starr, "New Communications Technologies," 37–38.
59. Skwierawski, "Polskie wideo rodem z Kasprzaka," 12. While the two companies manufactured their own VCRs separately, I was unable to find any evidence of their cooperation. Perhaps the reason for this puzzling and costly decision was the internal rivalry between two state enterprises and power plays within the UNITRA industrial federation of the electronics industry to which both companies belonged.
60. "Program rozwoju wideofilmów."
61. "Gaweł Główne kierunki reformy systemu zarządzania i programowania w kinematografii."
62. Sowińska, "Teatr w 'Kasprzaku,'" 7.
63. "Upowszechnianie filmów na kasetach wizyjnych."
64. Such claims can be found in Grzegorzewski, "Kroki we Mgle," 4; *Akcje Diory*.
65. Siwik, "Trzy Konstrukcje," 3. For a discussion of marketing surveys in the Polish electric appliance industry, see King, "Enterprise-Level Marketing Research."
66. The history of Diora's VCR project and privatization will be discussed in my upcoming book, Wasiak, *Home Technologies*.
67. Kotowski, "Wygrywa 'Panasonic.'"
68. For instance, Dąbrowski, "Elitarna czy egalitarna."
69. Mieczykowski, "TVC opium dla mas?"
70. Polskiewideo was extensively supported by *Ekran* editors; see, for instance, Skwierawski, "Polskie wideo rodem z Kasprzaka."
71. "Mieszkanko i co dalej?"
72. See, for instance, Skwierawski, "Magnetowid z 'Kasprzaka.'"
73. Divergent voices in such debates were regularly expressed on the pages of the periodicals *Życie Gospodarcze* and *Przegląd Techniczny*.
74. Stokes, *Constructing Socialism*.
75. Reid and Crowley, *Style and Socialism*, 3.
76. Slater, *Consumer Culture and Modernity*, 8.

REFERENCES

Abramson, Albert. *The History of Television, 1942 to 2000*. Jefferson, IA: McFarland, 2003.
Adas, Michael. *Dominance by Design: Technological Imperatives and America's Civilizing Mission*. Cambridge, MA: Harvard University Press, 2006.
Akcje Diory. PKF (Polska Kronika Filmowa), 90/04, 1990.
Bren, Paulina, and Mary Neuburger. "Introduction." In *Communism Unwrapped: Consumption in Cold War Eastern Europe*, edited by Paulina Bren and Mary Neuburger, 3–19. Oxford: Oxford University Press, 2012.
Chandler, Alfred. *Inventing the Electronic Century: The Epic Story of the Consumer Electronics and Computer Industries*. Cambridge, MA: Harvard University Press, 2005.
Chernyshova, Natalya. *Soviet Consumer Culture in the Brezhnev Era*. London: Routledge, 2013.
Collins, Robert. "Sony in Poland: A Case Study." *European Management Journal* 11, no. 1 (1993): 46–54.
Critcher, Chas. *Moral Panics and the Media*. Buckingham, UK: Open University Press, 2003.
Dąbrowski, Janusz. "Elitarna czy egalitarna." *Przegląd Techniczny*, October 18, 1981, 24–27.
Fehérváry, Krisztina. "Goods and States: The Political Logic of State-Socialist Material Culture." *Comparative Studies in Society and History* 51, no. 2 (2009): 426–59.
Fickers, Andreas. *"Politique de la grandeur" versus "Made in Germany": Politische Kulturgeschichte der Technik am Beispiel der PAL-SECAM-Kontroverse*. Munich, Germany: De Gruyter Oldenbourg, 2007.
Gaweł, Piotr. "Pierwsza runda dla Rocky'ego." *Polityka*, March 12, 1988, 1, 6–7. "Główne kierunki reformy systemu zarządzania i programowania w kinematografii." Ministerstwo Kultury i Sztuki; Wydział Kultury KC PZPR, November 1986, Archiwum KC PZPR, AAN, LVI 1694, 30–31.
———. "Rynek wideo w Polsce." *Aktualności Radiowo-Telewizyjne*, no. 8, 1987, 35–56.
Gołębiewska, Rita. "Bieg po wideo." *Tygodnik Kulturalny*, March 1, 1987, 6–7.
Greenberg, Joshua M. *From Betamax to Blockbuster: Video Stores and the Invention of Movies on Video*. Cambridge, MA: MIT Press, 2008.
Grzegorzewski, Zbigniew. "Kroki we mgle." *Życie Gospodarcze*, July 2, 1989.
Gumbert, Heather L. *Envisioning Socialism: Television and the Cold War in the German Democratic Republic*. Ann Arbor: University of Michigan Press, 2014.
"Jutro tworzy się dziś." *Ekran*, April 21, 1986, 4–5.
Keck-Szajbel, Mark. "Shop Around the Bloc: Trader Tourism and Its Discontents on the East German-Polish Border." In *Communism Unwrapped: Consumption*

in *Cold War Eastern Europe*, edited by Paulina Bren and Mary Neuburger, 374–92. Oxford: Oxford University Press, 2012.

King, Robert. "Enterprise-Level Marketing Research Activity in Poland: The Predom/Polar Experience." *Academy of Marketing Science* 11, no. 3 (1983): 292–303.

Kotowski, Paweł. "Wygrywa 'Panasonic.'" *Cinema Press Video*, October 1995, 72–73.

"Kupić nie kupić." *Ekran*, December 1, 1988, 10–11.

Mały Rocznik Statystyczny. Warsaw: Główny Urząd Statystyczny, 1989.

Mazurek, Malgorzata, and Matthew Hilton. "Consumerism, Solidarity and Communism: Consumer Protection and the Consumer Movement in Poland." *Journal of Contemporary History* 42, no. 2 (2007): 315–43.

Mieczykowski, Karol. "TVC opium dla mas?" *Przegląd Techniczny*, January 2, 1983, 14–16.

"Mieszkanko i co dalej. Cykl mała prognoza konsumpcyjna. Rozmowa z Januszem Dąbrowskim, pracownikiem Komitetu Badań i Prognoz Polska 2000." *Atut*, no. 3 (1989): 46–47.

Miller, Daniel. "Consumption as the Vanguard of History." In *Acknowledging Consumption: A Review of New Studies*, edited by Daniel Miller, 1–52. London: Routledge, 1995.

Misa, Thomas J. "The Compelling Tangle of Modernity and Technology." In *Modernity and Technology*, edited by Thomas J. Misa, Philip Brey, and Andrew Feenberg, 1–30. Cambridge, MA: MIT Press, 2003.

Morley, David. *Media, Modernity and Technology: The Geography of the New*. London and New York: Routledge, 2007.

Newman, Michael Z. *Video Revolutions: On the History of a Medium*. New York: Columbia University Press, 2014.

Oldenziel, Ruth, and Karin Zachmann, eds. *Cold War Kitchen: Americanization, Technology, and European Users*. Cambridge, MA: MIT Press, 2010.

Patterson, Patrick Hyder. *Bought and Sold: Living and Losing the Good Life in Socialist Yugoslavia*. Ithaca, NY: Cornell University Press, 2011.

Podwysocki, Tadeusz. "Kukła na targowisku." *Veto*, August 3, 1986, 5.

Pod każdą strzechą. PKF (Polska Kronika Filmowa), 88/03, 1988,.

"Program rozwoju wideofilmów i dotychczasowe działania dla jego wdrożenia." Wydział Kultury KC PZPR, March 26, 1987, Archiwum KC PZPR, Archiwum Akt Nowych (AAN), LVI 1706.

Radgowski, Michał. "Video i szafa." *Pan*, March 1989, 7.

Reid, Susan E. "The Khrushchev Kitchen: Domesticating the Scientific-Technological Revolution." *Journal of Contemporary History* 40, no. 2 (2005): 289–316.

Reid, Susan E., and David Crowley, eds. *Socialist Spaces: Sites of Everyday Life in the Eastern Bloc*. Oxford: Berg, 2002.

———, eds. *Style and Socialism. Modernity and Material Culture in Post-War Eastern Europe*. Oxford: Berg, 2000.
Roth-Ey, Kristin. "Finding a Home for Television in the USSR, 1950–1970." *Slavic Review* 66, no. 2 (2007): 278–306.
Siegelbaum, Lewis. *The Socialist Car: Automobility in the Eastern Bloc*. Ithaca, NY: Cornell University Press, 2013.
Siwik, Zbigniew. "Gorący kartofel w gardle." *Życie Warszawy*, August 23, 1987, 1, 3.
———. "Trzy konstrukcje." *Życie Warszawy*, January 30–31, 1988, 1, 3.
Skolimowski, Jerzy, dir. *Moonlighting*. London: Michael White, 1982.
Skwierawski, Franciszek. "Co kupić? Rynek magnetowidów i kamer." *Ekran*, May 26, 1988, 30–31.
———. "Polskie wideo rodem z Kasprzaka." *Ekran*, November 2, 1986, 2–3, 12–13.
———. "Telewizja traci monopol." *Ekran*, July 13, 1986, 2–3.
Slater, Don. *Consumer Culture and Modernity*. Cambridge: Polity, 1997.
Starr, S. Frederick. "New Communications Technologies and Civil Society." In *Science and the Soviet Social Order*, edited by Loren R. Graham, 19–50. Cambridge, MA: Harvard University Press, 1990.
Stokes, Raymond G. *Constructing Socialism: Technology and Change in East Germany 1945–1990*. Baltimore: Johns Hopkins University Press, 2000.
Trentmann, Frank. "Knowing Consumers—Histories, Identities, Practices: An Introduction." In *The Making of the Consumer: Knowledge, Power and Identity in the Modern World*, edited by Frank Trentmann, 1–27. Oxford: Bloomsbury, 2005.
"Upowszechnianie filmów na kasetach wizyjnych." Wydział Kultury KC, March 10, 1988, Archiwum KC PZPR, AAN LVI 1716.
"The Video Revolution in Eastern Europe." RFE Background Report 242, December 17, 1987, Radio Free Europe/Radio Liberty Background Reports, Open Society Archives, Digital Repository.
W nowej roli. PKF (Polska Kronika Filmowa), 83/11, 1983.
Wasiak, Patryk. *Home Technologies, Consumer Culture and Poland's Post-Socialist Transition*, forthcoming.
———. "Sony in Cracow." In *From Stalinism to Coca-Cola: A Source Collection*, edited by Mark Keck Szajbel, forthcoming.
———. "The Video Boom in the State-Socialist Poland." *Zeitschrift Für Ostmitteleuropa-Forschung* 61, no. 1 (2012): 27–50.
Wasser, Frederick. *Veni, Vidi, Video: The Hollywood Empire and the VCR*. Austin: University of Texas Press, 2001.
"Wideo w geesie." *Głos Wybrzeża*, November 10, 1986, 4.
Zachmann, Karin. "A Socialist Consumption Junction: Debating the Mechanization of Housework in East Germany, 1956–1957." *Technology and Culture* 43, no. 1 (2002): 73–99.

Zukin, Sharon, and Jennifer Smith Maguire. "Consumers and Consumption." *Annual Review of Sociology*, no. 30 (2004): 173–97.

AUTHOR BIO

PATRYK WASIAK is Associate Professor at the Institute of History at the Polish Academy of Sciences. He is a former visiting fellow at the Center for Contemporary History in Potsdam, Germany, and the Netherlands Institute for Advanced Study in Wassenaar. His last fellowship was sponsored by a grant from the Andrew W. Mellon Foundation. He publishes on the history of consumer culture in communist Poland, the cultural history of Polish market transition, and the history of electronic technologies.

SEVEN

THE ENCHANTMENT OF IMAGINARY EUROPE

Consumer Practices in Post-Soviet Ukraine

TANIA BULAKH

"Ukraine will be a European country when we have IKEA and H&M here," said my informant, Roman, in 2014, a few months after the Euromaidan revolution in Kyiv. His comments were not unique: the idea that H&M, IKEA, or Starbucks—routine realities for European consumers—were a means to measure welfare, modernity, and sociopolitical progress appears constantly in public discourse in Ukraine. Relatively affordable "fast-food fashion" brands signify the pleasures of possibilities and freedom of choice, both signature features of capitalist market systems. At the same time, the absence of these labels and their products in the reality of postsocialist Ukraine is understood as an abnormality, and a signal that the state has failed to make a full transition from socialism into capitalism. As a result, the lacuna of iconic Western consumer goods gains political meaning, since desires for commodities are less about the material objects themselves and more about belonging to a certain politico-economic system that allows for the satisfaction of consumer aspirations. In this context, desirable goods serve as indicators for political directions. Roman, an active participant in Euromaidan protests in 2013–14, did not risk his life for the first H&M store in Kyiv. However, like many Ukrainians, he was driven by a vision of the future in which having a consumer choice is not a privilege but a right.[1]

The historical shift after the dissolution of the Soviet Union set broad expectations for a transition from state socialism to Western-style capitalism with concurrent democratization and the liberalization of political regimes. Ukrainians living in the Soviet Union, and after, have long understood themselves as participants in an unequal binary—as members of a socialist world locked in a global comparison with capitalism. In this paradigm, for many postsocialist countries the West has served as a benchmark of modernization by which the modernity of socialism was measured.[2] Accordingly, the collapse of the Soviet Union is often seen as a turning point, with the expectation that former Soviet countries would adapt the economic and political principles of the West, such as the free-market economy and liberal democratic rule.

These processes of systemic change have been a recurring subject of academic inquiry, as scholars strove to find an appropriate conceptualization of ongoing developments. In Western political discourse, one of the dominant interpretations of the reforms that followed the collapse of the Soviet Union as a straight-and-narrow conversion to liberal democratic capitalism was politically motivated and served to point out the absence of alternative options. However, expectations of a linear transition from socialist order to capitalist system have increasingly been understood as too simplistic. Accordingly, the model assumed in so-called transitology studies, the belief that all post-Soviet transitions would necessarily lead to Western-style capitalism, was replaced by more critically conceived concepts of "uncertain transition," "obscured transition," or "transition without transformation."[3] These new paradigms enabled more fruitful discussions about a multiplicity of postsocialist realities, "multiple modernities," "multiple temporalities," and more nuanced understandings of the complexity of the post-Soviet milieu.[4]

Unlike the academic discourse that recognizes the complexity of transformations, the story of everyday life in post-Soviet Ukraine, as experienced by everyday Ukrainians, has not moved beyond the linear model. The transition is still very much understood according to an evolutionary master plan, whereby a combination of certain political maneuvers and/or economic reforms are supposed to result in the advancement from backwardness to modernity—that is, from socialism to capitalism. The state in this scenario is seen as a political entity responsible for introducing the necessary changes, akin to a Hegelian understanding of the role of the state as a mobilizing agent of progress.[5] This understanding places the state as the primary agent shaping a shared vision of the future and identifying a temporal framework for sociopolitical reality. While the role of the state in the renegotiation of historical narratives and manipulation of the past is well explored, its capacity to negotiate the future has not been examined enough.[6] Understanding the visions of the future and especially recognizing conflicting aspirations uncovers the rationalities that drive political changes and socioeconomic decisions.

The 2013 Euromaidan protests have brought much of this to the fore—this conflict can perhaps best be seen as a clash of contrasting visions of expected progress: while one side of the political spectrum aligned with Western modernization, the other argued for the restoration and reactualization of Soviet-type prospects, and thus, an alliance with Russia.

Whereas the ideas about progress in Ukraine can be fairly abstract, consumer goods give them concrete shape and form, objectifying political orders and materializing the notions of well-being and prosperity. This chapter builds on theories of material culture and, more specifically, of the role of mass-market production in shaping people's understanding of their sociopolitical systems. Focusing on consumption patterns in post-Soviet Ukraine, I argue that market reconfigurations in the country could not satisfy middle-class consumer aspirations and demands, which produced a specific type of detained temporality, apprehended in material things. Studying everyday consumer practices, I aim to explain how "backwardness" is experienced and how "modernity" is desired.

Similar to the pursuit of consumer goods in the era of late socialist shortages, pro-European middle-class Ukrainians often find themselves continually searching for European brands in order to participate in a European consumer reality and to project a modern, fashionable self-image. In this way, Ukrainian reality is experienced as a continuously delayed and on-going process of "catching up" with the West (similar to the narratives of competition with the West in times of socialism). To explore this pursuit of Western goods, I employ the concept of the "Imaginary West."[7] I narrow this concept to the idea of "Imaginary Europe," a more geographically specific reference, which the European Union epitomizes. I argue that Imaginary Europe shapes understandings of modernity and progress among middle-class Ukrainians. Drawing from their experiences with Western goods, Ukrainians still consider consumer satisfaction as the state's responsibility. An understanding of the state, inherited from socialist times, as an actor that should facilitate citizens' existence, is now reinforced by democratic doctrine, where *choice* is a key notion. Thus, the frustration with the lack of iconic consumer options and limited access to European goods, when translated into the political field, becomes an important trigger for major political upheavals, like Euromaidan. Along with corruption and social injustice, consumer displeasures contribute to the general dissatisfaction with the quality of life.

In my approach to consumerism, I analyze the consumer patterns of the middle-class urban populations of Kyiv and Odessa, based on ethnographic research, carried out in 2013–14. My focus was on active middle-class consumers of mass-market goods, not trendsetters or fashionistas. During the fieldwork, I conducted twenty-eight in-depth interviews that can be divided into two groups: (1) interviews with consumers about their shopping experiences and preferences and (2) expert interviews with business owners, retail specialists, and media representatives in order to gauge their understandings of the socioeconomic factors underlying Ukrainian consumerism. While selecting informants for the consumer sample, I looked for both men and women who regularly bought clothes (at least once every two weeks) and who self-identified as shoppers. Further, a snowballing method was used to recruit other respondents. The consumer habits of these informants were not limited to basic necessities and allowed for some flexibility of self-expression, specifically through the consumption of durable goods and goods highly dependent on changing fashion tendencies, such as clothes and accessories. In terms of age, I focused on the generation that experienced the post-Soviet transition—namely, people who were born in the Soviet Union (in the mid- and late 1980s) but who did not have the adult experience of it. In choosing expert informants, priority was given to those who were willing to share aspects of their undocumented economic practices and informal market processes. In addition to the interviews, I analyzed media materials and conducted participant observations. The combination of these methods provided insight not only into consumer motivations but also into the larger context of economic and cultural factors that shape consumer patterns.

This chapter is structured around five sections. In the first section, I outline the allure that an Imaginary Europe holds for middle-class consumers. I argue that the idea of Europe—which became so prominent in the political discourse during Euromaidan—is mediated not so much through the direct experiences of traveling or living in the European Union but rather via commodities and tangible experiences with goods that are associated with Western lifestyles. The second section describes the market reconfigurations in the post-Soviet years to explain the increased symbolic value of brand items and the demand for European brands. The third section provides examples of what I refer to as shadow consumer practices: ways to obtain desirable European goods that are not officially represented in Ukraine. The final sections discuss postcolonial modernity in Ukraine and Imaginary Europe as a reference point for this modernity. Associated with novelty, progressiveness, and freedom of consumer choice, the idealized concept of an Imaginary Europe shapes the understanding of local Ukrainian modernity as backward. Accordingly, the persistent narratives of approaching Europe and political approximation to the European Union are explained in consumer discourses as a phase of the evolutionary development of Ukraine that can be measured through consumer satisfaction.

GLAMOROUS WEST AND IMAGINARY EUROPE

Vika sits for our interview in an Odessa coffee shop. She puts her phone on the table, and, covered with rhinestones, it sparkles in the morning sunlight. "My jeans are from Italy. This top I got in Prague. And this Mulberry purse I got as a present in New York, and I love it so much." Vika goes through her carefully planned outfit, casually mapping its geography. She does her shopping mainly abroad and openly voices her frustration with the limitations of what the Ukrainian market can offer her in Odessa, one of the biggest cities in Ukraine. As she puts it, "It's extremely expensive in price and super cheap in quality." When Vika does not have time to travel, she visits her "shopping dealer"—a young lady who regularly travels to Italy, purchases discounted clothes, and resells them in a tiny "showroom" apartment in downtown Odessa. Similar buyers at boutiques and multibrand stores and entrepreneurs from Odessa travel to Western Europe and buy "bootleg" clothes for further reselling. Nowadays, there are also small online stores that claim to bring "true Italy" to Odessa consumers. Vika referred me to a local online forum that she explained was the place to look for such shopping arrangements.

As Vika explains, she developed her passion for imported clothes in her childhood. She did not see her sailor father often, but his frequent travels provided her with a constant supply of clothes and shoes from abroad. Dressed in exotic Mickey Mouse T-shirts, Vika looked noticeably different from other girls, whose parents chose from a limited variety of goods in state-run Soviet stores. Foreign clothes not only made Vika feel special but also significantly contributed to her family's social standing: if the size or the style of her father's "souvenirs" did not suit any family members, they were sold on the black market, which provided substantial financial support for the family.

During Soviet times, goods imported from an unpronounced "there"—capitalist Western countries—became important visual tools for social distinctions and acquired a high symbolic value. Commodities became mediators for Western experiences and the reification of what Alexei Yurchak calls the Imaginary West: a "place that was simultaneously knowable and unattainable, tangible and abstract, mundane and exotic."[8] However, as Yurchak shows, the exoticism of the goods did not necessarily contradict the ideology of the Soviet regime. Instead, commodities often represented an alternative and parallel reality, which constituted a disjuncture between the everyday practices of the Soviet citizens and the political ideology they adhered to. Consumption of Western goods during the late socialist era paradoxically did not contradict dominant Soviet values or demonstrate political resistance.[9] In this understanding, the idea of the Imaginary West correlates with Edward Said's notion of imagined geographies: the social construction of places, perpetuated by their perception through discourses, images, and knowledge.[10] But in late Soviet times, the imagined abstract West in Ukraine was embodied in the rare Western consumer goods. Concrete and real items represented the part of the world that was otherwise obscure and unexperienced.

At the same time, as scholars have explored through ethnographic research, the concept of the Imaginary West operates differently in the post-Soviet context.[11] With the fall of state socialism, the all-too-real Imaginary West gained strength, while most of the possible negative political undertones of the consumption of Western goods were dismissed. As Catherine Wanner points out, in present-day Ukraine, "Western goods and political values work in tandem to signal the determination of some Ukrainians to integrate themselves into Europe, if not as political citizens, then at least as consumers."[12] In this case, the quality of Western goods is metonymical for an overall quality of Western life, which nourishes fantasies about the West and has the potential to be a driving force for political change. Western goods are where the Imaginary West becomes tangible, while their absence or limited presence signals the gap between political desire and the real. The amalgamation of consumption patterns and a political agenda originated in Soviet times, when the all-encompassing role of the state in consumption marked goods as measures of the successes and failure of the regime and endowed members of socialist societies with the subjectivity of citizen-consumers.[13]

This phenomenon of an Imaginary West has survived in present-day Ukraine, despite the common assumption that the collapse of the Soviet Union would reveal a more realistic and critical picture of the West. In contrast to these expectations, this imaginative concept has been strengthened by the influx of new media and advertising. Images from the glossy pages of Ukrainian magazines depict the West through material symbols, new brands, and alluring lifestyles. The media portrays and promises a glamorous reality: "[An] enticing and seductive vision that is designed to draw the eye of an audience."[14] Rich with selective representations and appealing references, the media reconfirmed the West as "a land of material abundance and personal freedom."[15] Accordingly, media outlets depict the West as an image, as a future-oriented set of desires that are tangible, materialized, concrete, and, thus, attainable. The goods become a goal, a way of knowing, and a point of orientation.

The continuous construction of the Imaginary West is fueled by the fact that the West still exists only as a *mediated* experience for the majority of Ukrainians. Statistics show that 77 percent of Ukrainians have never traveled abroad.

Since most of those who do travel visit Russia and other neighboring countries, the percentage of Ukrainians who have visited Western European countries is quite low.[16] Most Ukrainians experience the West virtually, and their interactions with media outlets and consumer goods stand as potent sources for the construction of the fantasy of the West or, in the case of Ukraine, the narrower fantasy of a more proximate Europe. As in Soviet times, foreign commodities continue to hold additional symbolic value and serve as markers for elevated social status.[17] However, during Soviet times the symbolic weight of Western commodities largely stemmed from overall shortages and the poor quality of goods that were produced locally. In post-Soviet Ukraine, market configurations and particular aspects of economic development that led to the downfall of national industry and the influx of inexpensive imports from Turkey and China amplified the symbolic value of Western goods.

As the analysis of economic data by Anders Aslund shows, market reforms in Ukraine were particularly slow in coming in the 1990s and were overshadowed by a nation-building agenda.[18] While economic stagnation weakened national producers, the introduction of international players was complicated as well. High real estate prices, business risks associated with corruption, and the absence of retail facilities, such as shopping malls, in the 1990s hampered penetration by Western companies. As a result, in 2014 Ukraine had "the lowest ratio of physical presence of international brands among European countries," which signals that little choice of goods is available for Ukrainian consumers.[19] This relative deficiency has only increased the social significance of Western goods, as the demand for imported, branded commodities remains high.

THE HEAVY LEGACY OF LIGHT INDUSTRY: MARKET SPECIFICS IN POST-SOVIET UKRAINE

The restructuring of the post-Soviet economy in Ukraine in the 1990s led to complex and quite chaotic market modifications, seen as a switch from a state-regulated political economy to the competitive market alternative.[20] These processes had significant implications for light industry—particularly in the fashion industry. The fashion industry suffered not only from an overall decline in economic growth and from technological backwardness but also from being a low priority for (state-supported) development and capital investment. As a result, many Ukrainian enterprises closed down. In 1990, light industry's share of national industrial output was 10.8 percent, but by 2010 this had decreased to 0.7 percent.[21]

Another influential factor was that, as Ukrainian producers were restructuring their businesses, the Ukrainian market was opened to international competition. In the 1990s inexpensive clothing from China and Turkey flooded the country. Unable to compete on volume, price, or quality, by 2012 Ukrainian manufacturers had less than 10 percent of the national market share.[22] As of 2012, a year before Euromaidan, 92 percent of textile clothing sold in Ukraine was imported. China accounted for 60 percent of textile clothing and accessories imported, and Turkey, for 24 percent. Since these data do not include the informal economy and smuggling, the share of imports is likely to be even higher.

At the same time, while the quality and variety of Chinese and Turkish commodities are generally satisfactory for mass consumers, they often remain inadequate for middle-class patrons, especially as the latter have become more and more educated in global consumer trends and transfixed by burgeoning glamorous lifestyle images. Anton, who used to be a marketing manager and strategist for an international brand in Ukraine, explained it in the following way: "The middle class has discovered consumer pride. We have had enough of shortages [*defitsyt*] and Chinese-Turkish mass production [*shyrpotreb*], and now we are looking for other options" (Anton, 32).[23] European products serve as categories of modernity and are associated with innovation, progress, and the symbolic immaterial value of a brand (*firma*). Nonbranded Turkish and Chinese goods do not serve as markers of modernity: while they might replicate certain fashion trends, their main appeal is their low price and variety of styles. Accordingly, items by Western brands are placed higher in the "hierarchy of qualitative orders of goods."[24]

Though walking in the streets of Kyiv one can easily find certain Western brand stores, consumers express their dissatisfaction with either the price or the limited selection of available goods. Oksana, a midtier manager of a media company, summarizes her disappointment: "I do not shop in Ukraine unless it is an emergency" (Oksana, 32). Others admit that big urban centers like Kyiv, Dnipro, or Odessa are more likely to have luxury stores than shops selling unbranded items for middle-class consumers. "I do not understand how come you can buy a pair of Bally shoes in the middle of downtown Kyiv for several thousand hryvnias, but to get a reasonably priced pair of black pumps, you need to embark on a major quest and spend so much time," complains Maryna, a manager in a bank (Maryna, 34).[25] It is no surprise that luxury brands are more confident in exploring emerging markets, including post-Soviet countries, especially since new elites present a vast clientele for them.[26] At the same time, the prevalence of high-end stores over affordable middle-class ones reveals the unequal nature of market processes and sends mixed signals about the postsocialist transition itself. The uneven transformation in Ukraine supports the idea of multiple modernities. In the realm of consumption, some elements of the Imaginary Europe point to Ukraine's belonging to the current global consumer discourse. At the same time, the lack of others denotes the backwardness and underdevelopment in which middle-class Ukrainian consumers exist.

Frustration with the choice of stores in Ukraine stems from the complex and conflicting development of the Ukrainian retail market. Two factors that influence the price and retail market composition are at play: the informal economy, and the overall disposable income of Ukrainian consumers. The business environment in Ukraine raises significant concerns for present and potential business owners. Political instability in the country and opaque business practices create challenges for the retail industry in the Ukrainian market. Among the informants I interviewed were two experts: a senior manager of the largest distributor of several Western brands in Ukraine, and a business scout, who came to the country to estimate opportunities for launching an American middle-class brand. Both confirmed that economic uncertainty and corruption pose the main challenges to operating in the Ukrainian market. Companies often have to deal with a range of formal or informal fees and bribes, which they then pass on to the consumer. Informal, price-increasing fees are added to existing import and customs duties, resulting in a substantial markup in prices, making imported goods unaffordable for many middle-class consumers. An eloquent example of this situation was my informant's story of two identical suits of the same brand that were priced differently in Spain and Ukraine: "The difference in prices was equal to the plane ticket to Spain. Do they suppose that we are millionaires?" (Alina, 26). This price factor had a significant impact on the support of Ukrainian citizens for the Association Agreement in 2013, since the promise of free trade between the European Union and Ukraine was often understood to imply decreasing prices for European goods.

These hidden price components have demonstrably reduced overall consumer demand. According to a study by the GfK market research company, in 2013 the purchasing power of Ukrainians was one-fourth the European average.[27] This dynamic is significant, as it affects what international brands and distributors put on offer in Ukraine. Avoiding financial risks, distributors prefer to bring "secure" varieties of goods, such as basic, inexpensive collections. In turn, consumers interpret this move as an exclusion from the world of global fashion, as disrespectful, and, more generally, as a sign of Ukrainian underdevelopment. Several informants expressed their strong belief that Western goods sold in Ukraine are of a lower quality than those in the European stores. Catering to this perception, some online stores offer to order goods from Europe to be delivered in Ukraine. For instance, even though the Spanish brand Zara is present in the Ukrainian market, until 2019 it did not offer an online shopping option for Ukrainian consumers. Alternative pages, such as the Zarasite, invited Ukrainian shoppers to "order the best Zara items that are not available in Ukraine," for a price that is "two to three times lower" than in British stores.[28] This website, like many other similar ones, was not affiliated with the original Zara brand.

The absence of iconic European brands, such as IKEA or H&M, known globally for their affordable middle-class products, reinforces this discontent. The aforementioned trademarks are well recognized in Ukraine and are identified as an essential part of everyday European culture. Their absence in Ukraine stigmatizes the country as "not European enough." Accordingly, the prospects of opening these stores in Ukraine are often incorporated into political agendas and are interpreted as a symbolic integration of Ukraine into the European Union.

Interestingly, though not surprisingly, the fascination with famous Western brands is also prevalent in modern China. As LiAnne Yu explains, the appreciation of Western consumer culture in China is driven by the desire to distinguish oneself from the local crowd, which paradoxically ends up replicating global fashion trends. This principle of "standing out by fitting in" refigures the market and makes China one of the largest markets for European brands.[29] The similar ambition to be part of a global consumer culture in Ukraine is complicated by the underrepresentation of brands. In this way, Ukrainian consumers are partially left outside a larger consumer community and are marginalized in the Western consumer milieu. Even the alternative of online shopping is limited in Ukraine—many companies do not offer shipping options to Ukraine, or consumers find that shipping rates significantly and prohibitively increase the cost of goods. As a result, middle-class shoppers in Ukraine experience a consumer vacuum that is filled with emerging practices and alternatives to conventional shopping. Instead of shopping at malls, stores, or online, consumers deal with more time- and effort-demanding mediated practices, such as the use of the aforementioned middleman stores (fig. 7.1), petty smuggling, and shopping through friends and relatives, among others.

Consumers' desire to see brands like H&M and IKEA in Ukraine were particularly symbolic in times before Euromaidan, as the protests raised the issue of Ukraine's relationship to the European Union very dramatically. This was true both in terms of adopting European principles of democracy and social justice, and in terms of establishing closer economic ties, which many hoped would benefit Ukrainian consumers.[30] IKEA made the presence of "Europe"—and Ukraine's position outside of it—all too clear. In 2013, the

Fig. 7.1. An H&Mall store in Odessa uses a variety of mass-market brand signs. The store resells goods and—as it is not an official retailer—adjusts brand signs to be both recognizable yet not identical to the official branding. Photo by author.

Swedish furniture and home accessories retailer was named the most desirable European brand in Ukraine, followed by H&M.[31] However, corruption and an unfavorable economic situation made an agreement between the Swedish company and Ukraine difficult: the company's commitment to run a transparent business was stronger than its desire to expand to the Ukrainian market. In 2012, Petro Poroshenko, at that time the minister of economic development and later the president of Ukraine, defined IKEA's presence in Ukraine as a benchmark of success in state reforms and in achieving economic stability: "IKEA is a symbol. When IKEA is not able to enter the market, it is not the business that suffers, it is the image of Ukraine that is damaged."[32] The value of IKEA's presence in Ukraine was reiterated in 2015 by Aivaras Abromavicius, the minister of trade and economy, who represented a post-Euromaidan generation of government officials: "We hope that IKEA will open a store. It would be an important symbol, because of its good reputation and the fact that it doesn't pay bribes."[33] While opening IKEA seemed to be an inconceivable challenge for the government, web-based retailers filled the space by acting as middlemen, purchasing IKEA goods from Poland and other neighboring countries and reselling them in Ukraine.[34]

Thus, the aspirations for European brands in Ukraine have larger sociopolitical implications. Brand names are interpreted as essential tokens of "Europeanness." And their absence indicates the state's inability to create a "proper economic environment" and the rule of law required to facilitate a reorganization of consumer culture. Similar to socialist beliefs, the ties between consumer satisfaction and state legitimacy remain strong and unchallenged. From this perspective, the Ukrainian middle class is expressing what Kriszina Fehérváry describes as "waning faith in the state's ability to materialize an alternative modernity."[35] They understand Ukraine as "stuck" in the global consumer past. Pointing out the backwardness that consumers struggle with, several respondents called Ukraine a "third world" country.

SHADOW CONSUMER PRACTICES

As a result of this marginalization of the consumer, mass-market Western goods acquire additional symbolic meanings in Ukraine and are negotiated as luxuries and as material signs of modernity.[36] Echoing Soviet times, shoppers find alternative ways to obtain desirable goods in order to bridge the gap between a backward present and a glittering imaginary consumer future. The most visible of these alternative means are shopping tourism, small-scale smuggling, and secondhand shopping. I refer to these practices as "shadow," as they are neither integrated into the official economy nor regulated by the state. However, they are generally understood by most Ukrainians as legitimate, and, by and large, they do not violate Ukrainian laws or regulations.

"For Ukrainians, the Best Souvenir Is to Dress in Europe"

Shopping when traveling holds a significant place on the agenda of many Ukrainian tourists. Ukraine does not belong to the EU Schengen area, and as a result a trip to Europe is often an expensive and time-consuming endeavor, made more complicated by the application process to obtain an EU visa. In this context, shopping is not just a cosmopolitan leisure activity, but a compensation for the hardships of getting out of the country. Accordingly, purchases brought from Europe are not only better bargains, but trophies won against international bureaucracy.

Since traveling westward is a privileged experience, accessible for those with the economic means to travel and who have successfully navigated the visa application process, when travelers talk about their purchases, they often take a moment to point out where items were bought. Comments like "This top I got in Prague" categorize objects as symbols of places visited and proof of the owners' international mobility.

Bureaucratic difficulties are often understood as being "paid off" through shopping. The price of tickets and visas are made up in savings accrued by shopping abroad. A popular practice among tourists is to reserve a day or two exclusively for shopping during vacations in Europe. Some people, like Olesya, confess that it is a strong priority during leisure or business travels: "Whenever I go abroad, shopping is almost the primary goal of the trip. So I travel with empty suitcases but come back all packed" (Olesya, 27). While many informants mentioned the importance of shopping, its essence is crystallized in Dasha's explanation: "For Ukrainians, the best souvenir is to dress in Europe. I don't need another magnet on my fridge. I would rather spend a couple of Euros on a T-shirt that will cost much more here. Like most of my girlfriends I travel to Europe not only for sightseeing but also to replenish my wardrobe" (Dasha, 29). A friend's request to bring something back from a trip to Europe was also very commonly mentioned among respondents. This prioritization of shopping is reminiscent of Soviet practices, when trips across the border presented unique opportunities for bringing "foreign consumer delights," which were not available in the USSR.[37]

The practice of reselling used shopping bags well demonstrates the higher symbolic value carried by European commodities. The Ukrainian online marketplace OLX.ua sells empty brand-name bags for an average price of one to two US dollars, which is ten times higher than a regular bag bought in Ukraine. Since shopping bags are free with a purchase, the resale in Ukraine presents a monetization of brand value. As elements of brands, resold empty bags carry within them the desire to be part of the European lifestyles that the commodities (or the commodities' bags) embody and that the brand philosophies promote. And while it would be a stretch to state that this is a widespread practice, some informants admitted that they keep bags from stores either for further reuse or because they hold sentimental value.[38] In the late Soviet period, Catherine Wanner observed that consumers were saving the packaging of Western goods, such as beer cans and cereal boxes, in their households.[39] She explained this phenomenon as a political protest and a rejection of Soviet values. However, seeing how the elements of this practice have survived into contemporary Ukraine, it is clear certain Western goods continue to be exotic and fascinating objects in post-Soviet geographies. Since packages and shopping bags project a modern self in the everyday, their social lives are prolonged by consumers. Rather than representing a political protest, their continued use embodies the desire for alternative modernity and privileges Western tokens of it.

While shopping is an essential part of vacations for many Ukrainian tourists, designated shopping tours are also commonly arranged by travel agencies and listed in special sections of tour catalogs. In addition, private entrepreneurs in the western border regions arrange shopping trips to Poland lasting from one day to a weekend. A shuttle takes people to several big shopping centers and shopping malls, depending on their preferences.

Black Market in Suitcases

Another way to obtain European clothes is through petty smugglers. This type of trade can be considered a contemporary variation on the post-Soviet phenomenon *chelnochniki* (shuttle traders), small-scale traders who started their businesses when the Soviet Union collapsed. But if in the 1990s chelnochniki were trading all kinds of mass-produced goods from Poland and Turkey, contemporary traders target designer brands or underrepresented labels. In this way they act like store buyers: they travel to Milan, select items, and serve as fashion consultants for their clients. Often these businesses operate out of private apartments, where entrepreneurs arrange the existing rooms as showplaces. Elena, one of the top Ukrainian fashion bloggers and a regular client of petty smugglers, refers to this phenomenon as *elitnoe chelnochestvo* (elite shuttle trade). She emphasizes that these entrepreneurs have keen expertise in fashion brands: "When I was staying at home with my baby, this was my only way to get things. This is a pretty large business run by girls who have good fashion sense. They shape our Odessa style with an Italian flavor" (Elena, 25). The chelnochniki in the 1990s capitalized on the overall shortages, while "elite trade shuttles" and travelers today monetize the limited availability of European stores in Ukraine.

This phenomenon also exists on a smaller scale, when travelers purchase brand items to resell for profit in Ukraine. Individuals, mostly young women, visit their relatives in Europe, buy brand-name clothing at a discount (on sale or in outlets), and resell it for full price online or through friends. In this way travelers can recoup the cost of travel. "Girls just bring some dresses to *otbit'raschody* [cover travel expenses] from the trip. My former schoolmate visits her cousin in Italy regularly and she usually brings some stuff to sell" (Masha, 27). Thus, a discounted pair of Roberto Cavalli shoes originally priced for 380 USD and purchased on sale in Italy for 150 USD are resold for 260 USD. In this case, the seller makes a profit, but the purchaser also gets a good deal, paying less than the original price for an exclusive pair of Italian shoes. These market transactions are typically small in scale, conducted through personal networks or online forums and social media groups. As such, these business practices are neither registered nor legally regulated and pay no taxes.

Secondhand Stores and Brand "Outlets"

Secondhand stores were initially seen as marginalized outlets for underprivileged social groups, but soon after the collapse of socialism, they acquired new meaning due to the changed sources of goods and the range of brands sold. A 2010 survey showed that 39 percent of Ukrainians regularly purchased items from the secondhand marketplace.[40] Notably, secondhand shopping in Kyiv resembles similar practices of shopping at flea markets, thrift stores, and garage sales for bargain deals or in pursuit of unexpected experiences. As Fleura Bardhi and Eric J. Arnould argue, this type of shopping combines "thrift and treat aspects," satisfying both economic and hedonic desires.[41] However, the difference in secondhand shopping in Ukraine is that in addition to satisfying desires for luxury and collectible items, this practice also fulfills consumer demand for not-so-luxurious mass-market European goods. As the selection of goods in thrift shops includes Western branded clothing in relatively good or even new condition, these marketplaces have become sites for middle-class "safari" shopping. Lisnyi market in Kyiv, with its dozens of secondhand tents and piles of goods, is a key stop for secondhand shoppers. Recently, it was featured by the Italian *Vogue* online magazine as one of the gems of shopping in Kyiv, which further legitimized its place in the fashion discourse.[42]

The inner structure of Lisnyi has been developed according to the types of items that are on sale there. Some tents have piles of clothing and shoes that are sold per kilogram. Other tents have rows of hangers with selected brands or better-quality items that are priced individually. There are also so-called elite tents, where exclusive pieces from luxury brands like Christian Dior and Chanel can be found.

In the summer of 2013, I attended the market with one of my informants, Anton, who is a marketing manager with a stable income. Despite his comparatively high social standing, he prefers to replenish his wardrobe with secondhand commodities. Anton openly explained that he shops at Lisnyi for "inexpensive expensive brand things." He admitted that there is a strong adventure component to this type of shopping—you never know what you will find. But for many shoppers this type of market is a way to acquire basic things from Western brands (like solid cotton T-shirts or blue jeans). While I was accompanying Anton, he bought two plain dress shirts. In the process of selection, he paid attention primarily to the brand name, the item's condition, and the quality of the details and disregarded the cut and collar type, which generally change with fashion trends. For brand hunters like Anton, the novelty of the fashion style and its relevance to the current trends are less significant than the value of the brand name. The consumption of brands that are not available or affordable in Ukraine through official retail make these consumers "modern" and progressive.

These examples of shadow consumer practices are not exhaustive, but they illustrate how a desire for European and Western brands shapes consumer behavior among middle-class Ukrainians. Contemporary examples are evocative of the shopping practices that were common in Soviet times, even though now they exist within different socio-ideological and socioeconomic realities. At the same time, the high social and cultural value of brand names and their consequent underrepresentation in Ukraine produce a different type of temporality, quite distinct from Western "fast fashion."

Unlike the spinning styles of Western consumer discourse, the mode of Ukrainian temporality resembles what can be referred to as a *vintage temporality*: the lasting value of things is more entrenched in the significance of brand rather than contemporary fashion context. Goods are not necessarily bound to the "present" of fashion but are reactualized because of their belonging to the geographical and geopolitical notion of Europe associated with commodities. Goods represent material connectivity with the aspired to Imaginary Europe, unpacking modernity as a notion of belonging to this idea.

Over the past two decades, the fashion industry has significantly decreased the time between the introduction of styles into the high-fashion world and their adaptation by mass-market companies. A turnover that used to take approximately six months now takes no more than a few weeks. This modification is known as the phenomenon of fast fashion: a highly responsive, flexible fashion system with a short memory for tendencies.[43] Fast fashion is closely connected to processes of globalization and the advancement of production processes. Free trade and niche production coordinated by new communication technologies have allowed companies to decrease the time required for manufacturing even at higher volumes. Brands like Zara and H&M are prime examples of this type of operational system. Not surprisingly, this change in business model has caused a change in consumer behavior. The profit-driven fast fashion industry speeds up the cycle of mass-market consumption. It encourages shoppers to buy more things and to buy them more frequently.[44] Accordingly, mass-market fast fashion has transformed the perception of time and temporality for consumers. The change of seasons no longer dictates changes in a wardrobe, as commodities can become irrelevant and disposable sooner than the end of the season. This stimulates a "throwaway culture" and overconsumption.[45] Planned obsolescence is profit driven and reflects the essence of capitalist ideology. In the postsocialist context, where consumer patterns are reshaped after decades of state-planned consumption and the shortages of post-Soviet crises, the idea of throwaway turnout is still not widely acceptable.

Sales in Ukraine are based less on seasonal fashion trends than on the acquisition of brand names. Thus, to some extent, branded items are perceived as universal and atemporal. Things from H&M, for instance, are used not for a season but for a couple of years. "I have worn this blouse for about three years," says Zhenia (32) about her favorite item from H&M. "It is decent quality, not like the trash from the market." The social value of the brand makes items less exposed to quick changes in fashion, and the commodities also hold personal value, as significant time and effort were invested in acquiring them. In this way, the use of fashion items is more brand-name related, than style and context related. This does not mean that middle-class consumers do not follow fashion trends, but it indicates that within this particular temporality, the sense of modernity is captured in static labels that represent the Imaginary West for middle-class Ukrainian consumers. The idea of the West is fixed in a future that appears attainable for Ukrainian consumers through belonging, mediated by commodities. This understanding demonstrates how ideas about being modern are objectified in material objects. At the same time, it shows how modernity is unequal and therefore unevenly experienced in the world of growing market globalization and enhanced communication technologies. Ironically, while modernity and progress are associated with ideas of simplifying and making life easier for customers, Ukrainian middle-class consumers often multiply efforts and economic resources to catch up with the appeal of Western modernity.

POSTCOLONIAL MODERNITY

The desire to belong to the Western consumption world reflects something of a postcolonial logic of post-Soviet processes. As Olga Gurova observes, at some point the postcolonial turn in postsocialist studies allowed theorizers to conceptualize and explain processes in former socialist states by a different route.[46] This is particularly so in scholarly attempts to capture the hierarchal relationship between postsocialist countries and Western capitalist ones: "If postcolonial discourse was organized around dichotomies of 'colonies' and 'metropole,' the dichotomy in postsocialism was 'East' and 'West.'"[47] One of the pioneers of this approach, David Chioni Moore, suggests that postcolonial hermeneutics can enrich the understanding of post-Soviet processes. He points out that the end of state socialism caused significant effects on former Soviet cultures that are in many ways analogous to decolonization.[48] Within the opposition between the former Soviet states and Western capitalist societies, the latter are framed as modern and progressive, taking over the role of global metropoles. Global economic development strategies reinforce this dichotomy. Thus, in Immanuel Wallerstein's world-system theory, former colonial states became core countries that dominate the global economy and spur economic growth.[49] At the same time, former Soviet countries are positioned as semiperiphery states that are economically dependent on the core. Though the clear lines of this distinction can be contested, the underlying economic relations of the postcolonial world reproduce the unequal dynamics of colonial relations.

The postcolonial lens can be useful for understanding cultural power relations that occurred in the aftermath of the Cold War, where the dependency of "colonial" countries is not explicitly defined in direct political and economic subordination but rather implicitly constructed through culture, as in, for instance, the appropriation of fashion trends. In this light, the desire for Western commodities can be seen as an acknowledgment of cultural hierarchy. Arjun Appadurai argues that cultural homogenization is in tension with cultural heterogenization and states that "different societies appropriate the materials of modernity differently."[50] However, the important point is that these appropriations often lean toward the West and reveal material realities of global inequalities. In other words, the desire to be homogenized and to be part of the imagined community is associated with a developed and progressive West. Researchers like Peter Stearns see this tendency as a new form of Western predominance that can outlast more traditional military and colonial power.[51]

Ideas about Western modernity and postsocialist processes are heightened and clarified through the concept of civilization and "civilization competence," coined by Piotr Sztompka. Dissecting the challenges of Poland's postsocialist transition, he states: "The decades of real socialism not only blocked the appearance of civilizational competence, but in many ways shaped a contrary cultural syndrome of civilizational incompetence." Civilization competence is measured by the local approximation of Western forms. As a result, Sztompka claims that real socialism in its rivalry with capitalism produced a "fake modernity."[52] Quite often consumers follow the same logic, assigning the qualities of authentic modernity to Western brands and commodities. In a similar fashion, Sasha Newell argues that consumption in Côte D'Ivoire is a form of performing Western modernity, where "modernity act[s] as a kind of force or quality which inhere[s] in places, objects, and people, rather than a state of development."[53] In a similar way, for European-oriented middle-class consumers in Ukraine, modernity is bestowed and experienced through branded goods, while the unavailability of these markers of European modernity demonstrates Ukraine's continually delayed arrival as a modern and Western space.

In the field of consumption, the overcoming of "civilizational incompetence" can literally be narrowed through the possession of Western or Western-like things. Jennifer Patico's analysis of Russian consumer realities in post-Soviet St. Petersburg illustrates how the Russian middle class has adopted the concept of civilization. According to Patico, it is not just a set of cultural resources but tropes of value that are manifested in material respectability and in the preference for Western goods, which stand as signs of belonging to modernity. This ideology is reflected in the narratives of the "self-peripheralization" of Russian consumers, which reflect their self-identification in a global context.[54]

A similar consumer logic of self-peripheralization is evident in Ukraine: Western countries are labeled as "civilized," which is understood through material goods. Interestingly, this idea overshadows the fact that the major production facilities of Western brands are often located in Central Asia. So, while European brand names are automatically equated with "made in Europe," in reality they are "made in China" or "made in Turkey." The brand name eliminates the stigma and low social prestige of non-European mass-market production. This understanding is also evident in the fact that mass-market commodities bought in European stores are valued more than those bought in

Ukrainian ones: "Mass market here and there are two different words. European stores and the quality of things there are so different. It is as different as day and night" (Zhenia, 32). "Zara in Europe is very different. Pinkie, French store, NafNaf... We also have 'Made in China,' but their 'Made in China' is just better, much better" (Dasha, 29). These observations point out that the value assigned to goods is inseparable from place. In this case, that place is Europe, and its goods exist in a different, more progressive, yet unattained modernity. In the cosmology of consumers, this place is also associated with a future model for Ukraine.

IMAGINARY EUROPE AS A FRONTIER OF MODERNITY

In Ukraine, the Imaginary West is often substituted by the narrower concept of Imaginary Europe. Europe's geographical proximity and Ukraine's strong political aspirations to join the European Union play significant roles in this modification. At the same time, the concept of the Imaginary West remains a generalized model, a collective image that encompasses fragmented and selective knowledge about Europe. The concept is elusive particularly because of its abstraction and its lacking a specific referent. Imaginary Europe is all and nothing at the same time. In many discourses it stands for the widespread desire for well-being and social justice, referred to as "normal life" and contrasted with the "abnormality" of postsocialist reality.

The postindependence period in Ukraine can be seen as a continuous crisis: from the economic meltdown in the 1990s to major inflation in 2014, from the Orange Revolution in 2004 to Euromaidan in 2013. Like in many other former Soviet countries, in Ukraine "the crisis of socialism became a postsocialist crisis": durable and lasting.[55] Under these conditions, uncertainty is not an exception to the norm but constitutes a norm itself. The perception of these critical conditions resembles the eschatological model of time, when suffering is justified by the awaited salvation. As the idiosyncrasy of postsocialism is juxtaposed with the "normalcy" of Imaginary Europe, the salvation in this case is seen by pro-EU Ukrainians in political and economic association with the European Union. Hence, the concept of Imaginary Europe has significant political implications that, for instance, became articulated in the course of the Euromaidan revolution of 2013–14.

Euromaidan protests started when the former president of Ukraine, Viktor Yanukovych, and his government announced that it had suspended the signing of an Association Agreement with the European Union. The initial demand of the movement was to renew the negotiations with the European

Union to ensure closer economic and political cooperation with Europe. In my interviews with Euromaidan protesters, they offered different interpretations of Europe at that time. Their comments varied from "increased social welfare payments" and "better-maintained roads" to "affordable prices for goods" and "higher quality of goods." The decision to backpedal from signing the agreement was seen as a change of geopolitical course and also as a threat to a better quality of life. This correlated with the idea that the backward status of consumption and unsatisfied consumer desires undermined the legitimacy of the state, as the government was not able to provide its citizens with the right to choose and the right to buy.[56]

CONCLUSIONS

My exploration of consumer practices by middle-class Ukrainians maps the imaginative geography and temporality of modernity in Ukraine. Inquiring into consumer frustrations with the specifics of the retail market and interpreting the historically inherited symbolic value of European goods, I argue that the social imaginary of Europe structures consumer behavior and, in return, affects sociopolitical processes in the country. Imaginary Europe remains a highly idealized concept that Ukrainians look up to as a standard of "civilization" and "normal life," especially in light of the strengthening of political attempts for closer cooperation with the European Union.

By trying to achieve European standards of living, Ukrainians consume for stability. They prioritize and preserve the enduring quality of brand names rather than following fast-fashion throwaway culture. Ironically, these Ukrainian consumer patterns embody a slower temporality, which nevertheless copy fast-fashion trends of the West. In other words, the middle-class replication of European fashion is a bricolage, where the linear perspective of time is disrupted and reassembled. By obtaining commodities from the consumer "past" of Europe in secondhand stores and outlets or from previous collections and embedding them in contemporary fashion manifestations, middle-class consumers underline belonging to the desired modernity.

My study is mainly focused on the time that preceded the 2013–14 revolution and is colored by early conceptualizations of Euromaidan experiences. Importantly, the initial agenda of the Euromaidan protests articulated the demand to move closer to the European Union, which resonated with consumer desires to have IKEA or H&M in Ukraine, as the indexes of European consumer well-being. The displeasures of backwardness and exclusion from the global consumer culture were central as factors that informed middle-class dissatisfactions with the former political regime. The success of Euromaidan multiplied hopes and expectations for approximating European modernity among the supporters of a pro-European course for Ukraine.

In this light, the consumption of European goods retranslates the concept of European modernity, makes it tangible, and maps it as the way forward for Ukraine, as a signpost of aspirations and progress. At the same time, through the acquisition and consumption of signified commodities, consumers reimagine the signifier (Europe). Mediated through goods, the concept of Imaginary Europe is both idealized and influential for measuring development and prosperity. What is crucial in the contemporary Ukrainian milieu is that Imaginary Europe is one of the models for social and political visions of the future, based on the enchantment of the unknown, a "future perfect" desired in "present continuous."

NOTES

I would like to thank the editors of this volume, who have generously given up valuable time to review this chapter and provide comments and insightful suggestions.

1. As this chapter was prepared for publication, H&M opened its first store in Ukraine in August 2018 and announced the opening of the second store three months later.
2. Fehérváry, "Goods and States," 435.
3. See Burawoy and Verdery, *Uncertain Transition*; Chivens, "After Post-Socialism?"; and Burawoy, "Transition without Transformation."
4. See Thelen, "Shortage, Fuzzy Property"; Eisenstadt, "Some Observations"; Gurova, *Fashion and the Consumer*; Hann, "Anthropology's Multiple Temporalities"; and Humphrey, "Category 'Postsocialist.'"
5. Gross, "Temporality," 65; see also Shevchenko, *Crisis and the Everyday*, 39.
6. Berdahl, *Social Life of Postsocialism*; Pine, Kaneff, and Haukanes, *Religions, Politics and Memory*.
7. Yurchak, *Everything Was Forever*.
8. Ibid., 159.
9. This paradox is reproduced in contemporary Russia, where tense relationships with Western countries and trade sanctions coexist with the everyday consumption of Western goods and the presence of European brands.
10. Said, "Orientalism."
11. Humphrey, *Unmaking of Soviet Life*; Patico, "To Be Happy"; Klumbytė, "Soviet Sausage Renaissance"; Gurova, *Fashion and the Consumer*.
12. Wanner, "Money, Morality," 518.

13. Fehérváry, "Goods and States."
14. Gundle, *Glamour: A History*, 4; see also Douglas, "What Is Glamour?"; Dyhouse, *History, Women, Feminism*.
15. Prokhorova, "Material(ized) Desire"; Selivestrova, "Keeping Alive."
16. Korrespondent, "Tri Chetverti."
17. Patico, *Consumption and Social Change*; Humphrey, *Unmaking of Soviet Life*; Oushakine, "Quantity of Style"; Wanner, "Money, Morality"; Gurova, *Fashion and the Consumer*.
18. Aslund, *Market Economy and Democracy*.
19. Ernst and Young. "Retail Market in Ukraine," 11.
20. See, for instance, Dunn, *Privatizing Poland*; Burawoy, "Transition without Transformation."
21. Peltek, *Rozvytok Regional'noii Promyslovoii Polityky Derzhavy*.
22. State Statistics Department of Ukraine, "Ukraina v Tsyfrakh."
23. I use parenthetical text citations when quoting interviewees and include their name and age at the time of the interview.
24. Manning and Uplisashvili, "'Our Beer.'"
25. At the time of the interview, the currency exchange rate was 8 UAH (Ukrainian hryvnias) to 1 USD. The average price for Bally shoes was 500 USD.
26. As McKinsey research on luxury retail shows, the growth of the luxury market in 2014 was shifting to emerging markets in all categories of retail goods (fashion, spirits, and beauty). See Kim, Remy, and Schmidt, "Glittering Power of Cities."
27. Tovstyzhenko, "Rashody."
28. See zarasite.com.ua. At the time of publishing, the website was no longer available.
29. Yu, *Consumption in China*.
30. Interestingly, the Euromaidan initial demand of signing the Association Agreement with the European Union, which later developed into a broader agenda of state violence and corruption, was contrasted to the signing of the Customs Union with Russia.
31. "Dashed Ikea Dreams."
32. "Poroshenko obyasnil Bloomberg."
33. "Plea for Swedish IKEA."
34. At the time of writing, IKEA representatives had had an official meeting with the president of Ukraine, Petro Poroshenko, to negotiate starting business in Ukraine. President Poroshenko commented in his official Twitter account: "We finally have finalized 13 years-long procedure of Swedish company IKEA to enter Ukrainian market. With the support from the state, IKEA has found reliable partners and approved its important decision, which confirms that the investment climate in Ukraine has improved" (@poroshenko, September 12, 2018).

35. Fehérváry, "Goods and States," 429.
36. For instance, an unofficial store in Odessa that was reselling H&M items had a sign "H&M. Luxury style."
37. Chernyshova, *Soviet Consumer Culture*, 95–97.
38. In a similar way, used shopping bags can be found for sale on eBay and similar websites in other countries, but most often these would be bags by luxury brands, such as Gucci, Fendi, and Louis Vuitton.
39. Wanner, "Money, Morality," 515–37.
40. Rating Group, "Second Hand."
41. Bardhi and Arnould, "Thrift Shopping."
42. Satenstein, "Move Over, Le Marais."
43. Fletcher, "Slow Fashion."
44. Joy et al., "Ethical Appeal of Luxury Brands."
45. Gurova, *Fashion and the Consumer*, 140.
46. Ibid.
47. Ibid., 8.
48. Moore, "Post- in Postcolonial."
49. Wallerstein, "Rise and Future Demise."
50. Appadurai, *Modernity At Large*.
51. Stearns, *Consumerism in World History*.
52. Sztompka, "Civilizational Incompetence," 87; see also Buchowski, "Specter of Orientalism."
53. Newell, *Modernity Bluff*, 178.
54. Patico, "To Be Happy," 489; Gurova, *Fashion and the Consumer*, 69.
55. Shevchenko, *Crisis and the Everyday*.
56. Berdahl, *On the Social Life of Postsocialism*, 89; Bauman, *Intimations of Postmodernity*; Wilk, "Morals and Metaphors." The debates on the pro-European orientation of Ukraine actualized a conception of Europe that has a long history in the intellectual tradition in Ukraine. In the early twentieth century, the Ukrainian writer and public intellectual Mykola Khvyl'oviy was one of the most vocal advocates for what he called a "psychological Europe." Khvyl'oviy was a proponent of fighting Russian cultural hegemony with an adaptation of European tradition, both in literature and in the process of state building. He praised Europe as a "grandiose civilization," drawing an opposition between European modernity and Russian oppression. See Dziuba, *Mykola Khvyl'oviy*. At the same time, Khvyl'oviy emphasized the prioritization of the intellectual legacy of Europe. He encouraged the appropriation of European values and civil stances rather than "outer forms of European life." In contrast, narratives from Euromaidan point out that these "outer forms" became a tangible aspect of Imaginary Europe and a desirable material affirmation of European modernity.

REFERENCES

Appadurai, Arjun. *Modernity At Large: Cultural Dimensions of Globalization.* Minneapolis: University of Minnesota Press, 1996.

Aslund, Anders. *How Ukraine Became a Market Economy and Democracy.* Washington, DC: Peterson Institute for International Economics, 2009.

Bardhi, Fleura, and Eric J. Arnould. "Thrift Shopping: Combining Utilitarian Thrift and Hedonic Treat Benefits." *Journal of Consumer Behaviour* 4, no. 4 (2005): 223–33.

Bauman, Zygmunt. *Intimations of Postmodernity.* London: Routledge, 2002.

Berdahl, Daphne. *On the Social Life of Postsocialism: Memory, Consumption, Germany.* Bloomington: Indiana University Press, 2010.

Bloomberg. "Dashed Ikea Dreams in Ukraine Show Decades Lost to Corruption." *Kyiv Post*, March 31, 2014. http://www.kyivpost.com/content/ukraine-abroad/bloomberg-dashed-ikea-dreams-in-ukraine-show-decades-lost-to-corruption-341463.html.

Buchowski, Michal. "The Specter of Orientalism in Europe: From Exotic Other to Stigmatized Brother." *Anthropological Quarterly* 79, no. 3 (2006): 463–82.

Burawoy, Michael. "Transition without Transformation: Russia's Involuntary Road to Capitalism." *East European Politics and Societies* 15, no. 2 (2001): 269–90.

Burawoy, Michael, and Katherine Verdery. *Uncertain Transition: Ethnographies of Change in the Postsocialist World.* Lanham, MD: Rowman & Littlefield, 1999.

Chernyshova, Natalya. *Soviet Consumer Culture in the Brezhnev Era.* London: Routledge, 2013.

Chivens, Thomas. "After Post-Socialism? Transition's Obscured Inevitability." *Anthropology of East Europe Review* 23, no. 2 (2011): 26–29.

Douglas, Gordon C.C. "What Is Glamour? The Production and Consumption of a Working Aesthetic." *Mudot—the Magazine for Urban Documentation Opinion, and Theory*, no. 2 (August 2009): 44–63.

Dyhouse, Carol. *Glamour: History, Women, Feminism.* London: Zed Books, 2011.

Dunn, Elizabeth C. *Privatizing Poland: Baby Food, Big Business, and the Remaking of Labor.* Ithaca, NY: Cornell University Press, 2004.

Dziuba, Ivan. *Mykola Khvyl'oviy—"aziatskiyrenesans" I "psychologichna Evropa."* Kyiv: Kyiv-Mohyla Academy Press, 2005.

Eisenstadt, Shmuel N. "Some Observations on Multiple Modernities." In *Reflections on Multiple Modernities: European, Chinese and Other Interpretations*, edited by Dominic Sachsenmaier and Jens Riedel, with Shmuel N. Eisenstadt, 27–41. Leiden, Netherlands: Brill, 2002.

Ernst and Young. *Retail Market in Ukraine: Industry Trends.* Kyiv: E&Y LLC, 2014.

Fehérváry, Krisztina. "Goods and States: The Political Logic of State-Socialist Material Culture." *Comparative Studies in Society and History* 51, no. 2 (2009): 426–59.

Fletcher, Kate. "Slow Fashion: An Invitation for Systems Change." *Fashion Practice* 2, no. 2 (2010): 259–65.

Gross, David. "Temporality and the Modern State." *Theory and Society* 14, no. 1 (1985): 53–82.

Gundle, Stephen. *Glamour: A History*. New York: Oxford University Press, 2008.

Gurova, Olga. *Fashion and the Consumer Revolution in Contemporary Russia*. Abingdon, UK: Routledge, 2014.

Hann, Chris. "Anthropology's Multiple Temporalities and Its Future in Central and Eastern Europe." Max Planck Institute for Social Anthropology Working Papers no. 90, 2007. Accessed September 27, 2019. http://hdl.handle.net/11858/00-001M-0000-0011-984F-D.

Humphrey, Caroline. "Does the Category 'Postsocialist' Still Make Sense?" In *Postsocialism: Ideals, Ideologies and Practices in Eurasia*, edited by Chris Hann, 12–15. New York: Routledge, 2002.

———. *The Unmaking of Soviet Life: Everyday Economies after Socialism*. Ithaca, NY: Cornell University Press, 2002.

Joy, Annamma, John. F. Sherry Jr., Alladi Venkatesh, Jeff Wang, and Ricky Chan. "Fast Fashion, Sustainability, and the Ethical Appeal of Luxury Brands." *Fashion Theory* 16, no. 3 (2012): 273–95.

Kim, Aimee, Nathalie Remy, and Jennifer Schmidt. "The Glittering Power of Cities for Luxury Growth," September 2014. Accessed September 14, 2018. https://www.mckinsey.com/industries/retail/our-insights/the-glittering-power-of-cities-for-luxury-growth.

Klumbytė, Neringa. "The Soviet Sausage Renaissance." *American Anthropologist* 112, no. 1 (2010): 22–37.

"Tri chetverti ukraintsev nikogda ne byli za granitsey." *Korrespondent*, June 1, 2012. http://korrespondent.net/ukraine/events/1355598-korrespondent-tri-chetverti-ukraincev-nikogda-ne-byli-za-granicej.

Manning, Paul, and Ann Uplisashvili. "'Our Beer': Ethnographic Brands in Postsocialist Georgia." *American Anthropologist* 109, no. 4 (2007): 626–41.

Moore, David Chioni. "Is the Post- in Postcolonial the Post- in Post-Soviet? Toward a Global Postcolonial Critique." *PMLA* 116, no. 1 (January 2001): 111–28.

Newell, Sasha. *The Modernity Bluff: Crime, Consumption, and Citizenship in Côte d'Ivoire*. Chicago: University of Chicago Press, 2012.

Oushakine, Sergei. "The Quantity of Style: Imaginary Consumption in the New Russia." *Theory, Culture and Society* 17, no. 5 (2000): 97–120.

Patico, Jennifer. *Consumption and Social Change in a Post-Soviet Middle Class*. Washington, DC: Woodrow Wilson Center, 2008.

———. "To Be Happy in a Mercedes: Tropes of Value and Ambivalent Visions of Marketization." *American Ethnologist* 32, no. 3 (2005): 479–96.

Peltek, Liudmyla. *Rozvytokregional' noiipromyslovoii polityky derzhavy.* Mykolaiv, Ukraine: Petro Mohyla Black Sea National University Publishing House, 2010.

Pine, Frances, Deema Kaneff, and Haldis Haukanes, eds. *Religions, Politics and Memory: The Past Meets the Present in Contemporary Europe.* Berlin: Lit Verlag, 2004.

"Plea for Swedish IKEA to Set Up Shop in Ukraine." *The Local,* October 15, 2015. https://www.thelocal.se/20151015/plea-for-swedish-ikea-to-open-in-ukraine.

"Poroshenko obyasnil Bloomberg nedoverie investorov k Ukraine na primere IKEA." *Korrespondent,* April 10, 2012. http://korrespondent.net/business/companies/1338617-poroshenko-obyasnil-bloomberg-nedoverie-investorov-k-ukraine-na-primere-ikea.

Prokhorova, Elena. "Material(ized) Desire: Forging a Subject of Consumer Ideology in Post-Soviet Russia." *Studies in Slavic Cultures,* no. 1 (2000): 60–74.

Rating Group. "'Second Hand' in Ukraine: Public Attitude towards the Ban and the Possible Consequences of This Decision." *RatingGroup.ua,* October 19, 2010. http://ratinggroup.ua/files/ratinggroup/reg_files/rg_sekond_hand_ua_102010.pdf.

Said, Edward W. "Orientalism." *Georgia Review* 31, no. 1 (1977): 162–206.

Satenstein, Liana. "Move Over, Le Marais: Kiev Might Be the Coolest Shopping Destination in Europe." *Vogue,* February 2, 2016. https://www.vogue.com/article/best-shopping-kiev-ukraine.

Seliverstova, Oleksandra. "Keeping Alive the 'Imaginary West' in Post-Soviet Countries." *Journal of Contemporary Central and Eastern Europe* 25, no. 1 (2017):117–34.

Shevchenko, Olga. *Crisis and the Everyday in Postsocialist Moscow.* Bloomington: Indiana University Press, 2008.

State Statistics Department of Ukraine. "Ukraina u Tsyfrakh u 2012 Rotsi" [Ukraine in Numbers in 2012]. 2013. www.ukrstat.gov.ua.

Stearns, Peter N. *Consumerism in World History: The Global Transformation of Desire.* New York: Routledge, 2006.

Sztompka, Piotr. "Civilizational Incompetence: The Trap of Post-communist Societies." *Zeitschrift für Soziologie* 22, no. 2 (1993): 85–95.

Thelen, Tatjana. "Shortage, Fuzzy Property and Other Dead Ends in the Anthropological Analysis of (Post)Socialism." *Critique of Anthropology* 31, no. 1 (2011): 43–61.

Tovstyzhenko, Andrey. "Rashody ukraintsev v chetyre raza nizhe chem v srednem po Evrope." *Zerkalo Nedeli,* January 11, 2013. https://zn.ua/UKRAINE/rashody-ukraincev-v-chetyre-raza-menshe-chem-v-srednem-po-evrope.html.

Wallerstein, Immanuel. "The Rise and Future Demise of the World Capitalist System: Concepts for Comparative Analysis." *Comparative Studies in Society and History* 16, no. 4 (1974): 387–415.

Wanner, Catherine. "Money, Morality and New Forms of Exchange in Postsocialist Ukraine." *Ethnos* 70, no. 4 (2005): 515–37.

Wilk, Richard. "Morals and Metaphors: The Meaning of Consumption." In *Elusive Consumption*, edited by Karin Ekström and Helen Brembeck, 11–26. New York: Berg, 2004.

Yu, LiAnne. *Consumption in China: How China's New Consumer Ideology Is Shaping the Nation*. Cambridge: Polity, 2014.

Yurchak, Alexei. *Everything Was Forever, until It Was No More: The Last Soviet Generation*. Princeton, NJ: Princeton University Press, 2006.

AUTHOR BIO

TANIA BULAKH is a PhD candidate in the Department of Anthropology, Indiana University Bloomington. Her research interests cover humanitarian aid, consumer culture, state power, postsocialist transformations, and displacement. Her current research project looks at humanitarianism and material aid among internally displaced people in Ukraine and the construction of citizenship.

EIGHT

THE LATE SOCIALIST GOOD LIFE AND ITS DISCONTENTS

Bit, Kultura, and the Social Life of Goods

CRISTOFER SCARBORO

The historical task of relating consumption to ideology haunted late socialist Eastern Europe. This should not surprise us. From the beginning, communist readings of political economy were tied to the promise that industrial production would produce plenty, generating new and improved social relationships. Marx believed that the productive might of industrial capitalism was destined to result in tremendous surpluses, ending scarcity and creating the material foundations for the new historical epoch of communism. This map and quest served as the master plot of communism, holding together the Soviet Union and the socialist societies of Eastern Europe from beginning to end. Communism was to be an improved form of modernity, designed as a means to allow these societies to catch up and eventually surpass the West on the road to a just and prosperous society. This was the foundation of a new social contract for a new society: a series of promises of better tomorrows understood, in part, through consumption—groaning shelves of sausages and long vacations at seaside resorts. It was to be a fulfilling life, where all material needs had been met: a good life measured, in large part, through the relationship to goods.

Increasingly, as the socialist systems moved to middle age—into developed socialism—consumption became the measure through which both the state and its would-be subjects were to understand the good life in late socialism. The state socialist system's legitimacy, from above and below, was predicated on the promise of ever expanding horizons. This is also true of its chroniclers. Traditional understandings of the nature of the socialist system in Bulgaria, and elsewhere in Eastern Europe, have focused on questions of material consumption as a useful and seemingly obvious shorthand for the arrival (and ultimate collapse) of developed socialism and its concomitant middle class in Eastern Europe.[1]

The hard years of the 1980s in Eastern Europe and the ultimate collapse of the state socialist system rudely called the socialist model of consumption—and by extension, the promise of communism as a road to a just and prosperous society—into question.[2] Shortage indicted the promises of equitably distributed abundance; inferior consumer goods questioned the superiority of communism in its struggle with capitalism; rolling blackouts painted a drab picture of the late socialist good life. Economic growth declined (although at differing rates across the region), and indebtedness to the West increased in harrowing ways. Beginning with the literature of the "shortage economy" of János Kornai and culminating most recently in Paulina Bren and Mary Neuburger's excellent anthology *Communism Unwrapped*, the "backwardness" of the Eastern European socialist system has been understood as a given—no one asks if we use this categorization ironically.[3] As long as the promises seemed to correspond with lived experience, or as long as people were at least content enough to muddle through, the system was stable, or so the story goes. Once they did not, collapse was the result. Unsatisfied consumer desire, at least in the face of the glittering allure of Western consumption patterns, doomed communism in Eastern Europe. The second world rested safely ensconced behind the first as a failed model of development. For most writing about late socialism, the successes of the system, such as they were, were attributed not to the system's measureable (and immeasurable) achievements but rather to people's ability to find "pleasure in backwardness."[4]

Less obviously perhaps, pleasure in socialism has similarly been understood within the realm of the material. In the introduction to their edited volume *Pleasures in Socialism*, David Crowley and Susan Reid place the Enlightenment promise of the "pursuit of happiness" at the center of the story of socialism in the Soviet Union and Eastern Europe. It is worth noting, parenthetically, that, in the American context, this term is generally understood as underlining the right to property.[5] For Crowley and Reid, pleasure was a "fugitive phenomenon" under socialism, resulting from and in a series of contradictions and paradoxes—paradoxes that lay at the root of socialism's failure.[6] Pleasure in the present was placed on layaway—asceticism paying for the radiant future. Individual agency—for Reid and Crowley, a requirement for pleasure—had to find its way in a world of "compulsory happiness, official optimism, and highly regulated leisure."[7] State control of the distribution of luxury goods served both as a means of social control and as a set of questions: Were these goods properly socialist or a holdover from a decadent, bourgeois past? Was refrigerator socialism a proper goal for the socialist good society? If so, what exactly was *socialist* about it? The absence, or poor quality, of these very goods—refrigerator capitalism made better refrigerators after all—seemed to point to the inadequate fulfillment of the socialist social contract.[8]

As Reid and Crowley note: "The dominant paradigm for the analysis of ordinary people's everyday experience—both material and subjective—of state socialism has not been luxury, leisure, and pleasure, but on the contrary, need, command, and shortage."[9] So where *do* we find pleasure in socialism?

PLEASURE, DISPLEASURE, AND CONVERGENCE

One answer, one that flows from the dominant paradigm above, is to search for it within the paradoxes—in economies of scarcity and luxury, in the furtive personal fulfillment and autonomy in the face of centralized regulation, in happiness pursued in the slippages found within any system. For me, this idea is most compellingly put forward by Ivaylo Ditchev, who terms it the "erotics of stagnation." People locked in a permanent present tense were more or less free to pursue personal—and at times hedonistic—pleasures.[10] Workers pretending to work, students smoking cigarettes while on volunteer brigades or listening to rock and roll supplied by extralegal measures—this type of pleasure required navigating these contradictions, surviving the risk associated with transgressing correct behavior, and finding joy in lack.[11]

Contrarily, in her study of the era of normalization in Czechoslovakia, Paulina Bren gives us a greengrocer honestly comforted by his television. For Bren, normalization was defined most clearly by the struggle between the call to "live in truth," exemplified in the writings of Václav Havel, and the desire to live the "quiet life" (the life lived by the Czechoslovak silent majority, a majority that was, until it wasn't). This quiet life is perhaps best understood as a (slightly) socialist approximation of middle-class comfort as lived in the Western half of the continent.[12] Bren leaves us with a question: "What was wrong with the regime-endorsed quiet life?"[13] For Havel, the problem with the late socialist good life was that it resulted in a "post-totalitarian state," one in which people vacated their public and political lives for a pittance (the "vast cultural wasteland of television," private apartments, and cheap food).[14]

For Havel, post-totalitarianism results from an atomization of society brought on by the pursuit of individual consumptive pleasure. Ritual and political apathy replace real belief in ideology, leaving a Potemkin village. In his words: "In the foreground, then, stands the imposing façade of grand humanistic ideals . . . and behind it crouches the modest family house of a socialist bourgeois. On the one side, bombastic slogans about the unprecedented increase in every sort of freedom and the unique structural variety of life; on the other, unprecedented drabness and the squalor of life reduced to a hunt for consumer goods."[15] The grand promises of ideology—castles in the sky—were built on the muddy foundations of toaster ovens. It is worth noting that Havel saw the post-totalitarian state emerging as a product of mass consumer societies everywhere—for Havel it was as much a product of capitalism as communism. This problem is not unique to state socialism (which is, perhaps, why we in the West often focus on collapse as a result of material immiseration).[16]

For those focused on pleasure in material consumption—for those who read the "pleasures of backwardness" ironically—the moral of the story is that the societies of socialist Eastern Europe weren't nearly post-totalitarian enough.[17] The irony, of course, is that Bulgaria, circa 2019, isn't either.

This conception is problematic in two important ways: first, it repeats a set of dichotomies with genealogies traced to the Cold War; it also ignores the real appeal of socialist pleasure and middle-class values. In this account, the West is understood as a model of development, the East perpetually lagging behind. "Normalization" in Western Europe is contrasted to "sovietization" in the East (though as Bren and Havel point out, normalization in Czechoslovakia doesn't really look all that different than that in France). During the period of détente these differences seemed even less acute. Observers as varied as Aleksandr Solzhenitsyn, Andrei Sakharov, and Michel Foucault spoke of the convergence of these systems—and each would recognize Fukuyama's understanding of the end of history manifested through "easy access to VCRs in the economic sphere."[18] (And our colleague Patryk Wasiak points out that the Polish Communist Party worked hard—if sometimes at cross-purposes—to provide easy access to VCRs.)[19]

With all its contradictions, consumption and the development of a cultivated socialist middle class were clearly central to story of the development of communism in Bulgaria. Emerging from dueling progressivist and modernizing ideologies, historiographical traditions in both East and West during the Cold War focused on material development as the most important measure of the success of the Bulgarian socialist system. In official Bulgarian historiography, the system passed from its original socialist revolution (1944–48), through building the foundations of socialism (1948–58), to building a developed socialist society (1956/1958–80). The Eighth Party Congress of the Bulgarian Communist Party passed in 1962 called for the material technical base for communism to be built by 1980 with the gradual passage to communism to occur soon thereafter.[20] People would mark these passages by the quantifiable improvements in their daily life. Time itself would be rewritten: better tomorrows becoming happy todays.

This story of Bulgarian communism was echoed in Western commentaries most famously by John Lampe.[21] It also, of course, mirrored capitalist teleology and self-reflective understandings of historical processes. Those living and writing in West and East understood both the communist and capitalist systems most importantly as a set of promises of better tomorrows. A propulsive narrative logic was written into the process of communism (and, again, capitalism). All agreed that the central task of the system was to demonstrate that material realities met with the principles and promises of communism.

For many, the material realities of developed socialism provided ample evidence of new worlds being born—of promises being met. The economy grew at a healthy rate: John Bell claims it had the fastest growth rates in the Soviet bloc, growing at 9.6 percent annually from 1951 to 1967 and 7.5 percent from 1967 to 1974.[22] Demographic patterns pointed toward progressive transformation: over 1 million peasants (out of a population of around 8.5 million) moved from villages to the modern world of the city.[23] The Eighth Party Congress called for a vast expansion of consumer goods. According to the Five-Year Plan adopted at the congress 100 percent of homes were to have refrigerators by 1980; 97 percent would have televisions; 96 percent would have a vacuum cleaner; and each household would have 1.5 radios.[24] While these goals were never met under socialism, real progress was made, and planners and consumers continued to monitor purchasing power and to see it as a primary measure of progress under socialism. Personal consumption and opportunities for leisure were, for most people, the most important connection to these promises—a language easily understood and daily encountered. In his contemporary study of the Bulgarian family, Chavdar Kiuranov reflects the general tenor of the era: "Over the past 40 years the material living condition of the Bulgarian families and households have been dramatically changed. Suffice it to note that in 1982, 82 percent of families had television sets; 83 percent had refrigerators; 30 percent had private telephones; and 32 percent had their own cars."[25]

If convergence was the master plot in the story of development, Bulgaria, at least in the 1960s and 1970s, seemed to be doing its part nicely. Until the slowdown of the late 1970s, people continued to see their purchasing power and opportunities for leisure advance. The stability, social advancement, expansion of cultural outlets, and relative personal affluence of the era of stagnation were powerful sources of support for the system. State support of leisure and cultural activities, the promotion of consumption, and the development of the private and idiosyncratic interior lives of ordinary Bulgarians were, from the perspective of party planners, both a means of developing well-rounded socialist subjects (the central goal of socialist humanism) and a vehicle for delivering a real and existing version of the socialist good life, (thereby creating a middle class of contented supporters of the system).[26] As Patrick Hyder Patterson and others remind us, there was a socialist good life to be lost as the system disintegrated.[27]

Further, this socialist middle class was a *socialist* middle class: under late socialism a new middle strata developed alongside the production and distribution of televisions, a middle class that expressed and lived their own new visions about what the good life should look like.[28] Often, these visions coincided with the material pleasures of consumption under state socialism—a reduction of working hours, the increased emphasis on private life, and the gratifications of the domestic sphere—but often they did not.[29] Old communists bemoaned the lack of voluntary and collective enthusiasm of the postrevolutionary generations (and here, ironically, they share Havel's concern about the atomization of public life in late socialism).[30] And audiences in art galleries fretted about the socialist content of paintings and the meaning and message of an increasingly mechanized world.[31] Their pleasures, expectations, and fears of the new socialist middle class emerged in settings familiar yet foreign to the worlds of liberal, democratic capitalism.

BEING AND CONSCIOUSNESS

Bulgarian sources from the time of developed socialism reveal consumption as an alienating process along two primary trajectories. First, by moving toward consumer goods as the central legitimizing trope for the communist systems, the leaders of these regimes quickly discovered the impossibility of satisfying those demands. The tyranny of more—the insatiability of consumption—doomed the system to a Sisyphean attempt for new and better diversions (diversions that the West was simply better designed to fulfill). It also meant a change in understanding *what* was an important measure of the good society: televisions and automobiles eclipsed collective goods, universal health care, after-school clubs, and workers' poetry circles as a way to make sense of a life well lived. Western goods were more exhilarating in part, as Zsuzsa Gille and Diana Mincytė argue in this volume, because of their difficulty to acquire. They were ready-made for consumption, as opposed to Eastern goods that required work and creativity to produce, remake, and consume. In this story, the race to a satisfying life in socialist Eastern Europe was run against boredom. Would the goods provided by late socialism be good enough, diverting enough, to create fully realized human subjects?

Second was alienation born of toil and bewilderment. Consumption was designed to be a transformative process—changing both people's orientation in time and socialist ideology as it had previously been understood. People moved from the future-oriented, collectivist process of building socialism to the more sedentary, personal, and present-focused living in developed socialism. New worlds were indeed being born, and people had to know how to live this good life with all its successes and failures. Creating this good life would take work, education, and organization. It also meant finding meaning in the goods themselves. Refrigerator socialism was both a source of shabby solidity and revolutionary rage. The failures and successes of the late socialist system—measured in material terms—were premised on a designed insatiability: consumption required an ever increasing expectation of better goods resulting in more fulfilled lives (a difficult idea to measure in the best of circumstances). Thus, the era of late socialism was a time in which everyone involved was negotiating the relationship between the material and metaphysical promises of the system.

From the perspective of those living the socialist humanist system, the arrival of mass consumption was to mark the arrival at developed socialism manifested in the correct relationship between socialist humanist subjects and their consumer products. As such, the goods themselves represented both the potentials and the malfunctions of socialism. They were both profoundly satisfying and heartbreakingly alienating. Perhaps most worrying on the part of party planners was the understood lag between that most Marxist of concepts: being and consciousness. Socialism was to be about more than satisfying the material requirements of a good society. It was, equally importantly, to free people from the tyranny of the "alienated, consumerist outlook of bourgeois consumer society," allowing them to become "versatile, harmoniously developed, active, creative individuals." The goods were to be a means to an end.

Being and consciousness was to be brought into concert in Bulgaria by twin, staggered revolutions. The political and economic revolution of September 9, 1944, was to transform the material base of the country in order to bring about new outlooks and capacities within those living in the new society. As early as 1956, speaking to the Union of Bulgarian Writers, Todor Zhivkov articulated the beginnings of this difficulty: "The development of the nation's economy and of its productive forces, no matter how great it may be, does not, and cannot, exhaust the entire problem of the construction of the socialist society. . . . As you know consciousness always lags behind the economy in its development, it is refashioned much more slowly than the latter. On the basis of the great changes in economic and social relations, the work of communist education and re-education has to be stepped up. A socialist consciousness has to be instilled in the masses."[32] A second, cultural revolution was to follow closely behind the first, leading to a world in which, in the words of Liudmila Zhivkova at the Third Congress of Culture, "spiritual development and improvement should become an inner need and necessity, they should elevate the human spirit, expand man's horizons, and turn human labor into a joy in view of the infinite prospects and possibilities of human progress and evolution."[33] Material successes had to be appropriately tied to human fulfillment.

As material conditions approached the levels hoped for and expected under developed socialism, there was a real fear that the accompanying socialist consciousness was behind schedule. Ironically, this gap was understood to be the result of the successes of the socialist system. This was a particular problem as the story of communism's development in Bulgaria turned the page: moving from building the foundations of socialism to building a developed socialist society. Speaking to the Union of Bulgaria Writers in 1966, Todor Zhivkov noted that Bulgarian society was riven with two truths: "the truth of the construction of the new society, and the truth of the negative phenomena accompanying socialist construction." Developed socialism had created a society in which "many citizens can afford to buy a flat, many own country houses and cars. As a result, conditions are at hand for the emergence of another kind of reasoning, of a different mentality: indifference to politics, selfishness, a striving after a more luxurious life, self-seeking etc."[34] Here Zhivkov seems to be warning us against the emergence of a post-totalitarian state.

Developed socialism was producing both a middle class and middle-class angst. Philistinism was understood to be a real problem; the scientific-technical revolution held out the danger of alienation and estrangement from labor. The difficulty lay in determining whether these visions were the product of the remnants of bourgeois ideology or the result of developing socialism. Addressing these concerns, developing a correct consciousness and relationship to consumer goods, was of central importance for both state and society during the late socialist period. The First Congress of Culture in Bulgaria was convened in 1967—which reflected both the coming cultural revolution's inevitability and its resistance to planning. Reflecting on the process in 1971, Boris Tsenkov writes: "No decrees can compel people to substitute the socialist mode of thinking for the bourgeois one.... Not without importance, too, is yet another characteristic feature of the cultural revolution: its relative independence, inner logic and laws."[35]

This did not stop the Bulgarian party from trying. The culmination of these attempts was the 1975 Comprehensive Program for Nationwide Aesthetic Education enacted by the Committee on Culture, headed by Lyudmila Zhivkova.

The goal of this program was to "bridge the gap between the sphere of material production and the sphere of aesthetics," to develop a "harmonious multisided personality" against the "alienated, consumerist outlook of bourgeois consumer society."[36]

As Veneta Ivanova has convincingly demonstrated, the era of stagnation was anything but stagnant in Bulgaria. Communist theorists and ordinary men and women spent the 1970s and 1980s furiously thinking through the implications of living in the world of developed socialism. At least officially, the goal was to create a world in which Bulgarians would "live in beauty"; what this meant was a matter of some conjecture.

GOODS AND HOW TO USE THEM

Much of this tension is laid bare in the development of the Bulgarian trade journal *Kooperativna promishlenost* (Cooperative industry) and Bulgarian domestic encyclopedias—most importantly *Kniga za vseki den i vseki dom* (Book for every day and every home)—whose audience was to be those producing (and later consuming) domestic goods and services. The title of the journal, as it changed over time, itself tells an interesting story of the semiofficial transformation of Bulgarians' relationship to consumer goods. The journal was founded in 1951, and until 1953 it was known as *Zanaiatchiiska kooperatsia* (Craftsmen's cooperative); from 1954 to 1962 it was *Trudovo-proizvoditelna kooperatsiia* (Worker-producer cooperative); from 1963 to 1970, *Kooperativna promishlenost* (Cooperative industry). From 1971 to 1974 the journal was titled *Bit i kultura* (Daily life and culture)—reflecting a real shift toward the idealization of consumption. From 1975 until it ceased publication in 1984, it was titled *Mestna promishlenost i uslugi* (Local industry and services).

When it was first published as *Zanaiachiiska kooperatsia*, the journal's central focus was the question of production. In the first issue, a letter from Vulko Chervenkov, the general secretary of the Bulgarian Communist Party, outlined the mission of the publication. For him the big questions for cooperative industry were as follows: "How can we fulfill the plan; how can the cooperative fight for the diversification and high quality of assorted models of production; what savings can be made in raw material, fuel costs and administrative reorganization; how can we use regional raw materials; how can we rationalize production; how can we increase production and reduce costs; how can we fulfill our responsibilities as citizens."[37] Early articles in the journal followed Chervenkov's lead. Throughout the 1950s, articles focus on such topics as "studying and implementing the Stakhanovite way of work in the sewing industry" and provided instructions on how, "to learn from the experience of the Soviet Union: in employing Stakhanovite movement in manual shoe production" (which included a helpful schema for organizing the workplace)."[38] As they transformed themselves into rational, industrial labors, workers were given models to follow, reflected in such articles as "How I fulfilled the production plan and kept my promise to Comrade Vulko Chervenkov"[39] and "How I became a shockworker."[40] Early issues in 1952 are littered with mass promises sent in by readers to fulfill the newly outlined Five-Year Plan. Similar promises were made after the death of Stalin in 1953.[41]

Even in these early, heady days, there were echoes of the problems and opportunities posed by consumption. Each issue in the early 1950s ended with a section entitled "question and answers." Generally, these were questions about the rationalization of labor: questions about how one could best meet the plan. Even here, however, ideas of obligations were coalescing in tandem with new understandings of rights. Already by April 1951 an anonymous questioner asked: "Does a worker in the TZKS [collective farm] canteen have the right to eat there for free?" It turns out, they could.[42]

The shift at the Seventh Party Congress in 1958 (also called the Congress of the Victory of Socialism) and the adoption of the third Five-Year Plan (also of that year) declared that its goal was to build "an advanced socialist society." The Victory of Socialism entailed the completion of the material technical basis necessary for socialism: power was in the hands of the Soviets, the masses had been drawn into socialist modes of production, and the country had (more or less) been electrified.[43] Left unsaid but increasingly implied was the fact that the new social relationship to production was creating a new socialist middle class.

These transformations were reflected in the covers of the journals themselves over the course of the 1960s. Early covers with images of workers working—of producers producing—were replaced by images of consumers enjoying those products produced. Even when workers were given something of a star turn on the covers of *Kooperativna promishlenost*, the effect was somewhat muddled—hairdressers dressing hair, cosmetologists exfoliating customers' skin—there is little ambiguity about who is living the good life here. Images of workers on the covers ended in the mid-1960s—they were entirely replaced by images of consumers and products. One thing was clear: products were coming that would transform and improve daily life; the future was going to be fabulous.

These new Bulgarians would have to come to terms with their own subjectivity mediated through their relationships to the products of a new economic order.⁴⁴ Much work was done on the part of the editors of *Trudo-proivoditelna kooperatsia* to introduce these new modes of living and sets of expectations. The good life had to be modeled. Consider this tutorial on proper decorum at the dinner table:

> The food has to be served in plates of the exact same size and decoration. The silverware—knives, forks and spoons, have to be completely clean and of the same type. It is desirable for the plates to be equidistant from the hands of the people so that they can move freely. You should place the knives in a sharp, straight line along the right side of the plate. On the other side of the plate you should place the spoon for soup. To the left of the plate you should place the fork. Above the plate you should place a desert fork or spoon and a little to the left of that—a glass for water. The bread, sliced thinly, should be placed in a plate in the center of the table. Around it you will find the plates with salads, a pitcher of water and the salt and pepper. Many hosts are now using napkins [*kurpata za iadene*]. If you have them, place them to the right of the plate under the knife and spoon. Using them will save your tablecloths, your clothing and your hands from messes. A good impression is made on those around you if children from a young age learn to eat with their knives and forks. Be sure to teach them to hold the knife in their right hand and in the left (at a slight angle) the fork.⁴⁵

Instructions on the correct relationship with home, with food, and with others were paralleled by lessons on how to shape the body. Many observes feared that the arrival of developed communism had created a world where the "body is weak and obese. In this case the shoulders slump, the chest—sunken, the breasts—sag, the back curves, posture is slack and the overall appearance is like that of a wilted flower." For the first time, in February 1959, the magazine published what would become a recurring feature: "Lechebno gimnastika" (Healing gymnastics). For those who followed the instructions, "twinkle would return to their eyes," and they would "feel pleasant and happy."⁴⁶

These instructions on living the cultured life were echoed in the proliferation of self-help literature centered on the domestic sphere, like in the postwar United States. Books with titles like *Dom, semeistvo, bit* (Home, family, daily life), *1001 suvet za vseki den* (1001 everyday tips), and *Kniga za vseki den i vseki dom* (Book for every day and every home—which described itself as a domestic encyclopedia) promised a road map for how to make a good life in this new world. New homes for newly urban, cosmopolitan, and socialist Bulgarians were bewildering, ecstatic, and confounding spaces. These books provided a vision for what the late socialist good life should (and would) look like and how to properly live within it. Perhaps then, it should come as no surprise that the books were extremely popular. Among those with the widest circulation (and largest publishing run, ranging from 52,080 in 1967 to 100,000 in 1977) was *Kniga za vseki den i vseki dom*.

I have yet to meet a Bulgarian since I began working on this project who did not have a strong, almost visceral connection to this book. Everyone it seems had a mother or grandmother who turned to the book to figure out how to iron polyester pants, pot plants, sew clothes, and cook *iatsa Pangiurishte* (Pangiurishte style eggs). When I purchased my copies of the book from a second-hand bookseller on Ploshtad Slaveikov, I got an urgent call from him that very evening—he had sold me his mother's book, and she desperately wanted it back.

It is the gently paternalistic and highly gendered elements of self-improvement (a basic feature of self-help books and lifestyle magazines everywhere) that stand out from the texts. Instructions range from examples of monthly menus, to instructions in facial massage and the correct application of cosmetics, to instructions on exercise at home: a "vital necessity for the modern woman." The books are written with the expansive use of the modal verb—replete with advice for how the ideal home or person or flower arrangement "should be." The books are a promise. If these instructions are followed, in every house, every day could be this grand.

These were promises that Micki McGee (writing in the US context) would have understood as "belaboring." Women in particular in this genre of self-improvement were "continually asked to invent [and improve] themselves ... while paradoxically finding some way of cultivating an authentic self."[47] New, modern socialist life produced a new "citizenry that understood themselves to be defined by their consumption habits and modern lifestyles."[48] These domestic encyclopedias were also intended as a means to alleviate the alienation endemic to consumer society everywhere by promoting the active involvement of the citizen-worker consumer in building her world.

As the examples above demonstrate, creating this good life would take work, education, and organization. It would take exercise and sweat to develop a supple body. Confusion would have to turn to knowledge. The section on cooking (something, presumably, engaged in for generations) starts by asking if the reader knows how to cook (the assumption being that the reader did not, at least not in the kitchen of the future). Modern electrical conveniences—harbingers of comfort and an advanced socialist economy, measured primarily in labor saved—were befuddling. Labor-saving devices required labor to learn how to operate and care for them. In the domestic encyclopedias, much space was given to how to operate and repair refrigerators and washing machines. *Kniga za vseki den* provided answers about how time was to be spent, life lived, and meaning found in a world increasingly without labor and limned by consumption. Here we meet the model of the fully realized late socialist subject.

The model home—the *obratsov dom*—dominates all three volumes of *Kniga za vseki den*. Bright, modern, functional furniture—and incredibly expansive rooms—promise a world of rational leisure, a world devoid of work. Clutter is absent (as are people for that matter). Work is ensconced safely in the past tense: rugs freshly vacuumed, dustbins emptied. The chairs invite the viewer to sit down, dine by candlelight, or watch television on one of the comfortable velour or naugahyde sofas. It is a rapturous and universal vision—one of the future becoming—the appeal of living in a permanent present tense (as if on repeat): every day, in every house.

In the decade between the first and third edition (1967–77), questions about whether the reader knows how to cook are replaced by French recipes, cocktails, and debates over which resort to visit.

In the pages of *Trudovo-proizvoditelna kooperatsiia* the world had become more joyous as the future moved into the present. Products sparkled and enticed. An unnamed correspondent passed through the stores of the workers' manufacturing cooperative in a reverent daze: "We walked through the streets of the capital. One after another were the stores of different producer cooperatives. And all of them, more wonderful, more beautiful. In each of them were arranged all kinds of goods meeting the different needs of the consumer. The stores for TPKs had almost every kind of shoe: men's, women's, kid's. The display stand at the store resembled a well-ordered bouquet of flowers—so successfully had they arranged the dresses, pajamas, nightdresses, of all kinds of colors and styles." The correspondent gives the last word to Sia Balan, who had visited the store to pick up her order for sheets. Writing in the impression book (*kniga za vpechatlenie*), Balan exclaimed: "Not only did it please me, it made me happy for the first time in a long time."[49]

Consumer desire, closely tied to human happiness, became a primary means—perhaps the primary means—of measuring the successes and failures of the socialist project. This was often understood officially in terms of aesthetic appreciation and the idea of "living in beauty." "And one cannot live full-bloodedly without beauty," proclaimed the new feature *Nashata anketa* (Our investigation): "Beauty! More Beauty! These words have to ring throughout our socialist society. It has to show up in our homes, our public spaces, city buildings and parks and gardens. It has to show up in our daily life, in the higher quality and better production in our factories—in our shoes and clothes, in our rugs and furniture. We want everything we touch to be beautiful. We want even more goods in the store that satisfy good taste."[50] Making this life possible required new products for people to develop new relationships with. Two new sections appeared in the mid-1960s: Novo-novo! (New-new!) and Panorama, each designed to highlight these new products. These new features represent a larger thematic shift on the part of the journal, which moved from focusing on workers at work to the products they produce. Readers are introduced in 1964 to beautiful new machines to slice bread. Graters made with "elegant and beautiful lines from strong plastic" are omnipresent. Suitcases with built-in drink-mixing sets appear with the 1970s; as do two-sided electric fish fryers, egg slicers, designer soap dispensers, and Progres, a paste from Balkanhim that promises to clean cloth and other material of "dirt, blood, paint, urine and other things."

My favorite of these products—and this is mostly because it so closely resembles late-night basic-cable "sham-wow" commercials—is onion cutters, which appear in repeated articles: "Onion cutter: a circular enclosed knife—you can put in a whole head of an onion and quickly chop it to bits. No smelly hands, no more tears! Your sink won't smell. But that is not all. You can also chop almonds and walnuts (for cakes and soups). You are sure to find many other uses. Stand up grater, circular stand up grater; regular universal grater; plastic slicer; potato grater (and for making *kiufte* [meatballs])."[51] While I am unsure of the relevance, in 1972 the journal—now entitled *Bit i kultura*—published its first articles on toupees (for men) and, in 1973, stories on electric hair removal (for women).[52]

New consumers were born in this beautiful reverie—in this new world of happiness—and they brought in their train new sets of expectations. As early as 1964 Nasha anteka noted:

> The desire of our working people to live better continues to grow. They already expect to have beautiful clothes, shoes and other personal possessions. It used to be that an inside toilet was the preserve of the few. Today it is available to all. Our workers now have the required material necessities of life. As manufacturers and builders, who have laid the foundations for the economic transformation of our country, who have allowed us to catch up to the most advanced countries, they have imperceptibly and fully effectively changed their own tastes, desires and way of life. In the bazaars they don't buy anything they see, they now only purchase beautiful clothes, and useful tools to bring relief in household chores. Things that bring comfort, coziness and beauty to daily life. They don't search only for what they really need but search out things with the luxury label. More beautiful clothes, shoes, bags, hats, necklaces! More beautiful furniture! That is our task which will define the nature of our time. And the producers' cooperatives who are not only consumers but who provide the goods and services, are happy that along with the glorious working class are creating the beauty without which our new life is unthinkable.[53]

New, previously unthinkable worlds of beauty created both pleasure and anxiety. Consumer demand had to be fulfilled and understood. Taste had to be cultivated, refashioned, and restrained.

Even in this world of consumer beauty and (hoped-for) fulfillment, work still remained in the everyday world of every home in late socialist Bulgaria. There were walls to be built, fruit from the villages (or villas) to be made into juice, and diseased teeth to extract. New styles and new clothing—required in the transition from peasant dress and work overalls—necessitated work and knowledge. Fold-out instructions for dressmaking were included in each encyclopedia. It meant mothers sewing clothing for their families—and knowing how to do so. It meant washing and ironing—and knowing how to do so. The world of clean, spacious, well-apportioned apartments, of children in perfectly tailored outfits, of sumptuous French dinners, of vacations perfectly planned, required new relationships of consumption and production. Commodity fetishism loomed ominously over the expanding horizons.

The question of doing it yourself—a return to the era of the cottage industry, of making one's own clothing—was understood as a way to satisfy consumer demand. Do-it-yourself (*napravi si sam*) sections, where one could borrow tools ranging from sewing machines to beekeeping equipment, were a central component of the trade journals from the late 1970s. Doing it yourself—the combining of production and consumption—provided something of an ideological challenge: a return to the putting-out system did not seem to follow what was expected to be the path to communism. In the short article "Do It Yourself: Hobby or Necessity," an unnamed author seeks to contextualize the Bulgarian version of the global phenomenon:

> Many people incorrectly think that this kind of work is more often found in countries of lower levels of economic development. In fact, statistics show that this movement is more often found in countries with the highest levels of development. In these countries people can often find special stores or stands selling manual or electric instruments and machines, special details and spare parts. People here have the know-how and can ask the advice of highly qualified specialists in the repair of furniture, and small household maintenance. Maybe it is a hobby. Maybe it reflects a natural need for people to design and create their surroundings. It is clear, however, that is it practical and necessary when people are working on their home or villa to do some of the work themselves. More and more the new self-taught masters are demonstrating their abilities and improving their lives.[54]

Do it yourself is explained as a means of self-actualization: a sign of prosperity rather than dearth, and an enviable ability on the part of Bulgarians to control and improve one's environment and self.

Over the course of the 1960s and 1970s, in the pages of *Trudovo-proizvoditelna kooperatsiia, Kooperativna promishlenost, Bit i kultura,* and *Mestna promishlenost i uslugi*, this future realized competed with the future betrayed. A 1982 cartoon entitled "Do It Yourself" portrayed a person angrily walking up to a television set with an ax. Repairs (or destruction) were part of the process of late socialist diversion.[55] The journal revealed inconvenient truths: the absence of dry cleaning services, locksmiths, and shops for the repair of musical instruments, guns, and eyeglasses. There was a dearth of plumbing services and shops for quilting and bedding. Services for the "advanced state of daily life," including for radios, vacuum cleaners, typewriters, and light cars and motorcycles, were absent.[56]

Writers complained of heavy, outdated furniture and the difficulty of finding and consuming the simple pleasures of a new beautiful life.[57] From Sliven, Bozhidarka Dzhendova wrote:

> When will we have more beauty salons? Our working women love beauty. All of us want to have modern and pretty hairstyles. But when my friends and I try to get our hair done we can never get an appointment. That is because in the whole town of Sliven there are only two beauty salons. One can wait from morning until night and not get in (especially on holidays). We have often written of the need for more hair salons. In our time having a haircut is not a luxury—a person has to have one to be happy and it is unfortunate to have to wait 10 hours to get your hair done.[58]

Liliana Nikolvna (a teacher living on "N. Rilski" street no. 25) complained: "Skiing has become an incredibly popular sport in Bulgaria. What family with children doesn't have at least one or two pairs of skis? I wonder why then, in all of Sofia there is not one ski repair shop? Why don't carpenter shops pay attention to this problem and offer these services? To fulfill even better the people's needs we need stories like this in this magazine—it is the least you can do."[59] On a more practical level, Elisabeta Nikolova complained that "in our city there is only one store where one can buy men's shirts. I understand that Stara Zagora is a city of 80,000 people—this is absolutely inadequate." Ominously she concludes: "The same is true for underwear."[60]

Consumers complained about the quality of their products—dentists asking their patients if they were eating rocks are informed that, to the contrary, they were eating walnuts from the sweets cooperative.[61] Cartoons from the journal outlined shoddy products and dry cleaners spreading rather than removing spots from pants (resulting in a whimsical set of polka-dotted, Haight-Ashbury-style pants).[62] Television salesmen offer to have the newly sold television delivered to the customers house or directly to the repair shop, and plumbers make fountains out of showers. The plumber exclaims: "It may not be practical but it is aesthetic."[63]

Often poor goods and services were linked directly via deficiencies in the production mechanism—the idea that people were pretending to work. In one joke, an interviewer asks a brigade leader how many people work in his brigade. The answer: about half.[64] Two people sit in front of a chessboard. One asks the other: "How did you get so good at chess?" The answer: "Well, it's how I spend my time at work."[65] A wife is furious at her husband who has given her a dress for a holiday: "How could you give me such garbage?" He responds: "But, sweetheart, your brigade made it!"

It is also important to keep in mind that this scarcity and this dismay at poorly designed and inefficiently distributed goods are the results of expectations met and unfulfilled. Televisions that don't work are, after all (and this may be cold comfort), televisions. Showers more appropriately understood as fountains are a measure of the successes of the system. Half workers working, is half workers not. On one level we have to give the planned economies of the socialist world their due: by the mid-1970s they had created a consuming middle class whose expectations increasingly matched that of their cousins in Western Europe. However, these frustrations concerning the slipshod delivery on the promises of consumer modernity also carry within them a critique of those very promises. In another cartoon, a man jogs by while watching television on a stroller (echoing our own fears about alienation brought to us by Apple).[66] These images reflect the fear that the social good was falling away in the pursuit of individual consumptive pleasures. The difficulty, of course, is that this is precisely the metric we use to understand progress as we travel on our way to the good society.

Much of *Bit i kultura* and *Mestna promishlenost i uslugi* were spent questioning the cosmic meaning of the goods they were producing. Let's return to the shower-fountain. What we see here is the triumph of the uselessly beautiful over the practical: human need subordinated to the insubstantial. The woman working in the dry cleaner has, by at least one measure, made her customers' pants more fashionable (at least fashionable circa August 1966). Neither worker seems particularly chagrined at what they have done.

These journals return again and again to the seeming insanity of modern consumption. Modern transportation sees people moving off horses and under cars. Helicopters are required to place an elaborate wig on a woman's head (a pretty good metaphor for the triumph of the artificial over the natural). Men are also the victims of modern hairstyles—long hair causing them to drive their motorcycles into fire hydrants. Most tellingly, *Kooperativna promishlenost* and *Bit i kultura* have a recurring starring role reserved for Diogenes, who walks through its pages carrying a lamp in daylight searching for a human being (generally understood as someone living the thoughtful and self-conscious good life).[67]

Diogenes was a Cynic—Plato called him "Socrates gone mad"—who made it his life's work to challenge accepted customs and values. He claimed to live a good life, while experiencing much deprivation—including exile and enslavement. He lived in a tub (in Greek, *pithos*). He apparently spent his days wandering the streets with a lantern looking for a human being. Reincarnated in Sofia in the mid to late 1970s, Diogenes, searching for a human being, encounters these new middle-class socialists: a man looking for spare parts and an absurdly fashionable woman searching for a store selling household appliances.[68] Diogenes looks a little confused.

Zanaiatchiiska kooperatsiia and its descendants point to a world promised and only partly delivered. We (those of us writing the history of collapse) have thus far tended to focus on the inadequate fulfillment of those visions of the good life—the fairy-tale nature of the living rooms on display—to understand the collapse of communism as a result of dearth and repression. But these promises also carried within them the current of dissatisfaction with those very promises.[69] This is something the party itself realized and feared. This current was not unique to Bulgaria or the communist world; a worldwide generation reacted against the foundational premises of modernity—the last third of the twentieth century was a period when children refused to inherit the world of their parents. An "age of panic" dawned as the first postwar generation came of age across the globe: this generation saw the promises of modernity met and found themselves underwhelmed.[70]

NOTES

1. Patterson, *Bought and Sold*; Gorsuch and Koenker, *Turizm*; and Fehérváry, *Politics in Color and Concrete*. Specific to Bulgaria, see Kalinova, *Bulgarskata kultura i politicheskiiat imperative, 1944–1989*; Znepolski, *Bulgarskiiat komuminzum*. Much good work in Bulgaria is being done at the Institute for the Study of the Recent Past (Institut za izsledvane na blizkoto minalo). See Boiadzhieva, *Sotsialnoto inzhenerstvo*; Vachkov and Ivanov, *Bulgarskiia vunshen dulg, 1944–1989*; Znepolski, *Da poznaem komunizma*; Doynov, *Bulgarskiiat*

sotsrealizum, 1956, 1968, 1989; Elenkov, *Kultiniiat front*; Ivanov, *Reformatorstvo bez reformi*; Znepolski, *NRB*.

2. Kenny, *Carnival of Revolution*; Stokes, *Walls Came Tumbling Down*; Ash, *Magic Lantern*; Kotkin, *Uncivil Society*.

3. Kornai, *Economics of Shortage*; Bren and Neuburger, *Communism Unwrapped*. One notable exception is Moshe Lewin, who understood state socialism as a failure only when measured against the goals it set itself. See Lewin, *Soviet Century*.

4. See Bren and Neuburger, *Communism Unwrapped*; Crowley and Reid, *Pleasures in Socialism*; and Bren, *Greengrocer and His TV*.

5. The phrase comes to American ears from the Declaration of Independence (authored by Thomas Jefferson in 1776) via the Virginia Declaration of Rights: "that all men are by nature equally free and independent and have certain inherent rights, of which, when they enter into a state of society, they cannot, by any compact, deprive or divest their posterity; namely, the enjoyment of life and liberty, with the means of acquiring and possessing property, and pursuing and obtaining happiness and safety"; and John Locke's *Two Treatises on Government* argues that government exists to protect its citizens' "life, liberty and estate." Locke, *Two Treatises of Government*.

6. Note that Stephen Lowell in his account of the Soviet experience understands paradoxes as a source of strength and legitimacy for the system. Lowell, *Soviet Union*.

7. Crowley and Reid, *Pleasures in Socialism*, 4.

8. Patterson, *Bought and Sold*.

9. Crowley and Reid, *Pleasures in Socialism*, 10.

10. Ditchev, "Erotika na komunizma." This understanding bears much in common with Alexei Yurchak's seminal *Everything Was Forever until It Was No More*.

11. Genev, "Borsa."

12. Bren, *Greengrocer and His TV*. Approximation saw Eastern Europeans measuring the successes and failures of the socialist system (and their own internal lives) according to values alien to many of the expressed goals of the socialist system. The anger and ennui associated with this process of approximation was increasingly a source of destabilization within the state socialist system.

13. Ibid., 111.

14. The reference is to the speech "Television and the Public Interest," given by the chairman of the Federal Communications Commission, Norman E. Minnow, to the National Association of Broadcasters in 1961.

15. Havel, "Dear Dr. Husák."

16. Jeffrey Goldfarb makes the argument about a convergence in the depoliticizing effect of mass consumerism on both sides of the Iron Curtain. Goldfarb, *Beyond Glasnost*.

17. Kotkin, *Armageddon Averted.*
18. Solzhenitsyn, "An Exhausted West." This is the reprinted text of his famous commencement address earlier in the year. Sakharov, "Progress, Coexistence." Particularly useful is Foucault's simultaneous writings on the Iranian revolution. See Foucault, *Power*; Fukuyama, "End of History."
19. Wasiak, "Video Boom in Poland."
20. R. Daskalov, *Debating the Past*, 249.
21. Lampe, *Bulgarian Economy.*
22. Bell, *Bulgarian Communist Party*, 133.
23. Brunnbauer, "'Everybody Believes,'" 175–76.
24. Mineva "Razkazi i obrazi na socialistichesko potrebleniie."
25. Implicit in this is the question of Cold War competition. Kyuranov notes: "A comparison with the leading economic countries shows that the Bulgarian families are lagging behind. But if we note that in 1970 those figures were 42 percent for televisions, 30 percent for refrigerators, 4 percent for private telephones and 3.5 percent for cars, we can see how quickly these needs are being satisfied. Naturally these rapid rates will be decreasing as people's needs are being met but they are highly revealing." Kyuranov, *Bulgarskoto semeistvo dnes*, 23.
26. Brunnbauer, "'Everybody Believes.'"
27. Patterson, *Bought and Sold.*
28. This is perhaps best outlined in Krisztina Fehérváry's *Politics in Color and Concrete.*
29. How these pleasures relate to neoliberalism is, of course, a fraught question.
30. Scarboro, "Today's Unseen Enthusiasm."
31. Scarboro, *Late Socialist Good Life.*
32. Zhivkov, "More Among the People," 25–26. See also Obretenov, *Cultural Revolution in Bulgaria*, 17; Astradzhiev, *Bulkarskata sotsialisticheska kultura*; Avramov, *Kulturata i revoliutsiia*; Ganev, *Guidance of Bulgaria's Socialist Culture*; Stoikov, *Bulgarskata komunisticheska partiia i kultura*; Dikov, *Bulgarskata kultura pred praga na XXI vek*; Cenkov, *Socialist Revolution*; Boiadzhieva, *Sotsialnoto inzhenerstvo*; Doynov, *Bulgarskiiat sotsrealizum, 1956, 1968, 1989*; Elenkov, *Kultiniiat front*; Vasileva and Vaileva, *Bulgarskata kultura i evropeiskiiat XX vek*; Kalinova, *Bulgarskata kultura i politicheskiiat imperative, 1944–1989*; Znepolski, *NRB*.
33. Zhivkova, "Building the Culture," 192.
34. Zhivkov, "Work of the Ninth Congress," 130–31.
35. Tsenkov, *Socialist Revolution*: "Compared to the political and economic revolution, the cultural revolution is more prolonged because the bourgeois ideology, the bourgeois consciousness in general cannot be rapidly replaced by a completely new, socialist ideology and consciousness" (10–11).

36. Committee of Culture, *Comprehensive Programme*, 8.

37. "Kum nashite chitateli-kooperatori," inside back cover.

38. Kirilkov, "Izuchavane i vnedriavane na stahanovskite nachini za rabota v shivashkata promishlenost," 2–3. "Da se uchim ot opita na suvetskiia suiuz," 6.

39. Seizov, "Kak izpulniavam proizvodstvenia si plan i obeshtanieto sip red dr. Vulko Chervenkov," 25.

40. Panov, "Kak stanah udarnik," 25–26.

41. In 1952, *Trudovo-proizvoditelna kooperatsia* began publishing "Nashi stahanovtsi—purventsi" (Our Stakhanovites—shock workers). Typical of these early stories is that of Kiril Stoev, from the hat factory Svoboda, in Sofia. According to the story, he overfulfilled his norms by "176% realizing a savings of 6,924 leva during the third quarter of 1953." "Nashi stahanovtsi—purventsi," 15. These stories continued throughout the print run of the journal (though becoming much less central to the general tenor of the publication). As early as the 1960s, these shock workers were seen as a (somewhat nostalgic) product of a past historical epoch.

42. "Vuprosi i otgovori," 15–16.

43. Bulgarska komunisticheska partiia. See also Daskalov, *Debating the Past*, 249.

44. As Krisztina Fehérváry makes clear in socialist Hungary of the same period, "a distinctively socialist 'modern life' came to be produced during the 1960s and 1970s through new forms of housing and furnishing, and with it a new citizenry that understood themselves to be defined by their consumption habits and modern lifestyles." Fehérváry, *Politics in Color*, 78.

45. "Podrezhdane na vsekidnevna trapeza," 23. The example of how to host dinner parties expanded to cover all means of living in and through the products of developed socialism.

> The overall quality of the living quarters depends above all on the quality of the structure, on its relationship to its surroundings, the color of the walls and ceilings. This is the foundation—which furniture, what types of decorations—carpets, rugs, tablecloths, light fixtures, statues, and other things have to be in accordance with the general setting. Of real importance is built-in furniture which can take on many uses and fit into the niches of walls. Near the sink in the kitchen you should have the electric stove and the hot plates. Each house should have a good library and a wardrobe in the bedroom. Combination furniture—we constructed—is essential for every house. They fit well in tight spaces, and with a little manipulation can serve many functions. For example—this chair in the kitchen can transform into a practical step-ladder, this sofa folds out to become a bed for one or two people. This combination shelf, opens its horizontal door to become a practical table for writing.... The furniture is made of walnut, oak, elm, beech and other types of wood and is of high quality. The bedroom should have one double or two single beds of the same style as the

wardrobe. In some cases a fold out couch is favorable to a bed as it will give you a place to rest during the day. In the bedroom there has to be a toilette, though that might be moved if more convenient, and a mirror attached to the door of the wardrobe. The chairs in the room should be of a soft-form (i.e. armchairs) if need be you can add soft coverings to ordinary chairs. Presently many of us think that the best furniture can only be made of walnut. This idea is not true. There aren't good or bad types of wood—what matters most is how the furniture works harmoniously together. You should purchase furniture of the same color and style and this should apply to the sheets and tablecloths, rugs and everything else. Everything in the house should be part of a single whole creating a unified room.

Tellingly, these instructions ended with a plan for where to purchase the products required to create a unified and harmonious room.

1) Bedroom furniture of ash furniture consisting of a double bed, dresser and three door wardrobe (TPK "Stalin"—Sofia)

2) Living room of walnut furniture consisting of a combination shelf and library, a fold out couch, salon table and armchairs (TPK "1 mai," "Svoboda"—Sofia); 3) Furniture for a living room: wooden couch, two wooden chairs and a coffee table made from deciduous materials (shirokolistni materiali) (TPK "Narodna Mebel"—Sofia); 3) Furniture for a living room: Four chairs and a table made from elm with woven bulrush backing. Because of this is cheaper than usual upholstery (DVA—Sofia); 4) Walnut buffet with shelves for a library, pembroke table with four upholstered chairs (DVA—Kiustendil).

From, Atanasov, "Kak da uredi svoia dom," 20–21. See also Atanasov, "Kak da uredim doma ci," 22–23.

46. Kostov, "Za krasotata na choveshkoto tialo," 28–29. For the first time, in 1961, articles appear on yoga as a means of maintaining health. Kostov, "Fizicheskite uprazheniia na iogite," 28; see also Petrova, "Da bude zhenata zdrava i krasiva," 30.

47. McGee, *Self-Help*, 4–5.

48. Fehérváry, *Politics in Color*, 78.

49. "V magazinite na TPK," 16–17.

50. "Poveche krasota za asortimenta na stoki," 10.

51. "V pomost na domakiniiata," 16.

52. For toupees, see Konstantinesku, "Perukata," 25. For electric hair removal, see Kazanzhiev, "Obezkosmiavane s elektrichestvo," 28.

53. Kradlekov, "Krasota," 16.

54. "Hobi ili neobhodimost," 24.

55. Cartoon by Iliev, *Mestna promishlenist i uslugi*, 29.

56. "Izvodi i pouki or nashata anketa," 10–11.

57. Furniture was, apparently, a real problem. See the following complaints:

> Who among us does not want to have a beautiful bedroom, modern light furniture, a comfortable library? But it is hard to find furniture that fits the taste of the people. Still we have old, heavy, impractical furniture. Massive in construction. Take for example most people's buffet: three people could not move it from one side of the room to the next. We have wardrobes that can only be in one spot of the house because only the floor there will hold it. How much expensive wood has been spent on this furniture? Under the command of the party we are going to make up for the deficiencies in this respect. To make more beautiful, modern and light furniture. (Nikolov, "Za vseki dom," 8)

Again, the idea is that this would be the case *in every home*.

58. "Nashata anketa," 8.
59. Nikolova, "Nuzhda sa uslugi i za popravka na ski i sheini," an article published in the series "Nashata anketa" in *Kooperativna promishlenost*.
60. Nikolova, "I priematelni punktove." 12.
61. "Zhilo," 22.
62. Dragostinov, "Cartoon," 30. Dunkov, "Cartoon," 30.
63. Trichkov, "Cartoon" 30.
64. Stoianov, "Cartoon," 29.
65. Marinov, "Cartoon," 25.
66. "Bez dumi."
67. Hard, *Diogenes the Cynic*.
68. Daskalov, "Cartoon," 30.
69. It is very important to keep in mind that repression is foundational payment for any modern project. See Freud, *Civilization and Its Discontents*; and Foucault, *Discipline and Punish*.
70. This is Ivaylo Ditchev's phrase, which I find helpful. Tony Judt's great *Postwar* asks us to see, to take one example, the student revolts of 1968 in Prague, Warsaw, and Paris (and, for that matter, Mexico and the Unites States) as part of a similar phenomenon. See also Caryl, *Strange Rebels*. In this sense 1989 is merely one in a series of antimodern or postmodern trends that emerge in the period, including but not limited to the rise of religion as a (anti-)modern discourse, the move toward the postcolonial, the rejection of consumerism, revulsion against bureaucratization, and the general jettisoning of the idea of progress.

REFERENCES

Ash, Timothy Garton. *The Magic Lantern: The Revolution of '89 Witnessed in Warsaw, Budapest, Berlin, and Prague*. Reprint ed. New York: Vintage, 1999.
Astradzhiev, Penio. *Bulkarskata sotsialisticheska kultura*. Sofia: Nauka i izkustvo, 1967.

Atanasov, Georgi. "Kak da uredim doma si." *Trudovo-proizvoditelna kooperatsiia*, September 9, 1960, 22–23.

———. "Kak da uredi svoia dom." *Trudovo-proizvoditelna kooperatsiia* March 3, 1958, 20–21.

Avramov, Petur. *Kulturata i revoliutsiia v Bulgaria*. Sofia: Nauka i izkustvo, 1980.

Bell, John D. *The Bulgarian Communist Party from Blagoev to Zhivkov*. Stanford, CA: Hoover Institution Press, 1983.

"Bez dumi." *Bit i kultura*, no. 10, October 1973, 8.

Boiadzhieva, Penka. *Sotsialnoto inzhenerstvo: politiki na prien vuv visshnite uchilishta prez komunisticheskkia rezhim v Bulgaria*. Sofia: Institut za izsledvane na blizkoto minalo, 2010.

Bren, Paulina. *The Greengrocer and his TV: The Culture of Communism after the 1968 Prague Spring*. Ithaca, NY: Cornell University Press, 2010.

Bren, Paulina, and Mary Neuburger, eds. *Communism Unwrapped: Consumption in Cold War Eastern Europe*. New York: Oxford University Press, 2012.

Brunnbauer, Ulf. "'Everybody Believes That the State Does Everything for Him': An Essay on State-Society Relations in Communist Bulgaria." *Divinatio*, no. 31 (2019): 171–80.

Bulgarska komunisticheska partiia. *Sedmi kongres na partiia*. Sofia: Bulgarska komunisticheska partiia, 1958.

Caryl, Christian. *Strange Rebels: 1979 and the Birth of the 21st Century*. New York: Basic Books, 2014.

Cenkov, Boris. *Socialist Revolution and Socialist Culture*. Sofia: Sofia Press, 1971.

Committee of Culture. *Comprehensive Programme for Nationwide Aesthetic Education: Adopted at the 8th extended Plenum of the Committee of Art and Culture, Sofia, December 1975*. Sofia: Sofia Press, 1980.

Crowley, David, and Susan E. Reid, eds. *Pleasures in Socialism: Leisure and Luxury in the Eastern Bloc*. Evanston, IL: Northwestern University Press, 2010.

"Da se uchim ot opita na suvetskiia suiuz: stahanovskoto dvizhenie v ruchnoto obushtarsko proizvodstvo." *Zanaiatchiiska kooperatsiia*, June 3, 1951, 3–6.

Daskalov, Roumen. *Debating the Past: Modern Bulgarian Historiography—from Stambolov to Zhivkov*. Budapest: Central European University Press, 2013.

Daskalov, Zdravko. "Cartoon." *Kooperativna promishlenost*, no. 8 (August 1967): 30.

Dikovi, D., ed. *Bulgarskata kultura pred praga na XXI vek*. Sofia: NIN po kultura, 1982.

Ditchev, Ivaylo. "Erotika na komunizma." In *Ars Erotica*, edited by Orlin Spasov, 156–71. Sofia: Institute for Children's Literature and Art, 1992.

Doynov, Plamen. *Bulgarskiiat sotsrealizum, 1956, 1968, 1989: norma i kriza*. Sofia: Institut za izsledvane na blizkoto minalo, 2011.

Dragostinov, Kiro. "Cartoon." *Kooperativna promishlenost*, no. 11 (November 1965): 30.
Dunkov, Stoian. "Cartoon." *Kooperativna promishlenost*, no. 8 (August 1966): 30.
Elenkov, Ivan. *Kultiniiat front*. Sofia: Institut za izsledvane na blizkoto minalo, 2008.
"Hobi ili neobhodimost," *Mestna promishlenist i uslugi*, October 10, 1981, 24.
Ivanov, Martin. *Reformatorstvo bez reformi: politicheskata ikonomika na Bulgarskiia komunizum 1963–1989*. Sofia: Institut za izsledvane na blizkoto minalo, 2008.
"Izvodi i pouki." *Kooperativna promishlenost*, September 9, 1963, 10–11.
Fehérváry, Krisztina. *Politics in Color and Concrete: Socialist Materialities and the Middle Class in Hungary*. Bloomington: Indiana University Press, 2013.
Foucault, Michel. *Discipline and Punish: The Birth of the Prison*. Translated by Alan Sheridan. New York: Vintage 1995.
———. *Power*. Edited by James D. Faubion. Translated by Robert Hurley. Vol. 3 of *The Essential Works of Foucault, 1954–1984*, edited by Paul Rabinow. New York: New Press, 2001.
Freud, Sigmund. *Civilization and Its Discontents*. Edited and translated by James Strachey. New York: W. W. Norton, 2010.
Fukuyama, Francis. "The End of History." *National Interest*, no. 16 (Summer 1989): 3–18.
Ganev, Stefan. *Guidance of Bulgaria's Socialist Culture*. Sofia: Sofia Press, 1976.
Genev, Venelin I. "The Borsa: The Black Market for Rock Music in Socialist Bulgaria." *Slavic Review* 73, no. 3 (Fall 2014): 513–47.
Goldfarb, Jeffrey. *Beyond Glasnost: The Post-Totalitarian Mind*. Chicago: University of Chicago Press, 1989.
Gorsuch, Anne, and Diane Koenker, eds. *Turizm: The Russian and East European Tourist under Capitalism and Socialism*. Ithaca, NY: Cornell University Press, 2006.
Hard, Robin. *Diogenes the Cynic: Sayings and Anecdotes, with Other Popular Moralists*. New York: Oxford World Classics, 2012.
Havel, Václav. "Dear Dr. Husák." In *Open Letters: Selected Writings, 1965–1990*, 50–83. New York: Vintage Books, 1992.
Iliev, "Cartoon: Napravi sis am." *Mestna promishlenist i uslugi*, 1982, 29.
Judt, Tony. *Postwar: A History of Europe since 1945*. New York: Vintage, 2010.
Kalinova, Evgeniia. *Bulgarskata kultura i politicheskiiat imperative, 1944–1989*. Sofia: Paradigma, 2011.
Kazanzhiev, Rumen. "Obezkosmiavane s elektrichestvo." *Bit i kultura*, May 5, 1973, 28.
Kenny, Padraic. *Carnival of Revolution: Central Europe, 1989*. New ed. Princeton, NJ: Princeton University Press, 2003.

Kirilkov, S. S. "Izuchavane i vnedriavane na stahanovskite nachini za rabota v shivashkata promishlenost." *Zanaiatchiiska kooperatsiia*, May 2, 1951, 2–3.
Kornai, János. *Economics of Shortage*. Amsterdam: North-Holland, 1980.
Kostov, Konstantin. "Fizicheskite uprazheniia na iogite." *Trudovo-proizvoditelna kooperatsiia*, no. 3, March 1961, 28.
———. "Za krasotata na choveshkoto tialo." *Trudovo-proizvoditelna kooperatsiia*, January 1, 1960, 28–29.
Konstantinesku, Anda. "Perukata." *Bit i kultura*, no. 7, July, 1972: 25.
Kotkin, Stephen. *Armageddon Averted*. Updated ed. New York: Oxford University Press, 2008.
———. *Uncivil Society: 1989 and the Implosion of the Communist Establishment*. New York: Modern Library Chronicles, 2010.
Kradlekov, Ivan. "Krasota." *Kooperativna promishlenost*, June 1964, 16.
Kuranov, Chavdar. *Bulgarskoto semeistvo dnes*. Sofia: Jarastor, 1984.
Lampe, John R. *The Bulgarian Economy in the Twentieth Century*. New York: Palgrave Macmillan, 1986.
Lewin, Moshe. *The Soviet Century*. Reprint ed. New York: Verso, 2016.
Locke, John. *Two Treatises of Government*. Edited by Peter Laslett. Cambridge: Cambridge University Press, 1988.
Lowell, Stephen. *The Soviet Union: A Very Short Introduction*. New York: Oxford University Press, 2009.
Marinov, Simeon. "Cartoon." *Mestna promishlenist i uslugi*, November 1979, 25.
McGee, Nikki. *Self-Help, Inc.: Makeover Culture in American Life*. New York: Oxford University Press, 2005.
Mineva, Mila. "Razkazi i obrazi na socialistichesko potrebleniie—izsledvane na visualnoto konstrurirane na konsumativnata kultura prez 60-te gocini v Bulgaria." *Sociologicheski problem*, no. 1–2 (2003): 143–65.
"Nashata anketa: kakvi uslugi lipsvat vuv vashiia grad ili selo?" *Kooperativna promishlenost*, April 1963, 8.
"Nashata anteka: nuzhda sa uslugi i za popravka na ski i sheini." *Kooperativna promishlenost*, March 1963, 7.
"Nashi stahanovtsi—purventsi." *Trudovo-proizvoditelna kooperatsiia*, January 1954, 15.
Nikolov, Ivan. "Za vseki dom." *Kooperativna promishlenost*, February 1964, 8
Nikolova, Elisabeta. "I priematelni punktove." *Kooperativna promishlenost*, June 1963, 12.
Obretenov, Aleksandur. *The Cultural Revolution in Bulgaria*. Translated by Mihail Shipkov. Sofia: Sofia Press, 1966.
Panov, Spiridon. "Kak stanax udarnik." *Zanaiatchiiska kooperatsiia*, September–October 1951, 25–26.

Patterson, Patrick Hyder. *Bought and Sold: Living and Losing the Good Life in Yugoslavia*. Ithaca, NY: Cornell University Press, 2011.
Petrova, M. "Da bude zhenata zdrava i krasiva." *Koopertivna promishlenost*, November 1963, 30.
"Podrezhdane na vsekidnevna trapeza." *Trudovo-proizvoditelna kooperatsiia*, January 1958, 23.
"Poveche krasota za asortimenta na stoki." *Kooperativna promishlenost*, February 1964, 10.
Sakharov, Andrei. *Progress, Coexistence and Intellectual Freedom*. New York: New York Times, 1968.
Scarboro, Cristofer. *The Late Socialist Good Life in Bulgaria: Meaning and Living in a Permanent Present Tense*. Lanham, MD: Lexington Books, 2011.
———. "Today's Unseen Enthusiasm." In *Post-Communist Nostalgia*, edited by Maria Todorova and Zsuzsa Gille, 46–60. New York: Berghahn, 2010.
Seizov, Ivan. "Kak izpulniavam proizvodstvenia si plan i obeshtanieto sip red dr. Vulko Chervenkov." *Zanaiatchiiska kooperatsiia*, September–October 1951, 25.
Solzhenitsyn, Alexander. "An Exhausted West." *Harvard Magazine*, July–August 1978, 20–26.
Stoianov, Stoian, "Cartoon." *Mestna promishlenist i uslugi*, March 1982, 29.
Stokes, Gale. *The Walls Came Tumbling Down: Collapse and Rebirth in Eastern Europe*. 2nd ed. New York: Oxford University Press, 2011.
Tehnika. *Kniga za vseki den i vseki dom: Domakinska Entsiklopedia*. 1st ed. Sofia: Tehnika, 1967
———. *Kniga za vseki den i vseki dom: Domakinska Entsiklopedia*. 3rd ed. Sofia: Tehnika, 1973
———. *Kniga za vseki den i vseki dom: Domakinska Entsiklopedia*. 4th ed. Sofia: Tehnika, 1977.
Trichkov, Stefan. "Cartoon." *Bit i kultura*, April 1973, 30.
Tsenkov, Boris. *Socialist Revolution and Socialist Culture*. Sofia: Sofia Press, 1971.
"V magazinite na TPK." *Trudovo-proizvoditelna kooperatsiia*, October 1959, 16–17.
"V pomost na domakiniiata." *Bit i kultura*, February 1974, 16.
"Vuprosi i otgovori." *Zanaiatchiiska kooperatsiia*, April 1951, 15–16.
Wasiak, Partryk. "The Video Boom in Poland." *Zeitschrift für Ostmitteleuropa-Forschung*, no. 61 (2012): 27–50.
Yurchak, Alexei. *Everything Was Forever until It Was No More*. Princeton, NJ: Princeton University Press, 2005.
Zanaiatchiiska kooperatsiia, April 1951.
"Zhilo: stranitsa za humor i satira." *Trudovo-proizvoditelna kooperatsiia*, January 1957, 22.
Zhivkov, Todor. *The Cultural Policy of Socialism*. Sofia: Sofia Press, 1986.

Zhivkova, Liudmila. "Building the Culture of the Developed Socialist Society—Our Immediate and Historic Task: Report to the Third Congress of Culture, Sofia, May 18–20, 1977." In *Perfecting Man and Society*. Sofia: Sofia Press, 1980.

Znepolski, Ivailo. *Bulgarskiiat komuminzum: sotsiokulturni cherti i vlastova traektoriia*. Sofia: Institut otvoreno obshtestvo, 2008.

———, ed. *Da poznaem komunizma: izsledbaniia*. Sofia: Institut za izsledvane na blizkoto minalo, 2012.

———, ed. *NRB: Ot nachaloto do kraia*. Sofia: Institut za izsledvane na blizkoto minalo, 2011.

AUTHOR BIO

CRISTOFER SCARBORO is Professor of History at King's College in Wilkes-Barre, Pennsylvania. He is author of *The Late Socialist Good Life in Bulgaria: Living and Meaning in a Permanent Present Tense* (2011). His current research focuses on consumption and boredom in late socialist Bulgaria.

NINE

THE PROSUMERIST RESONANCE MACHINE

Rethinking Political Subjectivity and Consumer Desire in State Socialism

ZSUZSA GILLE

DIANA MINCYTĖ

Two opposing views exist in the journalistic and scholarly treatment of consumption under state socialism. The dominant one is that chronic—that is, systematically produced—shortage left most of the citizens of state socialist countries frustrated in their desire to consume. Routinely unfulfilled consumer desire then is used to explain the collapse of state socialism and/or the rush to embrace Western capitalism.[1] The other interpretation argues that low levels of consumption (which the proponents of this position are loathe to categorize as frustration or "going without") emphasize the positive consequences of the absence of consumerism while also recognizing the tremendous rise in living standards and the fairly universal fulfillment of basic needs during the decades of state socialism. Already, in the 1970s, Rudolf Bahro claimed a certain ideological and ethical priority for a dignified asceticism (today we would call it voluntary simplicity movements, except for him such simplicity would be enforced from above), and Krista Harper—echoing her many environmentalist research subjects—argues that because living standards were lower, which her subjects not quite logically attribute to low levels of industrialization, state socialism was less environmentally damaging than capitalism during the Cold War and certainly less so than post-1989 capitalism.[2] The two views are not necessarily mutually exclusive, but in general we can say that those who emphasize the significance of shortages and attribute the collapse of state socialism to frustrated consumption tend to view low-level consumption as a negative feature of central planning, while the latter tend to valorize it. However, even scholars in the latter camp admitted that the promise that living standards would continuously rise, and eventually surpass those of the West, had unintended consequences: because the state was the sole producer and distributor of all consumer goods, all problems with consumption came to be blamed on the party-state, thereby inevitably politicizing consumption.[3]

While we are sympathetic to any argument that finds some redeeming quality in existing socialism—if for no other reason than to add nuance to the dominant simplistic view of planned economies—we want to call attention to what these two otherwise radically different, if not opposing, perspectives share. First, both assume a linear and even teleological view of development and modernization that permutates the *differences* between Western consumer society and socialist central planning into *hierarchy*—that is, into a register of inferiority and superiority, expressed as lower and higher stages of development or modernization. For the first, dominant view, not only does this hierarchy imply that a higher level of development means higher levels of *individual* (as opposed to collective) consumption; it also suggests all societies need to evolve through the same stages of development in the same order and thus that state socialism was not so much a *different* kind of modernity but an *inferior* or backward one. With Judit Bodnár, we call this fallacy the *socialism package error*. As Bodnár states, "Everything that looked different in the state socialist part of the world could be accounted for by socialism. Differences came in a package, difficult to disentangle."[4] Later on, Bodnár explains: "Life was less glittery in the socialist part of the world not because it had been so even before [in great part due to the semiperipheral position of socialist countries in the world system] but because of socialism and, consequently, the lack of free markets. Methodology-conscious comparativists would say the comparison was not controlled."[5] But Bodnár contends that traditional and even properly controlled cross-national—or, in our case, cross-bloc—comparisons would also prove spurious because the units compared were not isolated, but rather they gained their distinctive features from being differentially positioned in the same global context.[6]

As a third common assumption, both perspectives operate with an essentialist and largely homogenous view of the socialist consumer. Even social scientists who are well versed in Western theories of consumption—whose foundational and enduring claim is the segmentation and differentiation of markets along various social variables (e.g., Pierre Bourdieu, Thorstein Veblen, Viviana Zelizer, Peter Corrigan, Colin Campbell, Douglas McCracken, Elizabeth Chin)—tend to only highlight one key dimension of differentiation or inequality, namely, the exceptional access to consumer goods the Djilasian new class(es) in all state socialist countries possessed. In a way, the figure of the socialist consumer tended to be a straw man or woman. It is only relatively recently that social dimensions—other than the us/them binary—have come to be researched using the concepts of Western sociology and anthropology of consumption.[7] In our personal experience in Hungary and Lithuania, as well as according to primary and secondary data, there were many different taste/status/norm groups and even consumer subcultures, and this is important because these moderated the alleged frustration of consumer desires quite significantly by generating different affective experiences of consumption.

Fourth, both views operate with a simplistic understanding of the relationship between desire and politics, that is, political subjectivity. Here again we can follow Bodnár, who in turn echoes Karl Polanyi's argument that the market means different things and operates differently depending on whether or how it is embedded in society.[8] A subsumed market's dynamic and logic, such as that of existing socialism, differed from that of developed capitalism, where it was disembedded or less embedded (though historically to a different degree). The same could be said about individual consumption. Even if we were to agree with the psychoanalytic assumption of a universal psyche, we would still have to admit that need fulfillment, libidinal energies, desires, and so on articulate differently with political consciousness in a society in which almost all needs are collectively fulfilled (or at least promised to be fulfilled) and largely appear to be free of charge and require no supplication.[9] Even beyond this basic recognition, however, we now have more sophisticated theories attending to the consumption–political consciousness relationship to allow us to treat with suspicion the mechanistic causality implied in arguments that explain political disagreement, passive resistance, or outright opposition to the party-state with low-level and low-quality consumption.

We want to unpack and problematize both ends of the causal link: consumption and political consciousness.

WHAT CONSUMPTION?

While it is almost obligatory for consumptions scholars (especially in studies calling for greater attention to consumption and for recognizing that it is not epiphenomenal or bourgeois to do so) to remind readers how even Marx did not separate production from consumption, the analytical depth to which the investigation of the relationship between consumption and production has gone to date is rather shallow. Recently this line of inquiry received a boost in the scholarship on alternative consumption. What it is an alternative to is mainstream consumption of industrially and impersonally manufactured goods, mostly quite disposable and causing social injustice and environmental degradation. To a lesser degree, in theoretical works these alternative ways of consuming are conceptualized as an allegedly new modality of capitalism.

First, with Elizabeth Chin and Jane Bennett, our point of departure in this endeavor of theorization is to see consumption as not reducible to the act of shopping, purchase, ingestion, or wearing, or what Bennett calls "the conquest model."[10] As Chin argues, "The consumption process is not limited only to the active: shopping and making purchases. Rather, it includes engagement with a diverse range of materials, images, and ideas."[11] She primarily means to broaden the study of consumption to its social and historical context in order to debunk racializing, if not racist, views of African Americans' consumer behavior. Bennett's objective is different: she wants to give some conceptual room in which we can start recognizing and understanding the agency of matter so that, rather than fully "conquering" what we consume, we come to be altered in various ways and to various degrees by what we consume. As she argues: "This material agency would include the negative power to resist or obstruct human projects, but it would also entail the active power to exert forces and create effects."[12]

For us the broader concept of consumption (yes, just like with Marx but also in the sense of the Derridean trace) includes a particular production-consumption relationship. That is, the reason why we consume the kinds of things we do—at the kinds of expense, in the kinds of quantity, with the kind of regularity or emotional investment—is because production necessitates a certain modality of consumption, and vice versa: what gets produced in what quantities, with what qualities or at what cost, is dependent on a certain modality of consumption. This relationship however is not only social (in the actor network theory sense of purely social) but also material and embodied. This hybrid and relational concept of consumption is the foundation of our argument.[13]

A growing scholarship across sociology, anthropology, and geography has focused on the emergence of new forms of, or alternative, consumption practices. The list is long and varied, including the following examples:

- Knowing the origin of the goods you buy
- Knowing the seller
- Being in the know in general (citizen-consumer)
- Practicing fair trade
- Sharing/collective consumption
- Reusing
- Recycling

- Repurposing/tinkering/upcycling
- Fixing/repair (producer responsibility)
- Buying locally
- Supporting alternative and local currencies
- Buying in bulk, no packaging (which on the whole necessitates a somewhat shorter chain linking producer and consumer)
- Using community supported agriculture (CSA)

While most likely this is not an exhaustive list, what these various types of sustainable, critical, political, or ethical acts of consumption share is a reconnection of the realm of consumption to that of production. People engaging in such projects are a far cry from the "passive receptacle" view of the consumer dominant in twentieth-century critical theory, such as the Frankfurt School's view critiqued in recent studies of consumption. Individuals and, less frequently, communities make conscious efforts to get to know the source of the goods they buy, the technologies they are made with, the inputs needed to produce them, the people or company that produces them and their way of treating employees, and their trade relations with suppliers in poorer societies, among others. They also choose more durable goods, fix and repair things, or up- and recycle them. Especially in CSAs, they get to know not only the farmers but also seek and receive information about how the harvest went, and they actually have less of a choice in what produce they get (because the contract only stipulates the value of the produce delivered and not its composition, thus giving CSA farmers security and flexibility). All of these practices challenge the underlying assumptions and organization of mass consumer society as we know it by rendering the boundary between producers and consumers more permeable.

There are however less progressive ways to suture these two realms as well. Recently several social scientists have taken up Alvin Toffler's concept of the "prosumer" to demonstrate a new modality of capitalism.[14] *Prosumption* is often defined as a set of practices that combine both production and consumption.[15] George Ritzer recognizes that previous societies were also based on prosumer subjectivity: "It was the Industrial Revolution that, to some extent, separated production and consumption, but he [Ritzer, in 'Correcting an Historical Error'] also contends that even at the height of the Industrial Revolution production and consumption were never fully distinct (producers consumed raw materials; consumers produced their meals)."[16] What previous societies Ritzer is referring to is unclear; he argues that they were premodern, but the actual evidence is sometimes from premodern societies, sometimes only Western, pre–Second World War societies. Our view is that state socialism is the only and first modernist suturing of production and consumption. In what follows we will provide empirical examples of state socialist prosumption. Many of these examples, of course, will be familiar to scholars studying Eastern Europe, but we now are placing them in a broader and analytically different frame with the goal of scrutinizing these practices for their political implications.

THE SUTURING OF PRODUCTION AND CONSUMPTION IN STATE SOCIALISM

From Above

Christina Kiaer in her excellent book *Imagine No Possessions* analyzes the many artistic and design experiments aimed at constructing objects that prevent the kind of alienation—or, in Walter Benjamin's words, "commodity phantasmagoria"—that characterizes Western capitalism.[17] The intellectual and artistic avant-garde, especially the constructivists (like Vladimir Mayakovsky or Aleksandr Rodchenko) and early Soviet ideologues, were envisioning a different relationship between humans and commodity, doing away with commodity fetishism but also with the objectification of humans in capitalism. The underlying goal of early productivism, as Kiaer shows in her analysis of the constructivist movement, was not only to "close the distance between art and life" and the object and the subject but also to consciously and purposefully revalorize daily human needs and everyday life (*byt*, in Russian).[18] While in the early years of the constructivist movement, the artists followed the Bolshevik reading of byt that emphasized the negative, even reactionary, effects of daily chores and objects on one's moral character, they later grew to embrace byt as the source of proletarian culture. In efforts to distinguish their approach from earlier meanings of byt, the artists introduced the notion of *novyi byt* (new everyday life) to underscore the unrealized potential of the socialist material culture. Novyi byt repoliticized the material in such a way that it was no longer positioned as the opposite to the spiritual or the moral. Rather, similar to Marx's materialism, the socialist object possessed transformative agency to generate human creativity and bring forth broader social changes. In practice that meant that artists were to become engineers preoccupied with designing mass goods, such as pots, beds, formulas for paints, or clothing patterns, a paradoxical move that brought them closer to the explicitly antimaterialist, ascetic ideals of the new socialist society.[19]

In addition to the visionary work aimed at reimagining the socialist object as "comrade," the socialist state promoted various forms of productive consumption activities by workers in their homes and public spaces. Examples of these efforts, especially in late socialism, include staging shows that displayed homemade artifacts, such as embroidered tablecloths, colorful teapot covers, or intricately knitted children's gloves, socks, or scarves. Showcased in museum spaces, these objects were transformed from simple handiworks made by socialist women in their spare time to works of socialist art intended to be admired and to serve as education and inspiration for others.

In a similar vein, specialty magazines, popular books, columns in newspapers, and TV programs provided advice on how to creatively furnish apartments, repair clothes, remove stains from carpets, bake cakes, or grow new varieties of fruits, berries, vegetables, and flowers in dachas. Not unlike today's alternative consumer movements in the West, these practices drew on the popular ethos of creativity, stewardship, and self-realization and were described as "do-it-yourself" (e.g., *pasidaryk pats*, in Lithuanian, *csináld magad* in Hungarian).

Yet another important example where the socialist state actively sought to create conditions for reinventing consumption and production comes from the organization of agricultural production on collective and state farms, where each household received a plot of land (approximately 1.5 acres) for subsidiary farming. Founded in the early years of socialism, these small farms were aimed as much at self-provisioning as they were designed to produce food for socialist industries and booming cities. Socialist farmers were allowed—and often contractually required—to raise such animals as pigs, cows, and chickens and grow vegetables. In all parts of the Soviet Union, subsidiary farms were tremendously important for the Soviet economy by feeding rural populations and supplying a significant proportion of food commodities to the urban market. Even as late as 1980, 75 percent of all pigs grown in Lithuania came from subsidiary farms.[20] Notably, the central feature of this subsidiary economy was the perfect melding of self-provisioning goals with industrial commodity production: the same chicken laid eggs for both collective farm employees and urban workers building Soviet industry.

This mobilization of household plots for meeting urban consumer demands in meat, fruits, and vegetables had first been tested in socialist Hungary. The experimentation of complementing state provision with private or semiprivate sources (in the latter, cooperative farms made arrangements with their members) went ahead with the explicit nod of Moscow and was later tried elsewhere in the Eastern bloc. In Hungary, by the end of the 1970s and early 1980s, the majority of nongrain produce originated in this sector, which indicates not only the objective importance of small nonstate producers for the centrally planned economy but which also sutured the spheres of production and consumption even further. First, citizens who were originally meant to be simple consumers of industrially produced alimentary goods were now becoming producers themselves (producing both for kin and the market), and, second, even consumers who did not partake in food production came into more frequent contact with small producers whom they saw everyday in open-air markets or on the streets and with whom they tried to cultivate good and personalized relations.

At the same time as various do-it-yourself and self-provisioning practices challenged the conceptual separation between consumption and production, the socialist approach also led to reimagining, if not eliminating, commodity fetishism. In our reading, fetishization has two opposites: (1) in the sense of objectification/reification and obscuring the social origins of the commodity, its opposite is subjectification (giving subjecthood to the commodity, as in "commodity as comrade"); (2) in the sense of idolatry and mystification, its opposite is politicization. The artistic or intellectual history of communism as it existed was a transition from the original utopia of subjectification to politicization. This is not the politicization we mentioned at the beginning of this chapter and what is usually meant by it in socialist and postsocialist studies. In those references politicization happens from below by citizens who are left frustrated in their ability to consume. Politicization however also happened from above, that is, by the party ideologues who throughout most of the socialist era advocated and demanded a certain responsible and even moral attitude toward individual consumption.

Defetishization from Below

It is quite likely that subjectification was the dominant attitude from below. An interesting example from a nonsocialist context is Michelle Schmidt's finding about Belizean Maya attitude to foodwaste: When it results from food they produced locally, wasting is taboo; you have to treat every morsel with respect (a kind of sanctification or sacralization). When the waste results from food bought with money and coming from elsewhere, it is not sacred and can easily be disposed of (or at least there are no prescriptions about how to dispose of it).[21] When you invest labor, you invest yourself, and the known human is always sacred to some extent. When the labor invested is that of an unknown entity (and most likely a machine or a company rather than a known individual), that sacred element is absent.

Similarly we could say that to the extent that in state socialism labor always had to be exerted in order to consume, mostly due to enduring shortages, there was no commodity fetishism of the kind Marx and neo-Marxists identified in capitalism. Instead there was sacralization. The description of how people living under communism revered Western goods, even just empty whiskey bottles, was not idolatry (which is fetishism) but a kind of sacralization.[22] That is evident in how they were reengineered (that is, invested with labor and creativity—such as how one of the author's neighbors turned whiskey bottles into lamps), how they were always narrated with a highly personalized story of coming into their possession, and how they were displayed, often in an altar-like fashion. Another widely cited example is that of imported blue jeans, especially Levi's. As with virtually all other clothing items, jeans were tailored, spared, and cared for by the consumers. Even after they were worn beyond repair, the jeans were kept at home for years, with the justification that somebody in the extended family might decide to use them. In Hungary torn or outgrown jeans were turned into shorts or haversacks that were just as highly coveted as the original pairs themselves.

More significant was the status of commodities that were domestic and were also sacralized both because of the need to invest labor in them and also because of the social relationships they expressed. In terms of labor, few commodities were consumed without altering or creatively reinventing them. From clothes and jewelry to food, furniture, cars, and dachas, socialist consumers put their time and effort into transforming mass-produced goods, raw materials, and discarded products into personalized objects endowed with meanings, memories, and markers of social relations. For example, patients in hospitals used IV lines to make ubiquitous macramé souvenirs, such as key chains or decorations. Presented as gifts to visitors and children, these artifacts embodied the values of productivity, resourcefulness, and creativity that were central to their self-respect as persons.[23] This was even more evident when people worked to bring back to life devices that had been deemed irreparable or build entire buildings from salvaged materials.

Another set of sacralization practices included gift giving, especially on the rare occasions when socialist citizens traveled to other bloc countries or the Soviet republics. Candy, bubble gum, pens and pencils, erasers, and calendars were routinely shared with neighbors, coworkers, and friends, signaling the precedence of such transactions over the actual act of ingestion or otherwise use. Notoriously difficult-to-procure gifts were central for celebrating birthdays, anniversaries, special occasions at work, or as signs of appreciation for favors. These included sets of utensils, glassware, dishes, small appliances, fragrances for women, rare books (such as novels by Western authors or encyclopedias), and tickets to cultural events, such as operas or theaters. Specialty alcohol and food items, including cognac, sparkling wine, coffee, boxes of chocolate, caviar, bananas, or even smoked sausages and game meats were rarely, if ever, consumed without company: they were designated to be shared with others. Following Jane Guyer's analytic distinction between the prevalent ideas in the West where material things in and of themselves were the repositories of wealth and the African principle of wealth in people, such an emphasis on gift giving in socialist societies suggests that the wealth might not have resided in the objects themselves but was accumulated and stored through performances reaffirming social relations.[24] By sharing special foods with others, presenting gifts that required labor and effort to acquire, and remaking commodities (sometimes even rejects) into objects imbued with meaning and affect, socialist consumers transformed them into vehicles of sociality.

Alternative consumption movements in the West/Global North today seek to resacralize commodities. They do this by suturing the realm of production and consumption (see our list above) and, by so doing, transforming the passive consumer to a conscious coproducer. By looking at actual practices rather than at ideologies of consumption in state socialism, we can see the advantages of the "backwardness" of state socialism/central planning, which eliminated commodity fetishism and the type of alienation often associated with capitalist modes of production and consumption well before similar current movements in the West. This claim upends the typical linear view we mentioned at the beginning of this chapter that sees the West as at the vanguard of all progressive experimentation in alternative consumption.

What we now have to answer is what the effects were (1) on political subjectivity and (2) on thrift/conservation, or the environmental benefits normally expected from a resacralization of consumption in today's alternative consumption movements or experiments.

WHAT POLITICS?

We have three points to make. First, this view of the relationship between consumption and political subjectivity also goes against writings by Jeffrey Goldfarb and Václav Havel, who argued for a certain convergence in late capitalist and late socialist domination (post-totalitarianism and domination through consumption à la the Frankfurt School) because both suggest a smooth and purely passive consumer: far from our empirical data and personal experiences.[25] Individual consumers in the West have few resources or reasons to creatively reappropriate the products they consume.²⁶ In a broader sense, because consumption in the West is equated with the act of shopping or using purchased goods and services, consumers find themselves at the receiving end of decisions made by marketers, retailers, industrial producers, investors, and regulators, as well as broader market forces. At the same time, in the context of a socialist society, consumption involves significant amounts of labor, from standing in lines to remaking the products, effectively producing consumers for whom consumption is inseparable from creative work and social transactions. In this sense, even mass-produced products obtained in stores may be transformed beyond recognition as they are remade by consumers and travel along social networks.

Similarly, as in Soviet Russia where environmentally minded scholars and practitioners carved out niches for openly debating and reenvisioning a different kind of socialist society (and nature), numerous Lithuanian intellectuals and professionals, especially the younger generations that came of age after the Second World War, were involved in what could be considered countercultural explorations.²⁷ But even before the movements of the late 1980s transformed Lithuania's political stage, there were less visible yet significant countercultural circles organized around artist workshops and music and clothing subcultures.

Echoing the constructivist artists' critiques of *meshchanstvo* (philistinism, in Russian), artists in Lithuania voiced strong critiques of the proliferation of kitsch in popular culture, such as the embrace of mass-produced objects (e.g., mass-produced copies of famous paintings, plastic souvenirs, or fake flowers) used to decorate the homes of the lower echelons of Soviet society.²⁸ In turn, many such artists—whom one of us met in the 1980s—lived and worked in studios that were significantly different from the cookie-cutter apartments built across the Soviet Union. (Think here of the famous 1974 Soviet romantic comedy *The Irony of Fate; or, Enjoy Your Bath!*, where a Muscovite protagonist wakes up in Leningrad after a long night of drinking and does not even realize he is not home because the lock, the apartment, the furniture, and the views from the window are so uniform.) Because the studios often lacked basic amenities, such as showers/bathtubs and kitchens, artists used them as a stage for reinventing modern infrastructures from scratch, resulting in unusual plumbing solutions, where, for example, water was delivered via an intricate hosing system, or novel uses of space, such as when eating/cooking areas were left open, without any walls to separate them from the rest of the space. Such a creative integration of living and working spaces served as both a manifestation of and a backdrop to the frequent debates about the future of art, culture, and politics. But even more important than these spatial arrangements or conversations was the formation of a counterculture that was critically engaged in questioning the proliferation of mass-produced goods.

As a side note, one can ask whether it was easier to be critical of consumerism when the things you could buy were not objects of desire, allowing these "activists" or experimenters to be inspired and freely borrow from synchronous countercultures rejecting consumerism in the West (one way to upset the linearity assumed in any talk of backwardness).[29]

The second point we want to make about the relationship between consumption and political subjectivity is the applicability of William E. Connolly's concept of the resonance machine, though in an admittedly different social context from the one in which it was coined.[30] Connolly is one of the many progressive political theorists in the United States who tries to remedy the American left's inability or unwillingness to aestheticize politics, to target hearts rather than minds, to use dogmatic rhetoric (see the attacks on Michael Moore), to mobilize affect especially through images, to hail people in their identity rather than in their interests.[31] While we have no space here to summarize the philosophical and political debates centering on this question, it is fair to say that Antonio Gramsci, Louis Althusser, Stuart Hall, Jürgen Habermas, Charles Taylor, Iris Marion Young, Nancy Fraser, and Wendy Brown have been key interlocutors. Connolly's initial objective was to understand the effectiveness of neoconservatism in the United States. Replacing the long-repudiated leftist concepts such as false consciousness, but even Theodor Adorno's concept of the culture industry or Benjamin's aestheticization of politics, he nevertheless does not reject the importance of the subconscious.[32] He relies on new research in neuroscience to understand more precisely the mechanisms of subconscious or subliminal (subcortical) processes. The idea here is that the brain, rather than having a set of biologically or anatomically determined operations, physically changes as a result of social impulses, which then affect the emotional and cognitive reactions people experience in their everyday lives. These effects and responses create layer upon layer of synaptic connections and other structures in the brain so that the brain-body-politics connection resembles interweaving layers of culture and nature, not one preceding and causing the other. This effectively debunks previous linear and mechanistic causal models of political consciousness formation, replacing it with what he calls the resonance machine. A key feature of this mechanism is that it is fast, so that it bypasses the conscious, and unpredictable. Connolly in his "The Evangelical-Capitalist Resonance Machine" article demonstrated that the relationship between neoliberalism and evangelicals is not causal; it is a matter of resonance, echoing back and forth. Equally importantly he argues—again relying on scientific discoveries—that the brain is malleable, which opens up the possibility of a new way of doing politics on the left, of whose politics of ressentiment he rejects.[33] Instead he favors creativity that would build a democratic, progressive counter resonance.[34] He is particularly hopeful of the analytical tools film theory has to offer in making ourselves aware of how this micropolitics (of the brain) affects us and how then to use that understanding toward progressive ends.

While Connolly never explicitly identified with what we in the social sciences call the practice turn, the similarities, at least in objectives between his framework and the more recent and more nuanced applications of Bourdieu's habitus and Elizabeth Shove's practice-oriented understanding of consumer behavior are striking, which invites us to provide a synthesis.[35]

At the core of such a practice-centered approach is a move away from the mentalist paradigm dominating the social theory at the end of the twentieth century and defined by its many isms, including "intellectualism, representationalism, individualisms (e.g., rational choice theory, methodological individualism, network analysis), structuralism, structure-functionalism, systems theory, semiotics, and numerous strains of humanism and poststructuralism."[36] Drawing on ethnomethodology, science and technology studies, feminist scholarship, and Pierre Bourdieu's writings, especially his concepts of field and habitus, scholars working in the tradition of the practice turn emphasize the place of nonpropositional knowledge, embodied experience, routines, intersubjectivity, and nonhuman agency as building blocks for articulating a theory of the social where power struggles, social relations, and political order are constructed through the body-activity-society nexus (in contrast to individual decisions, preferences, and behaviors, on the one hand, and social structures, on the other).

In her efforts to rethink consumption through the practice approach, Shove focuses on "inconspicuous routines and habits," such as laundering habits in modern Britain, to show how individual actions are shaped by historically situated collective conventions of what constitutes comfort, cleanliness, and convenience.[37] Shove's research brilliantly shows how daily routines (note the similarity to what the constructivist artists defined as byt) play a key role in normalizing and increasing the use of resources. In so doing, Shove's analysis points to the politicization of the entire set of public and private institutions that shape the evolution of conventions rather than of the individual consumer per se.

With this more sophisticated model of the relationship between consumption and political consciousness, we are now ready to explain some of our findings. The Communist Party in the early 1950s organized several material conservation campaigns in Hungary. Just to mention a few: the Utkin movement's participants wished to produce more or the same amount as others while using less material; the Gazda movement mobilized workers to reuse industrial scrap materials (mostly metals); and the Csorba movement, initiated by the Kossuth prize recipient, encouraged furnacemen to economize on coal use. While historians have treated these as yet another series of production-helping efforts to hasten plan fulfillment—along with the most notable such movement, Stakhanovism—the material-conservation and, especially, the waste-reuse campaigns enjoyed genuine popularity.[38] This is evident from the many letters ordinary people (who were not specifically asked to participate) sent in to the party or to the planning bureau about how to reuse certain discarded objects (bent nails, burned-out bulbs, beer bottle caps—to name just the weirdest/coolest examples). In my (Gille's) 2007 book, I talked about how these movements and campaigns *resonated* with ordinary citizens from all walks of life.[39] With Connolly's concept we can now provide a better understanding of the "mechanism" (which ironically is too mechanistic of a term for Connolly's intentions) by which the party's ideological goals created a desired but far-from-guaranteed positive reaction and action in people.

While in the United States sound/image/word associations are strategically developed by think tanks (the pro-life campaign is a case in point), in socialist countries, we would argue, such resonances were largely a hit-and-miss endeavor. What were the sound/image/word assemblages that moved and mobilized socialist citizens? And what implications do they have for understanding political consciousness under state socialism, which we now know must go beyond the accommodation/resistance binary?[40]

It is easy to use such examples to illustrate what has been said many times about the inevitable politicization of consumption in state socialism. However, we think it is the concept of the political that needs to be redefined. We advocate for a Connollian, practice-turn type of notion of politics, which starts not in ideology, identity, and culture but in everyday practice and materiality.

Third, we emphasize that we do not propose a "noble savage" view of the socialist consumer. Rather, our empirical claim could be viewed as an instance of what, since Thorstein Veblen, we call the advantage of the latecomer (the advantage of backwardness).[41] In this case, such a view would mean that a new post-1989 alternative could have built on this existing sutured producer/consumer, either in the interest of environmental sustainability or in the interest of avoiding the Western trap of mass consumerism. Instead, as happened in so many other realms, postsocialist societies first had to be thrown back to the past of the West. In my work on waste, for example, I showed that the above-mentioned institutions focusing on waste reuse and recycling had to be dismantled in the early 1990s as elements of excessive state intervention in the economy. As waste was no longer encouraged to be reused or recycled, eliminating waste by dumping or incineration came to be seen as the economically sensible solution, even if much less desirable from an environmental perspective. At the same time, the diminished capacity of the state made it possible for much of this disposal to take place without permission and without professional oversight. Until the European Union's waste policies were finally implemented—many with a fifteen-year-long derogation after accession in 2004— postsocialist Eastern Europe functioned as a veritable wasteland. Even more consequentially, because this was the period in which much of the foundations of capitalism were laid down, the domination of end-of-pipe policies and technologies (rather than the waste preventative practices of reuse and recycling) were locked in, rendering later efforts to switch to a greener pathway more difficult.[42]

Similarly, Johanna Bockman demonstrated how in several former socialist countries that had already privatized some state assets, employee ownership had to first be renationalized so that later they could be given to the "correct" owners through the managed privatization of the early 1990s.[43] Finally, Eva Fodor's work on gender inequality could also serve as an example of such a missed opportunity to build on the few redeeming qualities of state socialism. She showed how women's job participation has actually been higher in former socialist countries than in Western Europe, so the idea that postsocialist societies needed the tutelage of Western feminism—state or civic—was absurd.[44]

Analogously, we argue that to the extent that consumption was not alienated in the forms known in Western countries—where you have to invest labor to resacralize the consumer good—these societies missed an opportunity to enjoy the advantage of latecomers, to build on a kind of proto-postconsumerist or postmaterialist subject. That is, the backwardness paradigm/linear development paradigm in which stages of development cannot be skipped prevailed. This is the poverty of imagination not of postsocialist political subjects (as Habermas claimed) but of Western institutions and powerful entities managing the transition.

NOTES

1. For notable exceptions to these trends, see Bren and Neuburger, *Communism Unwrapped*; Reid, "Who Will Beat Whom?"; Berdahl, *Where the*

World Ended; for a critique, see Fehérváry, "Goods and States." Moreover, this "rush" is interpreted differently in different ideological camps. On the progressive end, we find Jürgen Habermas, who argued that the revolutions of 1989 were marked by a "total lack of ideas that are either innovative or orientated towards the future" (see Habermas, "What Does Socialism Mean," 5).

2. Bahro, *Alternative in Eastern Europe*; Harper, *Wild Capitalism*.

3. See Verdery, "What Was Socialism"; Burawoy and Lukács, *Radiant Past*, among others.

4. Bodnár, "Socialism Package Error," 1.

5. Ibid., 3–4.

6. The type of comparative method that can take into account such relationality is called incorporated comparison by Philip McMichael and relational comparison by Gillian Hart—see the introduction to this volume and McMichael, "Incorporating Comparison"; Hart, "Relational Comparison Revisited."

7. For example, see Berdahl, *Where the World Ended*; Bren, *Greengrocer and His TV*; Fehérváry, "Goods and States."

8. Bodnár, "Socialism Package Error"; Polanyi, *Great Transformation*.

9. The semblance of gratis services (education, school and workplace meals, housing, roads) and the heavily subsidized utilities and food were, of course, made possible by invisible taxation (see Burawoy, *Politics of Production*, on the political significance of invisible extraction of surplus, and Bodnár, "Socialism Package Error").

10. See Chin, *Purchasing Power*; and Bennett, "Edible Matter."

11. Chin, *Purchasing Power*, 7.

12. Bennett "Edible Matter," 143

13. Emirbayer, "Manifesto."

14. Toffler, *Third Wave*.

15. For a typology of prosumption practices, see Ritzer and Jurgenson, "Production, Consumption, Prosumption"; Dujarier, "Three Sociological Types"; and Graham and Thrift, "Out of Order."

16. Ritzer and Jurgenson, "Production, Consumption, Prosumption," 17; Ritzer, "Correcting an Historical Error."

17. Kiaer, *Imagine No Possessions*; Benjamin, *Arcade Project*.

18. Kiaer, *Imagine No Possessions*, 5.

19. Ibid., 52–53.

20. Vaga, *Lietuvos TSR Liaudies Ūkis*, 145–57; Mincyte, "Everyday Environmentalism."

21. Schmidt, "Respect and Humiliation."

22. See Berdahl, *Where the World Ended*; Berdahl, "'(N)Ostalgie' for the Present"; and Fehérváry, "Goods and States."

23. See also Fehérváry, "Goods and States," 403.
24. Guyer, "Introduction."
25. Goldfarb, *Beyond Glasnost*; Havel, *Power of the Powerless*.
26. Recently, however, the makers' movement and such popular pastimes as IKEA hacking have reintroduced remaking goods, not so much because of need but to express individuality.
27. Weiner, *Little Corner of Freedom*; Rinkevicius, "Transitional Economies."
28. Kiaer, *Imagine No Possessions*, 65.
29. See Havel's argument about living in truth (Havel, *Power of the Powerless*) and the Czechoslovakian countercultural/underground music group the Plastic People of the Universe's lyrics.
30. Connolly, "Evangelical-Capitalist Resonance Machine."
31. Although, as we are finalizing this, public debates in the wake of Trump's electoral victory suggest that when the left engages in identity politics—if indeed it does—it may backfire or whip up an even stronger white identity political backlash than previously.
32. Benjamin, "Work of Art."
33. Connolly, "Evangelical-Capitalist Resonance Machine."
34. Ibid., 870.
35. Bourdieu, *The Logic of Practice*; Shove, *Comfort, Cleanliness, Convenience*.
36. Schatzki, "Introduction," 2.
37. Shove, *Comfort, Cleanliness, Convenience*.
38. Pető and Szakács, *A hazai gazdaság négy évtizedének története*, 102.
39. Gille, *Cult of Waste*.
40. See Yurchak, *Everything Was Forever*.
41. Veblen, *The Theory of the Leisure Class*.
42. Gille, *From the Cult of Waste to the Trash Heap of History*.
43. Bockman, *Markets*.
44. Fodor, "State Socialist Emancipation Project."

REFERENCES

Bahro, Rudolf. *The Alternative in Eastern Europe*. London: New Left Books, 1978.
Benjamin, Walter. *The Arcade Project*. Translated by Howard Eiland. Cambridge, MA: Belknap, 2002.
———. "The Work of Art in the Age of Mechanical Reproduction." In *Illuminations: Essays and Reflections*, 217–52. New York: Schocken Books, 1968 (1936).
Bennett, Jane. "Edible Matter." *New Left Review* 45 (May–June 2007): 133–45.
Berdahl, Daphne. "'(N)Ostalgie' for the Present: Memory, Longing, and East German Things." *Ethnos* 64, no. 2 (1999): 192–211.

———. *Where the World Ended: Re-unification and Identity in the German Borderland*. Los Angeles: University of California Press, 1999.
Bockman, Johanna. *Markets in the Name of Socialism: The Left-Wing Origins of Neoliberalism*. Stanford, CA: Stanford University Press, 2011.
Bodnár, Judit. "The Socialism Package Error." *European Studies Forum* 39, no. 1 (2009): 23–28.
Bourdieu, Pierre. *The Logic of Practice*. Cambridge, MA: Polity Press, 1990.
Bren, Paulina. *The Greengrocer and His TV: The Culture of Communism after the 1968 Prague Spring*. Ithaca, NY: Cornell University Press, 2010.
Bren, Paulina, and Mary Neuburger. *Communism Unwrapped: Consumption in Cold War Eastern Europe*. New York: Oxford University Press, 2012.
Burawoy, Michael. *The Politics of Production*. London: Verso, 1985.
Burawoy, Michael, and János Lukács. *The Radiant Past: Ideology and Reality in Hungary's Road to Capitalism*. Chicago: University of Chicago Press, 1992.
Chin, Elizabeth. *Purchasing Power: Black Kids and American Consumer Culture*. Minneapolis: University of Minnesota Press, 2001.
Connolly, William E. "The Evangelical-Capitalist Resonance Machine." *Political Theory* 33, no. 6 (2005): 869–86.
Dujarier, Marie-Anne. "The Three Sociological Types of Consumer Work." *Journal of Consumer Culture* 16, no. 2 (2016): 555–71.
Emirbayer, Mustafa. "Manifesto for a Relational Sociology." *American Journal of Sociology* 103, no. 2 (1997): 281–317.
Fehérváry, Krisztina. "Goods and States: The Political Logic of State-Socialist Material Culture." *Comparative Studies in History and Society* 51, no. 2 (2009): 426–59.
Fodor, Éva. "Smiling Women and Fighting Men: The Gender of the Communist Subject in State Socialist Hungary." *Gender and Society* 16, no. 2 (April 2002): 240–63.
———. "The State Socialist Emancipation Project: Gender Inequality in Workplace Authority in Hungary and Austria Fodor." *Signs* 29, no. 3 (Spring 2004): 783–813.
Goldfarb, Jeffrey. *Beyond Glasnost: The Post-Totalitarian Mind*. Chicago: University of Chicago Press, 1989.
Graham, Stephen, and Nigel Thrift. "Out of Order: Understanding Repair and Maintenance." *Theory, Culture and Society* 24, no. 3 (2007): 1–25.
Gille, Zsuzsa. *From the Cult of Waste to the Trash Heap of History: The Politics of Waste in Socialist and Postsocialist Hungary*. Bloomington: Indiana University Press, 2007.
Guyer, Jane. "Introduction." *Journal of African History* 36, no. 1 (1995): 83–90.
Havel, Václav. *The Power of the Powerless: Citizens against the State in Central Eastern Europe*. Edited by John Keane. Armonk, NY: M. E. Sharpe, 1985.

Harper, Krista. *Wild Capitalism: Environmental Activists and Post-Socialist Political Ecology in Hungary*. Boulder, CO: East European Monographs, 2006.

Hart, Gillian. "Relational Comparison Revisited: Marxist Postcolonial Geographies in Practice." *Progress in Human Geography* 42, no. 3 (2016): 371–94.

Habermas, Jürgen. "What Does Socialism Mean Today? The Rectifying Revolution and the Need for New Thinking on the Left." *New Left Review*, no. 183 (September–October 1990): 3–21.

Kiaer, Christina. *Imagine No Possessions: The Socialist Objects of Russian Constructivism*. Boston: MIT Press, 2005.

Vaga. *Lietuvos TSR Liaudies Ūkis*. Vilnius: Vaga, 1981.

McMichael, Philip. "Incorporating Comparison within a World-Historical Perspective: An Alternative Comparative Method." *American Sociological Review* 55, no. 3 (June 1990): 385–97.

Merkel, Ina. "From Stigma to Cult: Changing Meanings in East German Consumer Culture." In *The Making of the Consumer: Knowledge, Power and Identity in the Modern World*, edited by Frank Trentmann, 249–70. Oxford: Berg, 2006.

Mincyte, Diana. "Everyday Environmentalism: The Practice, Politics, and Nature of Subsidiary Farming in Stalin's Lithuania." *Slavic Review* 68, no. 1 (2009): 31–49.

Pető, Iván, and Sándor Szakács. *A hazai gazdaság négy évtizedének története, 1945–1985. I.* Budapest: Közgazdaságiés Jogi Könyvkiadó, 1985.

Polanyi, Karl. *The Great Transformation: The Political and Economic Origins of Our Time*. New York: Farrar & Rinehart, 1944.

Reid, Susan E. "Who Will Beat Whom? Soviet Popular Reception of the American National Exhibition in Moscow, 1959." *Kritika* 9, no. 4 (2008): 855–904.

Rinkevicius, Leonardas. "Transitional Economies: Ecological Modernisation as Cultural Politics; Transformations of Civic Environmental Activism in Lithuania." *Environmental Politics* 9, no. 1 (2000): 171–202.

Ritzer, George. "Correcting an Historical Error." Keynote address at the Conference on Prosumption, Frankfurt, Germany, March 2009.

Ritzer, George, and Nathan Jurgenson. "Production, Consumption, Prosumption: The Nature of Capitalism in the Age of the Digital 'Prosumer.'" *Journal of Consumer Culture* 10, no. 1 (2010): 13–36.

Ryazanov, Elidar, dir. *The Irony of the Fate: Or Enjoy Your Bath*. Moscow: Mosfilm, 1976.

Schatzki, Theodore R. "Introduction: Practice Theory." In *The Practice Turn in Contemporary Theory*, edited by Theodore R. Schatzki, Karin Knorr Cetina, and Eike von Savigny, 1–15. New York: Routledge, 2001.

Schmidt, Michelle. "Respect and Humiliation: Mopan Conceptions of Food Waste in San Jose, Belize." Paper presented at the Future of Waste symposium, University of Illinois at Urbana-Champaign, March 2, 2013.

Shove, Elizabeth. *Comfort, Cleanliness, Convenience: The Social Organization of Normality*. Oxford: Berg, 2003.

Toffler, Alvin. *The Third Wave*. New York: William Morrow, 1980.

Veblen, Thorstein. *The Theory of the Leisure Class: An Economic Study of Institutions*. New York: W. E. Huebsch, 1899.

Verdery, Katherine. "What Was Socialism, and Why Did It Fall?" In *What Was Socialism and What Comes Next?* 19–38. Princeton, NJ: Princeton University Press, 1994.

Weiner, Douglas R. *A Little Corner of Freedom: Russian Nature Protection from Stalin and Gorbachev*. Berkeley: University of California Press, 2002.

Yurchak, Alexei. *Everything Was Forever, until It Was No More*. Princeton, NJ: Princeton University Press, 2006.

AUTHOR BIO

ZSUZSA GILLE is Professor of Sociology and Director of Global Studies at the University of Illinois at Urbana-Champaign. She is author of *Paprika, Foie Gras, and Red Mud: The Politics of Materiality in the European Union* (2016) and *From the Cult of Waste to the Trash Heap of History: The Politics of Waste in Socialist and Postsocialist Hungary* (2007—recipient of honorable mention of the AAASS Davis Prize), coeditor of *Post-Communist Nostalgia* with Maria Todorova (2010), and coauthor of *Global Ethnography: Forces, Connections and Imaginations in a Postmodern World* (2000). She was the special guest editor of a thematic cluster on "Nature, Culture, Power" (2009) published in the *Slavic Review*.

DIANA MINCYTĖ is Associate Professor of Sociology at the City University of New York's New York City College of Technology. She publishes on the environmental and social dimensions of agro-food politics in Eastern Europe. She coedited a number of special issues in journals, including a thematic cluster with Ulrike Plath on environmental and food politics in the Baltic states that received the Vilis Vitols best publication award from the Association for the Advancement of Baltic Studies and was republished as *Food Culture and Politics in the Baltic States* (2017).

INDEX

aesthetics, 36, 198
affect, 121, 170, 182, 220, 227, 229, 230
agrarian, 34, 36, 37
alcoholism, 34, 94
alienation, 8, 18, 196, 197, 201, 206, 223, 227
Angola, 112–13
Appadurai, Arjun, 8, 179
Austerity, 121, 68, 95, 96, 111
Austria, 2, 3, 121
Außenhandelsbetrieb (AHB) Genußmittel, 114
autonomy, 11, 15, 33, 53, 60, 192

backwardness, 1–5, 8, 11, 18, 25–27, 31–32, 36, 39, 41, 42, 52, 55, 138, 154, 163–64, 168, 170, 173, 182, 191, 193, 227, 29, 231, 232
Balkanturist, 40
bananas, 13, 105, 108, 111, 115, 121–23, 227
barter, 58, 61, 106, 111–16
Belgium, 2
Bennett, Jane, 221
Berdahl, Daphne, 14, 109, 118
Betts, Paul, 119, 122
Beziehungen, 109
Bit i kultura, 198, 203, 205–7
Black Sea Coast, 40, 42
Bockman, Johanna, 83, 232
Bodnár, Judit, 9, 219–20
bolshevism, 37–38, 223
boredom, 5, 195
Botev, Khristo, 33
Bourdieu, Pierre, 219

bourgeois, 5, 6, 14, 38, 73, 191, 193, 196–98, 220
Brus, Włodzimierz, 85–86, 90–92, 96
Bulgaria, 2, 5, 7, 10, 15, 17, 18, 30, 32–42, 58, 190, 193–98, 204, 205, 207
(Bulgarian) national revival, 32
Bulgarian Agrarian National Union, 36–37
Bulgarian Communist Party, 17, 36, 193, 198
business, 53–54, 104, 112, 114, 141–44, 147–48, 165, 168, 170, 173–76, 178
byt, 223–24

capitalism, 5–6, 8, 12, 18, 26, 34, 37, 40–41, 58, 69–71, 83, 86, 90, 92–97, 118, 154, 162–63, 180, 190, 195, 218, 220–24, 226, 232
capital accumulation, 86, 87, 89, 96, 97
Certeau, Michel de, 106, 116–17
Chervenkov, Vulko, 198–99
Chin, Elizabeth, 219, 221
China, 58, 168–69, 171, 180, 181
citrus fruits, 105, 107, 112–16, 122
citizens, 6, 8–11, 14, 15, 17, 18, 31, 39–41, 53–54, 58–61, 64–65, 69–74, 105–7, 109, 111, 116–23, 144, 164, 166–67, 170, 182, 197–98, 218, 225–26, 231
citizenship, 14, 17, 53–55, 57, 61
civilization, 25–26, 57, 180, 182
civilization competence, 180
class, 29, 31, 39, 109, 141–42; artisan, 34–5; classless society, 142; consciousness of, 5; high, 121; lower, 29; middle-class, 2, 5–6, 12, 18, 28, 94, 142, 152, 164–65, 169–73,

class (*continued*)
176–79; new, 220, 235; working-class, 5, 10, 34, 63, 86, 141, 149–50, 203
coffee, 6, 17, 28, 104–14, 117–23, 166, 227; Coffee Agreement between the GDR and Ethiopia of 1977, 113; crisis of, 109, 111–14, 121. *See also* Kosta, Kaffee-Mix, Mocca-Fix, Mona, Rondo, Westkaffee
collapse, 1, 5, 27, 66, 83, 93, 148, 163, 167, 175, 176, 191, 193, 207, 218
Commercial Coordination Division (*Bereich Kommerzielle Koordinierung*), 111
commodity, 10–15, 26, 105, 107, 109, 112, 117–18, 122–23, 135, 137, 141, 144–47, 150, 162, 165, 166, 168–69, 174–78, 180–83, 224, 226; defetishization, 225; fetishism of, 18, 28, 204, 223, 225, 226, 227
Communist Party, 1, 4–6, 9–10, 15–16, 36, 56, 59–61, 65–70, 91, 104, 105, 107, 108, 111, 120, 123, 193–99, 207, 219, 220, 225, 231
Committee on Art and Culture, 7, 197
Comprehensive Program for Nationwide Aesthetic Education, 7, 197
Comprehensive Program for Social Economic Integration (1976), 115
Connolly, William E., 229–30
constructivism, 223, 228, 230
consumer, 4, 11, 58, 60, 66, 70, 86, 94, 104, 106–16, 122, 123, 132, 133, 137, 140, 142, 143, 144, 148, 150, 152, 162, 164–68, 171, 175, 178, 180, 181, 183, 194, 202, 203, 205, 222, 225, 226–28, 230; abundance, 63, 74, 82; advertising, 61, 69; aspiration, 142, 162, 164; bargain of, 72–73; beauty, 204; bourgeois, 198; choice, 162, 164, 165; citizenship, 17, 40, 52, 121, 167, 221; consumer behavior/practices, 17, 18, 27–29, 31–32, 37–38, 40–41, 106, 117, 123, 135, 164–65, 173, 175, 177, 178, 180, 182, 221, 230; consumer–friendly economic policy, 57, 62, 64, 65, 68; consumer good, 232; consumer goods, 6, 8–9, 12, 27, 39, 40, 62, 64, 68, 82, 86–87, 105, 107–9, 119, 121, 132, 138, 139, 140, 141, 143, 147, 149, 150, 153, 154, 164, 168, 191, 193–99, 219; consumer preference, 59, 69; consumer pride, 169; consumer-producer, 222; consumer strategies, 107–8, 118, 121;

consumer trends, 169; consumer turn, 39; cooperatives, 37; culture, 18, 26, 28, 31, 55–57, 62, 82, 107, 114, 132–36, 138, 154, 171, 173, 182; demand, 10, 17, 53–54, 71, 84, 92–93, 105, 107, 108, 121, 139, 170, 176, 204, 224; desire, 5, 17–18, 26, 29, 40–41, 59, 68, 93, 106, 123, 132, 139, 143, 144, 148, 153, 171, 182, 191, 202, 218, 220; dialogues/discourse, 1, 5, 40, 165, 170, 177; displeasure, 15, 16, 34, 37, 41, 68, 111–12, 117, 118, 164, 182; elite, 143; excess, 41; experience, 54; fear, 119; future, 193; guides, 147; identity, 73, 134–35, 144; logic, 180; middle-class, 165, 169, 179, 180, 182; model, 41; modernity, 206; movement, 150, 224; needs, 40, 89; passive, 227; past, 173, 182; pleasure, 15, 18, 61; policy, 105, 107–8, 152; production, 83, 83, 87, 90–91; protection, 144; protests, 121; reality, 180; republic, 73; restraint, 37; revolt, 118; revolution, 28; satisfaction, 60, 72, 164–65, 173; scarcity, 112, 118; sector, 67; socialist, 11, 18, 62, 71–72, 114, 118, 123, 133, 137, 152, 153, 219, 220, 226, 227, 231; society, 5, 6, 56, 104–5, 114, 123, 141, 193, 196, 198, 201, 222; sovereignty, 105; status, 149; struggle, 173; subculture, 220; voices, 106; welfare, 69; well-being, 182; Western, 12, 14, 28, 34, 41, 69, 121, 139; worker-consumers, 64–65, 67, 72
consumerism, 10, 15, 27, 58, 62, 69, 82, 105, 107–8, 164–65, 218, 229, 231; absence of, 218; socialist, 62; Western, 10, 27, 69, 231; Yugoslav, 58; consumerist culture, 54–55; consumerist ideology, 6, 14, 26, 29, 31, 60, 69, 196, 198; consumerist policy, 64, 68
consumption, 2–18, 25–33, 34, 38, 54, 56–58, 63, 67–68, 70–96, 104, 108–9, 111, 115, 123, 132, 135, 138, 139, 141, 143, 144, 147–52, 164–67, 170, 177, 179–80, 182, 183, 190, 194–96, 198–99, 201, 202, 204, 206, 108, 219–32; affluent, 132, 133, 143, 153; alienation, 18, 196, 201, 223, 227; alternative, 220–25, 227; capitalist, 11, 16, 18, 61, 82, 138; collective, 3–4, 7, 9, 18, 67, 149, 153, 219, 221; conspicuous, 94; Eastern, 31; identity, 132–33, 135, 136, 141, 148, 153; ideology, 190; mass, 40, 62, 73, 80, 132–33, 136, 140, 142,

144, 149–54, 169, 178, 196; modern, 136, 206; moral economy, 32, 36; Ottoman, 32; patterns of, 26–28, 32, 38, 109, 123, 143, 164–65, 167, 178, 191; personal/individual, 4–5, 8,–10, 59, 60, 68, 70, 72, 82, 86, 92, 94, 106, 117, 132, 149, 192, 194–95, 206, 220, 225, 227, 230; policies, 9, 38, 53, 59, 60, 62–65, 107–8, 135–36, 139; politics, 28, 28, 132–33, 136, 142, 151–52, 222, 231; pleasure of, 6, 8, 12–18, 34, 71, 73, 121, 142, 162, 191–93, 195, 204–6; practices/habits, 11, 14–15, 17–18, 25–29, 31, 33–34, 38, 40–41, 106–7, 111, 116–18, 123, 135, 138, 141, 143, 149, 164–65, 173, 177, 182, 201, 221; and production, 83, 153, 204, 220, 222–25, 227; rational, 11, 27, 41, 84, 89–97, 202; socialist, 2–18, 64, 90; Soviet, 38; state-planned, 178; welfare, 58; Western, 11–12, 14–15, 28, 31, 36, 37, 61, 82, 179, 191
contract, 6, 17, 39, 52–74, 107, 111, 123, 190, 192. *See also* social contract
cooperatives, 36–37, 138, 198, 202, 203, 205
creativity, 28, 195, 223, 224, 226, 230
Cold War, 1, 3, 5, 18, 27, 40, 52–53, 67, 82, 84, 97, 105, 114, 133, 136, 138, 179, 193, 218
convergence, 192–94, 227
Council for Mutual Economic Assistance (COMECON, CMEA), 112, 114
Council of Ministers, 108, 118
Cuba, 104–5, 107, 112, 114–16
Czechoslovakia, 2, 12, 14, 15, 56, 61, 66, 91, 192–93

desire, 5–7, 12, 17–19, 26–29, 32, 38–41, 53, 54, 59, 63, 65, 68, 69, 72, 86, 87, 92–97, 106, 117, 132, 135, 141–44, 148, 149, 153, 162, 164, 167, 171, 173, 175–77, 179–83, 191–92, 202–3, 218, 220, 229, 231
debt crisis of the Eastern bloc, 111
Delikat, 104, 109
Dependency, 15, 86, 179
Derg, the, 104, 109
developed socialism, 2, 105, 132, 137, 190, 194–98
development, 2, 5–8, 18–19, 40, 89, 90, 92, 138, 153, 165, 168, 170, 173, 179, 180, 183, 191, 193–98, 204, 219, 232
Diogenes, 207

Diunov, Petur/Diunovtsi, 34–35
do-it-yourself (DIY), 15, 18, 204, 224–25
Drakulić, Slavenka, 57–58, 73

East/Eastern(ers), 4, 12, 15, 27, 31, 32, 40, 60, 136, 193
Eastern Bloc, 39, 40, 41, 83, 107, 108, 111, 116–17, 122, 133, 142, 154, 224
Eastern Europe, 1, 2, 5–9, 15, 17, 18, 25–27, 29, 31, 37, 39, 41, 52–54, 63, 67, 68, 83, 108, 118, 122, 133, 136, 137, 146, 148, 154, 190–91, 193, 195, 223, 232
East Germany. *See* German Democratic Republic
economic liberalization, 52, 53, 162
Eigen-Sinn, 123
Eingaben, 119, 122
environmental, benefits, 227; economic calculations, 232; degradation/problems, 219, 221
equilibrium, 83, 93
erotics of stagnation, 192
Ethiopia, 107, 112–14
Euromaidan, 162–65, 169, 171, 173, 181–83
Europeaness, 10, 173
Exquisit, 104, 109

famine, 38
fascism, 14, 37
fast fashion, 177, 178, 182
Faust, 52, 55, 75n20; Faustian, 55–56; Faustian bargain, 17, 64
Federal Republic of Germany, 108
Fehérváry, Krisztina, 19n12, 62, 142, 173, 210n44, 233n1
Five-Year Plan, 2, 72, 107, 194, 199
Fodor, Eva, 232
Foucault, Michel, 193, 209n18
France, 2, 193; French; 13, 14, 29, 181, 202, 204; French Revolution, 57
Fulbrook, Mary, 124n12, 124n16
Fukuyama, Francis, 193

German Democratic Republic (GDR)/East Germany, 3, 4, 17, 59–61, 66, 68, 77n43, 77n46, 104–23, 131, 134, 137, 153, 155n12

globalization, 18, 42, 178, 179
Gomułka, Władysław, 59
good society, 6–7, 10, 192, 195–96, 206
Gurova, Olga, 179

H&M, 162, 171–73, 178, 182, 183n1, 185n36
habitus, 29, 118, 126n72, 230
happiness, 1, 7, 191–92, 202, 203, 208n5
Harper, Krista, 218
Havel, Václav, 14–15, 56, 192–93, 195, 227
hoarding, 117–19, 123
Homo sovieticus, 17, 90
Honecker, Erich, 60, 104, 106, 107, 108, 111–13, 122
Hungary, 2, 3, 4, 12, 14, 39, 61–62, 66, 67, 125n37, 210n44, 220, 224, 226, 231; Hungarians, 13, 16, 76n34

ideology, 9, 11, 16, 20n18, 63, 96, 132, 136, 137, 166, 178, 180, 190, 192–93, 196, 197, 209n35, 231
IKEA, 162, 171, 173, 182, 184n34, 234n26
Imaginary Europe, 164–66, 170, 177, 181–82, 183, 185n56
Imaginary West, 164, 166–67, 178, 181
International Bank for Economic Cooperation, 112
Intershop, 104, 109, 134
Iron Curtain, 10, 11, 40, 138, 155n4, 208n16

Judt, Tony, 60, 212n70

Karavelov, Liuben, 32
Kaffee-Mix, 111, 121
Kádár, János, 16, 61–62
Keynes, John Maynard, 83, 91, 97n3, 99n43; Keynesian, 84, 91, 94, 97; Keynesianism, 91, 93
Khrushchev, Nikita, 9, 39
Kiaer, Christina, 223
Konsumsozialismus (consumer socialism), 124n16
Kniga za vseki den i vseki dom, 198, 200–2
Konstantinov, Aleko, 35–36, 44n30, 45n55
Kooperativna promishlenost, 198–99, 205, 207

Kornai, János, 68, 191
Kosta, 109–10, 111, 118
Kuba-Orange, 116

Lamberz, Werner, 113
Laos, 112, 113
Łaski, Kazimierz, 86, 91–93, 94
leisure, 2–4, 7, 55, 135, 142, 148, 174, 191, 192, 194, 202
Lenin, 38, 85
Leninism, 5, 11, 26, 56, 58, 65, 66, 73, 84
Lithuania, 220, 224, 228

market, 9, 17, 42, 52–54, 59, 68–69, 71, 73, 83, 89–90, 91, 92–93, 95, 105, 106, 110, 111, 114, 118, 120, 133, 134, 138, 140–41, 143, 145, 146–49, 151–52, 162, 163–65, 168–70, 171, 173, 176–77, 179, 182, 219–20, 224–25, 228; black, 118, 145, 166, 175; mass, 164, 172, 173, 176, 178, 180
marketing, 69, 77n43, 113, 145, 147, 157n65, 169, 177
material culture, 6, 164, 223
Marx, Karl, 20n17, 28, 190, 220, 221, 223; Marxist, 5–7, 56, 58, 63, 65, 66, 69, 73, 77n45, 83, 137, 196, 226; Marxism, 26, 27, 92
material agency, 221
materialism, 11, 37, 223
Mengistu Haile Mariam, 112
Merkel, Ina, 117, 126n72
Mestna promishlenost i uslugi, 198, 205, 206
Mittag, Günter, 113
Mocca-Fix, 109
modernity, 6, 11, 18, 25–28, 32–34, 36, 37, 93, 132, 133, 136–39, 142, 153–54, 162–65, 169, 173, 175, 178–83, 190, 206, 207, 219
Mona, 109
Mount Vitosha, 36
Mozambique, 112

needs, 1, 6, 7, 10, 11–12, 15–16, 39, 40, 41, 58, 84, 85–91, 93–94, 97, 107, 136, 139, 141, 142, 190, 202, 205, 209n25, 220, 223, 231; basic, 11, 39, 218

neoclassical economics, 83, 97n2
New Economic Policy, 38
normalization, 61, 147, 149, 192–93

obratsov dom, 202
Ogaden region, 112
orange, 10, 104–7, 109, 111, 114–16, 121–23. *See also* Kuba-Orange
Orange Revolution, 181
Orient, 27, 51; Oriental(ist), 28, 29, 32, 45n41, 45n55; Oriental luxury, 29
Orientalism, 16
orthodoxy, 34, 68, 74n2
Ottoman, 29, 31–34; Balkans, 29; Empire, 10, 31, 33

panic buying, 105, 118
Parteilehrjahr, 104, 123
participatory dictatorship, 106
Patico, Jennifer, 180
peasant, 32–38, 44n38, 45n56, 121, 141, 194; peasantry, 63
petition, 107, 116–17, 119–23
Philippines, the, 112–13
philistine, 141, philistinism, 197, 228
Plastic People of the Universe, 14, 234n29
pleasure, ix, 1, 5–8, 10, 11–15, 18, 21n31, 25, 34–36, 40–42, 53, 55, 57, 71, 73, 107, 120–21, 135, 142, 162, 191–93, 195, 204–6, 209n29; displeasure, 164, 182, 192
Poland, 14, 16, 18, 29, 58–59, 67, 82, 86, 88, 93–95, 102, 103, 108, 125n37, 132–36, 138–49, 153–54, 161, 173, 175, 180; Polish, 10, 11, 17, 71, 82, 86, 87, 91, 97, 103, 108, 132–41, 143–44, 146–54, 161, 193
Polish People's Republic (PRL), 17, 82, 83, 85, 87, 89–90, 93, 95, 98n15
Politburo, 104–5, 124n16
Polanyi, Karl, 220, 233n8
political economy, 1, 6, 85, 168, 190
politicization, 225, 230–31
populists, 31, 33
post-Soviet transition, 41, 152, 162–63, 165, 169, 180, 232
postcolonial modernity, 165, 179–81
Poznański, Kazimierz, 95–96

practice turn, 230–31
Prague Spring, 56, 60–61, 212n70
production, 1, 7, 20n19, 60, 62, 68, 71, 75n9, 82–96, 98n15, 115, 137, 141, 150–54, 164, 169, 178–80, 190, 195, 198–99, 202, 204, 206, 220–27, 231
progress, 2, 3, 8, 16, 25, 28, 42n4, 52, 55, 58, 77n39, 136, 138, 162–65, 169, 179, 183, 194, 197, 206, 212n70
prosumer, 222–23, 233n15
Protestantism, 28, 34–35, 45n49
Provisional Military Administrative Council (PMAC), 112

reunification, 14, 105
rationalism, 7, 27, 76n36, 83, 89–91, 93, 96–97, 99n26, 199, 202
resonance machine, 229–30
reuse, 175, 221, 231–32
rewards (for socialist citizens), 19, 63–65, 68
Rila Mountains, 35
Rilski, Ivan, 35, 205
Ritzer, George, 222
Romania, 16, 58, 96, 125n37
Rondo, 109, 114, 118–19
Russia, 26, 29, 33, 34–35, 42n1, 42n2, 44n31, 45n41, 45n51, 67, 164, 168, 180, 184n30, 185n56, 228
Russophile, 34
Russo-Turkish War of 1877–78, 33

sacralization, 225–27
Sakharov, Andrei, 193
scarcity, 5, 9–26, 29, 30, 41, 55, 57, 59, 82, 106, 107, 110, 111–12, 117–22, 124n11, 144, 147, 164, 168–69, 176, 178, 190–92, 206, 218, 226
Schalck-Golodkowski, Alexander, 111, 124n32
Scott, James, 122–23
secondhand, 173, 176–79, 182, 183n1
self-peripheralization, 180
self-provisioning, 224–25
shadow consumer practices, 165, 173–77
shopping, 12, 14, 18, 165–66, 171–78, 221, 228
shopping tourism, 29, 143, 146, 155n4, 173–76

shortages. See scarcity
shortage economy, 82, 106, 123, 191
Shove, Elizabeth, 230
shuttle trade, 175–76
Slavophiles, 31, 34
social contract, 6, 17, 39, 54–74, 75n18, 75n21, 77n45, 107, 190, 192
socialists, 31, 34, 36–37, 207
socialist humanism, 91, 77n45, 85, 195–96
Socialist Unity Party of Germany (SED), 104, 106–9, 113, 116, 123n1
soft budget constraints, 68
Solzhenitsyn, Aleksandr, 193
Soviet Union (USSR), 1, 21n31, 26, 38, 42n1, 63, 114, 125n37, 138, 162–67, 175, 190, 191, 199, 224, 228
stagnation, 168, 192, 194, 198
Stalin, 38–39, 59, 85, 199
Stalinism, 26, 38, 39, 63, 82, 85–87, 96, 98n10, 98n18; de-Stalinization, 39, 136
Stamboliski, Alexander, 37, 46n56
Stambolov, Stefan, 34
standards of living, 3–9, 16–17, 54, 62–73, 84–89, 95–97, 105, 107, 139, 218–19
State Council of the GDR, 119–20
state socialism, 1, 5–18, 52, 63, 66–67, 70, 73–74, 75n9, 105–6, 133–42, 148–50, 152, 154, 162, 167, 179, 190–95, 208n3, 208n12, 218–27, 231–32
Strandja, 35
subjectification, 225. See also subjectivity
subjectivity, 167, 199, 22; political, 11, 15, 18, 75n9, 218, 220, 227, 229, 232
subsidiary farming, 224
surplus, 190; surplus capital, 96
surplus value, 98n15, 233n9
supply-side economics, 17, 83–84, 92–97

Technisches Kontrollorgan (TKO), 120
Toffler, Alvin, 222
Tolstoyan (philosophy), 34–35
transfer ruble, 112
Treaty of San Stefano, 33

tropical fruits, 10, 105–7, 109, 111, 115–23
Trudovo-proivoditelna kooperatsia, 198, 202, 205, 210n41

Ukraine, 10, 18, 162–83, 183n1, 184n34, 185n56
Ulbricht, Walter, 76n25, 107
United States, the, 3, 14, 28, 33, 35, 41, 67, 69, 73, 84, 112, 142, 156n35, 200, 229, 231

Value, 6, 56, 61, 64, 69, 70, 73, 75n20, 77n39, 89, 118, 119, 120, 132, 138, 139, 141, 148, 150, 165–69, 174, 175, 177–82, 185n56, 193, 207, 208n12, 226; economic, 92, 134, 141–42, 175, 177, 222. See also surplus value
Valutamark, 108, 113
Vazov, Ivan, 35–36
VCRs, 10, 14, 18, 132–57, 193
Vietnam, 58, 112, 113, 126n55
vintage temporality, 177–79

Wanner, Catherine, 167, 175
welfare dictatorship, 107, 124n13
West/Western(ers), 1–18, 26–28, 31–37, 39–42, 42n1, 44n22, 45n44, 59–60, 65, 72, 75n3, 77n45, 94, 105, 118, 132–36, 140, 144–54, 163–64, 167–68, 178–80, 182, 190–93, 195, 219, 224, 227–29, 232
Westkaffee, 109, 126n69
White Brotherhood, 34
World's Fairs/trade fairs, 40, 145, 147

Yasna Polyana, 35
Yom Kippur War, 124n29
Yugoslavia, 2, 3, 17, 42n1, 53, 57–58, 63, 66, 68, 75n1, 75n9, 77n45, 91, 141, 148
Yurchak, Alexei, 77n39, 166, 208n10

Zanaiachiiska kooperatsia, 198
Zappa, Frank, 14
Zhivkov, Todor, 196–97
Zhivkova, Lyudmila, 197–98

www.ingramcontent.com/pod-product-compliance
Lightning Source LLC
Chambersburg PA
CBHW031806220426
43662CB00007B/546